# Biracial Br_____

## A Different Way of Looking at Race

Remi Adekoya

CONSTABLE

CONSTABLE

First published in Great Britain in 2021 by Constable

1 3 5 7 9 10 8 6 4 2

A CIP catalogue record for this book
is available from the British Library.

ISBN: 978-1-47213-345-8 (hardback)

Typeset in Minion Pro by SX Composing DTP, Rayleigh, Essex

Printed and bound in Great Britain by Clays Ltd, Elcograf, S.p.A.

Papers used by Constable are from well-managed forests
and other responsible sources.

Constable
An imprint of
Little, Brown Book Group
Carmelite House
50 Victoria Embankment
London EC4Y 0DZ

An Hachette UK Company

www.hachette.co.uk

www.littlebrown.co.uk

This book is dedicated to the memory of my parents
Remi Adekoya Snr and Elizabeth Zirkwitz-Adekoya.

To my wonderful wife Omosede Adekoya, I can never thank you
enough for your unconditional love and support in everything I do,
not just writing this book. It is wonderful to be married to the best
person you know, and you are certainly the best thing that's ever
happened to me.

# Contents

# Introduction

'Mixed race? What's all this mixed-race nonsense? If you're not white, you're black.' Thus asserted a legendary black British broadcaster to Sunder Katwala, a mixed-race Briton I interviewed for this book, during a conversation they had on identity a few years ago. The pronouncement appears even starker if you consider Sunder is of Indian-Irish heritage with no black roots of which he is aware. So goes the binary way of thinking about identity that continues to shape attitudes towards mixed-race people, even though most would couch it far more diplomatically today. Ideas that have become truly influential no longer need to be articulated that explicitly or emphatically, their power lies in appearing so obvious they barely require saying. They are simply silently assumed.

The notion of a stand-alone mixed-race identity that is not in effect an offshoot of one of the more familiar identities such as 'black', 'white' or 'Asian' is not something Britain and the world generally takes seriously as of yet. It is why Meghan Markle self-identifying as biracial sparked confusion and debate in Britain as to what exactly that meant and whether or not it was appropriate for her to do so. It is why, if Barack Obama had asked to be called the 'first biracial president of America', the world would have frowned in confusion, some even in hostility. What exactly is he trying to say here? 'First black president' we get, but 'first biracial president'? What's *that* all about? America's newly elected vice-president, Kamala Harris, has presented a unique challenge to identity declarers as she is an even lesser understood kind of mixed race, one with no white parent in the background. The default has been to mostly label her a 'black woman'.

Symptomatically, in the cases of both Obama and Markle, it is monoracial people who have dominated the public debates about what their identities are or should be. As the son of a Nigerian father and Polish mother, I found it somewhat odd watching discussions about Markle's identity on British TV in which everyone on the panel was monoracial, either black or white, with no mixed-race voices. That's like an all-white panel discussing what blackness means or vice versa.

As annoying as they can be, I understand these attitudes. In the career of humanity, we have always divided ourselves into in-groups and out-groups. The only things that change with time are the labels and the logic of division. We used to have Romans and Aztecs, now we have Italians and Mexicans. We used to divide into kingdoms and religions, now we divide into nations and races.

We also divide into classes, ethnic groups, ideological tribes and countless other in-groups and out-groups we've invented. Perhaps this century will bring new types of human divisions we can't even imagine today. But for now, social construct or not, race is a popular basis for human divisions. What matters is what people believe matters. But in the logic of race, mixed-race people are problematic because we muddy the picture of what would otherwise be a neatly-divisible world. One where it is very clear who the *We* are and who the *They* are. No ifs, no buts. None of this mixed-race nonsense.

However, there are now too many of us to continue be ignored as a stand-alone demographic force. Currently the fastest-growing minority group, there are already up to two million mixed-race Britons today, according to some estimates. Meanwhile, demographic projections in political scientist Professor Eric Kaufmann's book, *Whiteshift*, suggest that if current rates of interracial marriage continue, and there is little reason to think they won't, Britain will be 30 per cent mixed race by the end of this century, with that figure rising to nearly 75 per cent by 2150. We quite literally are the future.

Paradoxically, however, the greatest-ever interracial mixing is happening in a world that is becoming more racially polarised. While America has historically been divided by race and Britain by class, there is now a discernible trend in this country towards an American-style culture of race as the most significant, or at very least, most emotive, dividing line in society. The fact a terrible event that happened in faraway Minneapolis last year – the killing of George Floyd – sparked Black Lives Matter protests and heated debates about race here in Britain was but one recent manifestation of this trend, which is especially visible among younger ethnic minorities.

A 2020 survey by Hope not Hate asked Britain's minorities how they defined themselves: while 64 per cent of respondents aged over 65 described themselves simply as *British* with 15 per cent opting for Hyphenated British (e.g. Black British, Asian British), in the 16–24 age group, the number defining as British drops to 36 per cent while those identifying as Hyphenated British doubles to 30 per cent. An overwhelming 82 per cent of respondents described their racial/ethnic identity as 'important to who I am' and 2 in 3 believe we do not discuss race and racism enough in Britain.

As someone who now calls this country home, I suggest going forward that our energies will be best spent not on trying to render racial identities irrelevant, but on trying to figure out how we can navigate our identities and divisions in a manner offering the greatest opportunity possible for the individual to thrive. We must never forget that stuck in the middle of all these group conflicts is the individual trying to survive. Grand narratives and big-picture theories are sometimes needed to make sense of complex human realities, but for the individual, the small picture *is* the big picture. I am thus most interested in how individuals are dealing with the racial divisions of our times.

For self-interested reasons, the divisions I am most concerned with are those affecting mixed-race people like myself. Where do I and other mixed-race folk in Britain today fit in with all the ongoing polarisation around us? Considering the rate at which our numbers are growing, we are increasingly going to be a factor muddying Britain's racial waters. Do we get to choose our in-groups, are they chosen for us or can we play for various teams, so to speak? In real life, identity is not just about who you identify with, it is also about who identifies with you.

In the twentieth century, blackness was clearly defined by the one-drop rule, expressed in the 'if you're not white, you're black' claim. The child of a white father and half-white/half-black mother was seen as black even if they might have *felt* white. Does the one-drop rule still apply in today's Britain? If so, what is the twenty-first-century logic behind this? If the child of a black and white parent feels a closer affinity to their white identity, should such a person be derided for 'trying to be white'? Alternatively, if such a child feels black, do they still face questions about how authentically black or not they are?

An important point worth emphasising here is that, as the example of Kamala Harris shows us, 'mixed race' is not just about mixed black and white even though that is the single most common mix. Roughly half of Britain's mixed-race population is nevertheless of a different configuration. So how does it work if you were born to a white English father and Pakistani mother or vice versa? Can you count on being accepted by any of those communities? What about

4

if you have a white English father and Chinese mother? How are you seen by English and Chinese people?

What about the offspring of a Jamaican-Indian or Pakistani-Lebanese couple in Britain? How does that work today? And what about those who have parents with multiple racial identities, how do they navigate things? Also, considering the fact 75 per cent of mixed-race Britons have a white parent, does that mean the 'white side' of mixed-race Britons will acquire increasing significance to their self-identification as their numbers multiply and they intermarry with the white population?

Should racial identity go the way of sexual identity, now chiefly based on self-identification? Is it the parent who is more dominant in the mixed-race child's upbringing that determines which race or culture he or she will identify with or does the society they are brought up in play a bigger role?

It is high time we developed a new understanding of mixed-race identity better suited to our century. This book is an effort in that direction. As someone who has researched identity academically, I've come to the conclusion that while academic theories can tell us a lot about how identities are socially constructed, they are woeful at explaining how identities are *felt*.

Thus, in order to write this book, I spoke to mixed-race Britons of various ages and racial configurations from different regions of Britain to hear their stories about what it's really like navigating a mixed-race identity in the 21st-century. The oldest person I spoke to was 73, the youngest 6. I asked only one thing of each of them – that they speak frankly about their experiences no matter what. The only thing worse than not discussing an important issue like race is discussing it disingenuously. I spoke to regular people, not public figures, people with no grand narratives to push, no personal images to burnish, no ideological agendas to pursue. People who would simply say it like it is. The overwhelming majority spoke under their real names, but a handful preferred to speak under an assumed name if I wanted them to be *that honest*.

This book contains the stories and comments I felt were the most revealing about the mixed-race experience. Even though the stories emerged in conversations, they are presented in the first person. I wanted people to voice their own experiences rather than me doing it for them through the filter of my subjective interpretations. It is only outside their stories that I comment on the issues they raise and share some of my own personal experiences as a mixed-race person who has lived in Nigeria, Poland and now Britain. My aspiration is to broaden and (hopefully) deepen the discussion on race in Britain from an unapologetically mixed-race perspective. I think this perspective is a much-needed one in the wider discussion on race, identity and the future of twenty-first century societies in general.

Identity gives us a vantage point from which to observe the world. Being mixed race gives you at least two potential vantage points, or more in the case of those who are multiracial. I think these various vantage points from which we get to see the world can provide valuable observations to the overall discussion on race and identity in twenty-first century Britain.

The book is divided into three parts. The first part contains stories from Britons of mixed black and white heritage who constitute roughly half of Britain's mixed-race population, according to the last census. The second part tells the stories of the second-largest category of mixed-race Britons, namely those classified as 'mixed white and Asian'. The third part reveals the experiences of the category of mixed-race people we know and hear the least about, the so-called 'mixed other'.

I will always be grateful to the people who agreed to share their stories with me even when doing so took them to uncomfortable places, places of vulnerability, something none of us find easy. Without them, none of this would be possible. I stand on their shoulders. While our experiences have been individual, what we have learnt from them is not. Because there are others like us out there who are facing or will face similar situations to those we faced. Our search for identity, like everyone else's, is a search for a story about our life that makes sense to us. Something that explains why we feel the way we feel and where we fit in this world. An identity is a story. It is a story we tell the world about who we are, and a story the world tells us about who we are. These are our stories.

# Part 1

## Between black and white

# Chapter 1

# Why me?

Roughly half of Britain's mixed-race population is of mixed black and white heritage. There is no relationship quite like the relationship between black and white. The history of slavery, colonialism and racism, combined with a persistently huge power imbalance in the present, make for a very specific psychological dynamic.

To be born to black and white parents is to have to navigate this difficult dynamic; to be thrust in between two worlds that often fear and mistrust each other; that often see themselves as vastly different from each other; that sometimes even openly resent each other. In this no-man's-land is a child trying to figure out who they are and where they fit in. Trying to make sense of it all.

I can think of no society where being the offspring of a black and white couple comes with no particular tensions and complications. Growing up in Nigeria, I experienced these complications in an African setting. But how does it work in Britain? How have mixed-race Britons navigated this rocky terrain between black and white in the past, and how are they doing it today? I started my questions in Southampton where I spoke to Rita. Rita was born in 1946.

I was a war baby. My father was an African-American soldier stationed in England during the Second World War. He met my English mother at a dance in Eastleigh, which is in Hampshire, sometime in 1944, and they started a relationship. They were together until my dad left England less than a year after the war ended. He had a fiancée waiting for him in America. I don't know at which point of their relationship my mum found out about this. I was born the month after he left. My mum decided to keep me, which was not always the case with brown war babies at the time. In fact, it was rarely the case.

We lived in my grandma's house in Eastleigh, the town where I spent most of my life. My mum worked so it was my nan who really raised me. My mum never wanted to talk about my father. Even when he'd send me sweets from America, she'd say they were from my uncle. It was only much later I found out they were from my father. I think she just wanted to forget about him.

Growing up, two things distinguished me from all the other kids around me. The first was that I didn't have a dad like everyone else did. The second was of course my skin colour. I got a lot of abuse. The other kids would call me 'nigger', 'blackie', 'monkey', things like that. I tried to ignore them. I usually walked with my head down, trying not to attract any attention.

When I'd be passing a group of kids who'd called me names before, I'd say a silent prayer, 'God, please don't let them see me or if they see me, please don't let them say anything today.' I literally held my breath anytime I passed a group of boys. It was always boys who'd call me names and always when they were in groups. They made me feel scared. They made me feel like a nobody. They made me want to be invisible.

Even though my mum was white, back then there was nothing like being 'mixed race'. I never even heard the term until much later in my life. To everyone in 1950s Eastleigh I was black, so that was how I saw myself, as a black girl.

My mum eventually got married to a Polish man who became my stepfather. It started when I was eight, the sexual abuse. The first

time he touched me, I told my nan about it. She said the worst thing
you can ever say to a child being abused. 'You mustn't let him do
that to you again,' she told me. That made me think it was my fault,
that I was somehow making him do what he was doing. The fact he
would always give me money after touching me only made the whole
thing more confusing and made me feel even dirtier.

I often wondered whether he was doing it because I was a black
girl. Maybe that was why he didn't like me? For a long time, I
believed it was because of this. Because if not that, then why was this
happening to me? But there was a girl my age nearby whose mum
had also married a Polish man after the war. We were in the playground one day and out of the blue it just popped into my head to
ask her if her Polish stepdad touched her. She said he did.

I remember feeling a sense of relief. At least I wasn't the only one
it was happening to. And it wasn't just something that happened
to black girls like me. When I think about it now, my reaction was
crazy because terrible things were happening to that girl as well and
you wouldn't wish that on anybody, but that was how I felt back
then. I started thinking perhaps this was simply something Polish
men did to their stepdaughters.

I didn't tell my mum about what was going on. We were never
close. She never showed me any affection. I don't remember her
ever telling me she loved me or even hugging me. Not once. She had
three children with my Polish stepfather, so I have two brothers and
a sister. She would tell them she loved them, but never me. Again,
I wondered whether this was because I was black. Sometimes I
wondered why'd she even kept me at all. My nan showed me much
more affection than my mum did. The worst thing was that my
mum knew what my stepfather was doing to me. I sensed this for a
long time but found out for sure when I was fifteen.

I was going for a job interview at the railway station and I was
with her and my stepdad. He was having a go at me and suddenly

13

I lost it and yelled back at him. I said I knew he was having a go because I hadn't been letting him touch me of late. I looked at my mum when I was saying this. But she didn't react. She just told me to hurry up, not to be late for my interview, pretending she hadn't heard what I'd said. That's when I knew she knew but didn't care enough about me to do anything about it.

After this incident, situations from earlier years started making sense to me. There were times she'd be going to the laundrette or grocery shopping and I'd beg her to let me go with her because I knew my stepfather would want to touch me once we were alone. But she never let me go with her. She'd take my siblings but tell me, 'No, you stay at home.' Now I understood it was because she wanted to give my stepdad the opportunity to do what he willed with me. I felt very alone. I'd go for walks near the river all by myself and sit down in the grass, playing with a stick, wondering why all this was happening to me. Back then, there was nobody you could speak to about this kind of thing, no counsellors or whatnot. I had friends but I couldn't speak to my friends about this.

School was my only escape. I don't think any other kids liked school as much as I did. The teachers treated me like everyone else. They never picked on me or spoke to me meanly because I was black. I don't remember the other kids ever calling me racial names at school either. Maybe it's because I went to an all-girls school. Like I said, the racial abuse always came from boys. School was my favourite place to be. I was away from my stepfather and I wasn't getting called 'nigger' and 'blackie' all the time. I loved playing on the netball team. I was quite good at the sport and being on that team was the first time I'd ever felt a part of any group. Unfortunately, I had to leave school at fourteen as my mum and stepdad expected me to earn my keep. From then on, I worked in factories, bakeries, for the railway line, that sort of thing.

There were a handful of coloured boys around when I was growing up, but I'd never date any of them. I know this may sound weird, but the truth is all I wanted was to blend in and not be noticed. I knew that if I went out with a coloured boy and we were walking down the street we'd stand out because there'd be two of us who were black. Then people would probably start calling us names or taunting us. They'd see my colour more. But if I were walking down the street with a white boy, we'd draw less attention. That was how I figured it in my head. And as it happened, I don't recall ever getting any racial abuse or taunts from anyone when with my white boyfriends, so that just affirmed me in my choice. I tried to hide my colour by only dating white boys. I would never have even considered marrying a black man.

It sounds crazy, no? I know I shouldn't think like that, but blackness has always felt like a stigma to me, and that feeling is still there, to be honest. Being called a nigger when I was little, all the negativity associated with being black, those things stay with you. I don't think you can ever really get them out of your system. You can pretend you have because you want to look strong and act as if you don't care. But deep down, it's there, always at the back of your mind. You don't think about it all the time, but you know you're black and there are times you feel ashamed of that.

There was another girl in Eastleigh who was also coloured, mixed like me. We've been friends since childhood. If you met her, you'd think she is a very confident person. When we were kids, she used to jump round the playground making monkey noises, just to prove she didn't care about the other kids calling her a monkey. But I knew she did. She was always all bravado on the outside, but as her close friend I knew how insecure she really was about being black.

I'm a bit too old to start hiding my insecurities now. When I was a young girl, I straightened my hair because I wanted to look the way the white girls looked. I always wished I could swish my

15

hair the way they could. I really envied them that. I still straighten my hair. Sometimes my hairdresser will say, 'Maybe something different today, Rita? Maybe some curls?' I always say, 'No, just keep it straight.' Always straight because then I'm like a white person. I know this sounds silly, but it's the truth.

Growing up in 1950s England, there was no one who looked like me on TV. In general, there were no black people on TV then. It wasn't until the late 1960s when I was in my late twenties that I started seeing a few black actors on TV. Sidney Poitier was the first black movie star, of course. Denzel came along much later. It meant a lot to me to see the likes of Poitier on TV in the 1960s. For the first time, I saw black people being presented as normal human beings, doing the same kind of things white people did. They looked accepted. That made me feel better about myself. Though clearly not better enough.

I ended up in an abusive marriage with a husband who used to hit me. Once he even punched me in the stomach when I was pregnant. I took it for many years before finally divorcing him. We had three children. At the time I was raising them, I remember there was a lot going on with the civil rights movement in America. I was very proud of people like Martin Luther King for standing up against what was going on. But I was a young mother working jobs, raising kids, just living my life. I wasn't thinking about politics. Sometimes, I feel bad about that. I feel like I never did anything to change the situation of people like me. But that's how it was, I just focused on living my life.

I am close to my daughters, but I have a very complicated relationship with my son. One incident with him I'll never forget. He was around sixteen. One day I saw him in town in Eastleigh with his mates and stopped to tell him something I wanted him to do at home. When he got back that day, he said to me, 'Mum, next time you see me in public, please don't speak to me.' That felt awful. This was my son saying that to me. 'Why not? Are you ashamed of me?' I asked him. He said nothing, but he obviously was. My son looks white, you see. My daughters are visibly mixed. But my son looks white. When he was growing up, until people saw me and knew I was his mother, they'd think he was white. And I guess that's what he wanted people to think.

Our relationship has always been strained. I recently saw him at a family funeral, and he greeted me, 'Hello, mother.' That's how he always refers to me – 'mother' – not 'mum' or 'mummy', just 'mother'. He hasn't yet introduced me to his son, my grandson, even though he's two years old now. I think he's a bit ashamed of me up till today. It's a terrible feeling to know that, but like they say, as long as they're happy and healthy, it's fine. At least I have a great relationship with my daughters. As for my white siblings, I've always got on very well with one of my brothers; he's always been sweet and affectionate with me, always been there for me. But I have never been close to my sister and other brother. When we were adults, I told my sister her dad had molested me. She told me to my face she didn't believe me. 'He never touched me,' she said.

I've talked a lot about how self-conscious I've always been of my skin colour. But of course, sometimes you forget the colour thing and just live your life. Until someone says something or gives you a look. Then it all comes back. In my case, even though I've had years of counselling to get me where I am today psychologically, my experiences with my stepdad only made things worse regarding my feelings about being black. It's interesting the way the colour thing works, though. After my marriage broke up, I once dated a guy who, in the middle of an argument we were having, referred to my daughter as a 'little black nigger'. I dumped him immediately. But I later heard he married a black nurse. That's funny, isn't it?

Sometimes when I'm out about town and someone looks at me, I start getting weird thoughts in my head. It could be just a look of curiosity, but I start asking myself, 'Why are they looking at me?

Is it because I'm black?' A few years back, one of my daughters was in a relationship which seemed to be going very well. The man she was dating was an upper-class white English guy. After being with him for a few months, she introduced him to me. A few days later he texted her saying he didn't think the relationship would work out.

I remember wondering to myself, 'Was it because he had met me? Was it because he saw I was black?' I'm sure my daughter must have told him about me, but perhaps it hadn't hit home till he actually saw me. Then again, perhaps his breaking-up with my daughter had nothing whatsoever to do with me. My point is that I still get these kinds of thoughts in my head.

At moments like that, I feel very self-conscious and well, honestly speaking, ashamed of being black again. I wish I could shake that feeling. But I just can't. I still can't take compliments. People will often say, 'Hey Rita, you look beautiful today.' I say, 'Aww thanks!' But truth is, I never believe those compliments. When I look in the mirror, I don't see a beautiful person. I've never been able to think of myself as beautiful. It's all about what you've got in your head. I realise that, but I am seventy-three now, so I think it's a bit too late to change how I think about myself.

I do feel the situation of black and brown people in Britain has improved very much since when I grew up. I live in Southampton now and there are many more black and brown people here than there used to be. I still feel most connected to Eastleigh where I spent most of my life, though. It's interesting how we can feel so connected to the place of our childhood even if most of our childhood memories are bad. I find today's discussion about how it is being mixed race very interesting. But like I said, I've always thought of myself as black because that is how I was seen. Apart from black, I also feel British because I've lived my whole life in Britain. But it didn't really hit me I was British until I went to America after locating my biological father. I was sixty at the time.

Americans would ask me the time just to hear me speak because they liked my accent. That made me feel good and made me feel British. Meeting my biological father and his American family was also a wonderful experience. When my dad would walk with me and hold my hand, it was wonderful. It was like I'd lived next door to him all my life. His wife was so nice to me. His brother, my uncle Carl, instantly loved me to bits, as I did him. I'd never felt so loved. I felt wanted for the first time in my life when I was with them. It felt like proper family.

They told me stories about how my grandparents had been among the first freed slaves to buy land in Mississippi. That land is still in the family. It felt amazing to think I had ancestors who did amazing things. I didn't tell them anything about the abuse. My dad was in his eighties when I found him, so there was no point in bringing all that up, it would have upset him too much. Unfortunately, I only met my father once as he died not long after my trip. The counselling I've been through to help me make sense of my experiences, especially the sexual abuse, has helped me a lot. What matters is that I survived it all. But if I could go back and do it all over again, I'd definitely tell myself, 'Rita, don't let them get you thinking you're not good enough. Don't let them rule your life.'

On my train-ride back from seeing Rita, I couldn't get out of my head the picture of a young brown girl, sitting by a river near her home, poking a stick in the grass and wondering why all this was happening to her. I imagined how excruciatingly alone that girl must have felt in those moments. No one to protect her. A mother she couldn't rely on and a biological father far away in America. That Rita remains standing after all the sexual, racial and physical abuse she endured, and managed to raise three children in the process, is something of a miracle to me.

She survived, but her experiences left scars. The crude racism she was subjected to growing up in Eastleigh left her with the racial complex she spoke so frankly about. There was no navigating between black and white in Rita's case. Even though she grew up in an all-white home in an all-white town, having no contact with anything resembling black culture, she was never allowed to think of herself as anything but 'black'.

I felt grateful for her honesty about the shame she still occasionally feels about her skin colour. It is easier to admit having had a racial complex in the past than to admit having one in the present. Because that lets the world know you remain vulnerable. And there are few things we fear more than appearing vulnerable. I think the main reason Rita felt safe enough to let me see her vulnerability is because I am mixed race too. Many people of black heritage do not feel safe enough to appear vulnerable in front of white people, especially not in the context of racial insecurities.

The truth here is that, in the context of race, Rita's story offers us no triumphant punch-your-fist-in-the-air moment of overcoming. Despite her amazing resilience in surviving the many evils life brought her way, her story is also one of white racism achieving its objectives. Succeeding in making her feel 'less than'. It is important we are honest about our complexes, racial or otherwise. While we may feel very vulnerable revealing them to others, hiding them behind a brave face only gives the world an opportunity to do nothing about the conditions that produced them in the first place. This guarantees they will be reproduced in others after us.

I know those white boys who used to call Rita 'nigger' and 'monkey' in 1950s Eastleigh. The ones who made her hold her breath whenever she would walk past them, praying they wouldn't notice her. I met them on the streets of Warsaw, where I moved after finishing secondary school in Lagos in the mid-1990s. Like Rita, I too held my breath anytime I walked past them. I too would say a silent prayer hoping they wouldn't notice me that day or perhaps I'd just be lucky enough they wouldn't be in the mood to call me nigger or monkey or tell me to 'fuck off back to Africa'.

Those boys, and it is always boys, have the same agenda everywhere; to intimidate you into willingly accepting their right to be above you. On the basis of their white skin colour. Luckily for me, unlike Rita, I met those boys after a childhood spent in Nigeria, one that had given very different ideas about my place in this world.

While I did feel humiliated when those Polish boys yelled abuse at me and authentically dreaded those moments, I was a bit too full of myself ever to feel 'less than' them. I'm not saying I was the most confident teenager in the world – I wasn't – but I had been brought up in a society that nurses its own superiority complex. One not based on any notions of racial superiority, but on the idea of Nigerian exceptionalism, best expressed in the popular national claim Nigeria is 'the giant of Africa'.

Nigerians firmly believe they are a special people, endowed with a unique intelligence, resilience and creativity that predestines them for greatness. This is the gospel I was raised in, and I was a firm believer. So the idea my blackness, which I equated to my Nigerianness, somehow made me worse than those Polish kids was never one I could truly take seriously. If anything, quite the opposite. My Nigerianness shielded me from those boys' attempts to assert their superiority over me in my own head. But that still leaves the question of *why*.

Why did those boys in 1950s Eastleigh and 1990s Warsaw feel the need to say the things they said to Rita and me? 'Racism' is just the beginning of the answer. The deeper question is what emotional need racism satisfies in humans to make it so attractive to so many people in the first place?

I think what the kind of racism Rita and I experienced offers people emotionally is an opportunity to experience a sense of power over others. Those boys felt they had the power to humiliate us, and they enjoyed that feeling. Cruelty is the most explicit exhibition of power over another human being. Unambiguous proof you *can*. Hurling those abuses at us must have made those boys feel strong and dominant, feelings humans crave because they make it appear impossible we will die.

Racism is often discussed today as if it is a phenomenon unique in human behaviour. But far from it, racism is just one of the countless ideologies humans have developed to dominate other humans. Racism is not the result of prejudice, but of the capacity to dominate. The prejudice exists to justify the domination. Those boys wanted to let me and Rita *know* they had the capacity to dominate us. Many religions have ended up ultimately feeding this human need for domination, as have economic systems, systems built on the idea of some people possessing 'royal blood', (whatever that is), or ethnocentric ideas that say we may be the same skin colour, but I am better than you because I'm from ethnic group X and you're from group Y.

The most pressing question I see is not why racism exists but whether we are capable as humans of weaning ourselves off our addiction to these feelings of power and domination? Because if not, we will continue inventing all sorts of new ideologies in our search for that high. Racism will simply be replaced by something else.

Chapter 2

# No thing

My next chat was with Eugene, who has lived in Liverpool all his life, though he has travelled widely. His father, too, was an American soldier, stationed in Britain following the Second World War. But Eugene was born in 1955, almost a decade after Rita.

My father was African-American while my mother was of German-Scottish ancestry but born and raised in Liverpool. My father was stationed in Liverpool following the Second World War. He met my mum there, they dated and eventually got married. In 1958, when I was three years old, my dad was redeployed to Japan and left us behind. Interracial marriages were illegal under US law at the time, so he couldn't take us with him.

My mum raised foster children, so I grew up with siblings of Egyptian, English, Greek, Indian, Irish, Jamaican, Malaysian, Nigerian, Welsh and Yemeni descent. Our household was a proper melting pot. My mum studied the cultures and religions of all the nations represented in her children. She learnt how to cook dishes from all the countries so everyone could feel at home in our house. Multiculturalism was a normal everyday thing for us. The problem was once we stepped out of the house, there was a whole different world out there, one that did not see all this as something normal.

I was popularly referred to as 'Gene the nigga' by the white kids in my neighbourhood. They didn't think they were being racist. This was simply how people spoke back then. I myself was well aware it was racist. Whenever you single somebody out as the other in a group, it is always an attempt to establish a hierarchy, one in which you automatically assume a superior position to that person and show everyone else you can do that.

However, the main identity marker in 1960s Liverpool was not race but religion. This was largely due to the influence of the Irish in the city. I grew up in Everton and, outside my multicultural home, the neighbourhood was virtually all Irish. Liverpool is the most Irish of English cities. Some 1.5 million Irish moved here during the potato famine of the mid-1800s, bringing with them their religious divides. All the families in our area identified as either Orange Lodge or Catholic. We were Orange Lodge, so we weren't allowed to play with the Catholic kids and vice versa. The Catholic areas had pavements painted white, orange and green like the Irish flag. The Protestant areas were painted red, white and blue like in Northern Ireland. I was Gene the nigga in little Belfast.

Liverpool's black communities bought into the religious divide. Most were on the Protestant side and had their own Orange Lodges, dominated by people who had come from West African coastal states like Ghana, Nigeria and Sierra Leone before the Second World War. These people identified as Protestant Liverpool black. They'd fly the Union Jack and all that.

But there were hardly any black people in the area where I lived. There was a Chinese guy opposite our house, though, who was very much into the whole Motown thing. He had an Afro, looked like Smokey Robinson and kind of identified black. This was not so unusual in those days. Back then, anyone who wasn't white was black. And 'white' meant white. I remember once visiting a friend in Aberdeen. When his neighbourhood buddies saw me, they said, 'Oh, we have a black guy here too. He's called Sammy.' So we all went looking for Sammy. Turned out Sammy was Spanish. But the Scottish boys considered him black too!

When I say religion was the main identity marker in 1960s Liverpool, that doesn't mean my skin colour wasn't used against me. I went to a grammar school where I was the only black kid in class. Being a grammar school, Latin was an important subject. The Latin word for 'black' is *'niger'*. I still remember when I was around eleven how my teacher would always pick me to recite all the grammatical forms of 'black' in Latin. I'd have to sit there and go *niger, nigra, nigrum, nigrarum, nigrorum, nigras*, etc. The whole class would be roaring with laughter, my teacher along with them. I had to develop a thick skin because that was just the way it was back then.

By my teenage years, I'd made friends with some of the other mixed-race boys around Liverpool whose fathers had been black American soldiers, too. Like me, they were virtually all being raised by their white mums. We tended to stick together, united by our shared situation. Those who liked to call themselves 'Liverpool black', the descendants of West Africans who'd come before the war, turned up their noses at us mixed kids as well as at the Windrush generation arriving from the West Indies then. They thought they were better than us mixed-race kids and called us 'half-breeds'. They thought they were better than the Jamaicans because they'd been in Liverpool for longer. They felt Liverpool was 'their' city while the Windrush folk were outsiders. Go figure.

It was my mum who kept me sane during those years. Despite having so many children to take care of, she would always listen carefully to whatever bad experiences I'd had and speak with me about them for a long time. She couldn't really help me much with the discrimination I was facing from black people in Liverpool, but she gave me books to read by black thinkers on race in general. She taught me about Malcolm X and the civil rights movement. She helped me understand what was going on at the time in terms of race. She got married to a Cuban man when I was five, so I did have a father-figure growing up. He was a kind man. But it was my mum who was my rock.

When I was seventeen, we moved to Toxteth, a rough inner-city area of Liverpool. In this neighbourhood, there were all sorts of people: blacks, Chinese, Irish, Welsh, Yemenis, Somalis, people from the Caribbean and probably the largest mixed-race community in England at the time. You needed allies to survive in Toxteth, on your own you were done for. My group of friends consisted of black kids, some mixed-race kids and a couple of Yemeni kids. In the neighbourhood, we had to fend off our own predators, mostly black bullies and gangsters. But leaving the neighbourhood was also dangerous. By the 1970s, race had become a big deal in Liverpool. There were skinheads all over the place. If you ventured outside your zone at the wrong moment, you'd get jumped and beaten senseless or worse. You had to watch your back all the time.

Then there was the police. Once, me and my mate Keith got stopped by the police for no good reason. We were both around eighteen. In no time, eight policemen had appeared. They beat the shit out of us and then charged us with causing grievous bodily harm. Funny thing was, a couple days later, a white mate of mine was talking to his uncle who was a policeman. This uncle was boasting about how he and his police buddies had put keys in their gloves and battered two black guys recently. My mate said, 'So you was the one that done it. That was me mate you beat up. He was from around here, you know.'

Imagine his uncle, a policeman, boasting about beating up two eighteen-year-old kids. That was how it was. For some reason, the white policemen seemed to particularly dislike us mixed-race boys. 'You dirty fucker, at least we could make the niggers work. You'z half-caste didn't used to do nothing. You'z lot think you're something special,' they'd say to me.

When I was twenty-four, I left Liverpool for college in Wrexham, northern Wales. There I delved into sociology, psychology and politics as part of my Youth and Community studies. I read Saul Alinsky's *Rules for Radicals* and Paulo Freire's *Pedagogy of the Oppressed*. By now, I'd started playing music for a living and was a drummer in a band called Keh Tuh, named after the mountain. We played a punkier roots-rock-reggae type of two-tone. I was a Malcolm brother with dreadlocks. One love and black radicalism rolled into one. Music was a beautiful escape for me. Music was pure.

Both Wrexham and Cardiff where I went on placement were generally fine. At the time, Bluetown in Cardiff, also known as Tiger Bay, was home to the only other mixed-race community anywhere near as large as the one back in Toxteth. I felt quite at home there and in Cardiff generally. The city was more integrated than Liverpool at the time. Black people in Cardiff seemed happy to be Welsh. The city was full of rugby-playing Rastas. In general, it was quite good being a Rasta in Wales back then. There were loads of hippies, and the hippies loved us Rastas, so that was cool.

There were many African students in my Wrexham college, mostly Nigerians, but also from some other African countries. The only trouble we had was with some white ex-policemen who'd returned to college to play rugby. One day, me mate, a Rasta, Jamaican parents but born in Birmingham, he comes up to me and tells me some of these rugby players put up a poster in the student union hall, saying 'Niggers out, British education for the British.'

'But they don't mean us,' me mate says, 'they mean the Nigerians.'

'Fuck that,' I said, and we gathered some brothers and went over to where these guys were. I put my reggae music loud on the boombox and told them we'd bash their heads in if they didn't take the poster down. They eventually did and apologised. That's how we had to deal with these things back then. We either stood up for ourselves or we got bullied. But I generally enjoyed Wales. You'd wake up in the morning surrounded by beautiful hills. It was great.

In 1981, I made my first long-dreamed-of trip to Africa. It was a pilgrimage seeking my ancestral black roots. I chose Morocco for the practical reason it was the easiest and cheapest place to get to at the time. The trip was a transformative experience which eventually led to me becoming a Muslim. My skin colour is the shade of most Moroccans so for the first time in my life, everyone assumed I was a native and I was the one who had to tell them I wasn't. I felt what it was like to be in the majority. To be the norm. One day, I saw a woman begging for money on the streets. I gave her something and moved on. But for some reason, as I was walking away, my heart filled up with a strong feeling I needed to go get some more money and give it to that woman. So I did.

Afterwards, this guy comes up to me and says, 'You're a good Muslim, brother.' 'I'm not a Muslim, I'm a Rasta,' I said. He asked me why I gave the woman money twice. I said I'd never seen a sister looking so destitute before. 'This is the sign of a Muslim,' he said. That really moved me.

Another time, after a conversation we had, my friend's dad said to me, 'There are people who are Muslims who don't know they are Muslims.' I knew he was referring to me. What I felt in Morocco was people judging me on my character, not on appearance. Over there, everyone was brown like me, so no one was interested in how I looked. They were interested in who I was. It's in places like that you realise you're not really like the English, that you're more like these Moroccans because you identify with them and they identify with you.

I went through an identity crisis for much of my life. I'm in my mid-sixties now, and if there's one thing I regret, it's that I wasted so many years trying to be accepted by various groups that can reject you if you're mixed race. Black people would tell me I wasn't black enough, so I spent years trying to be the black man, trying to be Malcolm X. Today, I realise that even my embrace of Islam was part of a search for belonging in some kind of wider group. So I went out of my way to try to show other Muslims how Muslim I was.

It was not until my mid-fifties that I realised what really matters in life is developing your own individual personality. People sacrifice their individuality to groups too easily. They stop being themselves and start being a stereotype, being the kind of person the group says they should be. The bravest thing to be is an individual. Many people pretend to be individuals, but they're not really. They're just doing what a particular group expects them to do in order to be accepted. Bruce Lee used to say being an artiste means being totally yourself. But to do that, you have to be totally honest with yourself as well. My search for group acceptance lasted most of my life, which is way too long. But that's how life is. You spend most of it searching for the wrong things, and by the time you realise what's truly important, you're about to die.

I don't like dealing with race issues any more. It's a lot of bullshit. A lot of fucking bullshit white people put on us that we've been carrying all these years. The way people were categorised during slavery was crazy. You had mulattos, quadroons, octoroons; if you were even down to a sixty-fourth black, you couldn't own land or marry a white woman and you could be bought and sold. But while slavery is gone, the identity problems it left continue. Like the question about who can be considered 'black'.

In today's Britain, there are some very light-skinned people who identify as black. But I often hear people who've recently come here from Africa, for instance, say things like, 'Why is that person calling himself black? He's not black. We wouldn't call him black in Africa.' This kind of talk gets me angry. I'm thinking, 'Don't you come here and tell me what black is because you have no idea. If you don't know diaspora history, just shut the fuck up because you're just adding more confusion through your lack of understanding.'

Apart from this confusion being part of the legacy of slavery, one of my saddest observations over the years is that people from Africa, especially West Africa, tend to be very tribalist in their thinking. You'll see Nigerians prejudiced against other Nigerians because they're from different ethnic groups. Sometimes, I'll be sitting around a table at a gathering with people from a West African nation and they'll start speaking to those from their ethnic group in their language, knowing perfectly well the rest of us at the table don't understand it. They are basically excluding us, saying if you don't speak our language you stay out of the conversation. That's worse othering than the kind you get from the British these days.

When I complain about this kind of behaviour to my African friends, they tell me that's the way it is over there; it's all about hierarchies and ethnic identities, about which group you belong to. I guess this is how the human species functions much of the time. I've travelled around the world a bit, from America to the Middle East. When you visit many places, you start to see repetitive patterns of behaviour.

Truth is, we will always identify with the people we feel are closest to us, who are most like us. It's easier for me to speak to a mixed-race person about being mixed race because I know that person will get what I am saying. But even though we will always identify with certain types of people more than with others, we shouldn't treat that as an excuse or reason to separate ourselves from those we identify with less. We have to overcome those differences and accept them as part of our human existence.

When we were growing up, we used to think all of us with similar skin colour needed to be living together, hanging out with each other. I know now that is nonsense. What you need is to be with like-minded intelligent people. People you can learn from and grow with. Hopefully, that group will be mixed enough so there's all kinds of people from different backgrounds, black, white, whatever. You don't want to be hanging out in all-black groups because like any group of one kind of people, they tend to develop an insular nature. The consequence of that is groupthink.

I do feel a certain paradox, though. On the one hand, I feel I've transcended cultural identity politics. But on the other hand, it was cultural identity that moulded me. It was immersing myself in the traditions of the African diaspora, black spirituality, black music, black dance and black poetry that led me to my current state of mental awareness. If I had followed the Orange Protestant tradition of my childhood neighbourhood, I would not be who I am today. I'd just be a guy who hates Catholics. It was the black thing in me that led me to be someone I'm happy to be today. There is also no doubt that the uniting black cultural identity the diaspora developed aided in our liberation from slavery and segregation.

However, I see now that other cultures have their own paths and their own truths. I became a Muslim in my search for identity. But while all religions have a mishmash of outward manifestations encouraging tribal-like conflicts, at the core of them all is the same message of love and compassion. Love is the cohesive force that binds humanity together. It took me a long time to truly internalise this. As recently as six or seven years ago, I still had a lot of anger and hate in my heart towards white society. But I am free of that now and feeling free feels great.

What I tell young people of colour today is to make full use of the opportunities they have that were absent in my day. Get out of where you were born. Travel. Learn about other places and other cultures. Don't get caught up in a ghetto mentality. When we were growing up, only the upper classes could travel. The rest of us couldn't afford it, including the white working classes. Today, almost everyone can travel. It's crazy not to take advantage of that.

On my third birthday, my father sent me a birthday card. After that, I didn't see or hear from him for forty years. Then, about twenty years ago, a Liverpool woman with a similar story to mine told me she'd traced her dad through a lady from Birmingham. I went to see this lady. Two years later, she sent me two possible addresses for my father in America. I knew immediately which one was his because his middle name was the same as my first name. Turned out my dad lived in Texas.

I got in touch with him and, after some phone conversations, finally went to see him. He welcomed me like the prodigal son. He'd been a chaplain in the air force and was very religious, so for him a key thing was to introduce me to his church members. And so here I am at this church elders' meeting in Texas. We're all sitting there in suits and ties and everyone is introducing themselves. 'Hi, I'm Darren Johnson from Indiana, I believe in Jesus Christ as my Lord and Saviour.' And me, of course, I'm a Muslim, so when it gets to my turn, I introduce myself with my Muslim name Muhammad Kamil and say I believe Jesus was a prophet and so was Mohammed. And then my dad tells them in his southern drawl, 'This is my son from England, he's a Muslim.' But it's all good, they hug me and kiss me and welcome me into their church.

During the sermon, the pastor talks about perseverance and says there's a young man in the audience who travelled thousands of miles to meet his daddy after forty years. And I stand up and speak to the church briefly. They all show me a lot of love. It was beautiful. I felt accepted. In my dad's town, I experienced something I'd never experienced before. People would stop me on the street and say, 'Hey, you must be little Eugene, I see your dad in you, I'm your cousin.' That felt great.

Things are much better today in Liverpool in terms of race, but I can't say racism has disappeared from the city's institutions. In July 2019, the Lord Mayor of Liverpool was forced to resign after it emerged he'd shared a WhatsApp video comparing a black person to a monkey. Derek Hatton, a famous local politician in the 1980s, once said, 'When the bottom fell out the slave trade, everyone scarpered down south. Only the blacks and Irish were left behind in Liverpool.' At its heart, scouse culture is a blend of black and Irish. Yet Liverpool remains in denial of the contribution of its black citizens in shaping the city's culture, a bit like Spain and its denial of Moor influence there.

The regular folk of Liverpool are cool, mostly friendly people. It's the ones at the top who are the problem, the ones running the city. They're just a bunch of rednecks. But my focus now is to be what Sufi Muslims describe as 'La Shay', meaning 'No Thing'. Nothing other than I am. Don't put anything after those words because when you do you are reducing yourself to a label.

We were both in stitches when Eugene told me the story of Sammy, the Spanish kid in Aberdeen who the Scottish boys said was their 'black' friend. Sometimes you have to see the comical side of this race madness. Under what sort of cuckoo logic does a Spanish guy become black?

I instinctively hugged Eugene tight after he saw me off to the station. I'd done the same with Rita. During our conversations, I'd felt an instant connection with both of them and I like to think they felt the same way with me. I think in both cases the mere fact I was mixed black and white was enough for them to feel sure I would understand. That I knew 'what it was like' even though I'd grown up on a different continent and in a different era. Sensing they had that feeling around me felt beautiful. It was the joy of mutual identification. That feeling when you see yourself in others and know they see themselves in you too.

I think Eugene was absolutely spot on when he said, 'we will always identify with certain types of people more than with others', but the point is not to treat that 'as an excuse or reason to separate ourselves from those we identify with less'. The problem is not in feeling a particular pull towards a particular kind of human being, but in being incapable of identifying or empathising with other kinds of human beings as well.

I don't feel I have the right to be offended if someone doesn't instinctively identify with me. Eugene rightly pointed out there is a difference between who Africans consider 'black' and who is considered black here in Britain. In Nigeria, people don't look at me and see a black person.

The Nigerian who hasn't had much contact with people of different races looks at me and sees an *oyinbo* (white person). I was, and still am, often referred to as an *oyinbo* in Nigeria. The Nigerian with a keener eye for racial subtleties looks at me and sees a mixed-race person, someone who is definitely not white, but not someone they would describe as 'black' either. Not someone they would instinctively feel is 'one of us'.

They may often come to see me that way, after a conversation, after my Nigerian accent has told them I grew up there, after they discover we have many shared experiences, after they discover my pidgin English is tiptop. The Nigerian can often come to see me as his 'brother', which is the Nigerian way of saying we are one. But it will take some interaction, it won't be instinctive. And I get that. When you are mixed race, you are contrasted with the majority population of whatever society you are in. My skin colour and features make me look like a white(ish) other to many Nigerians. For some, maybe even too much of an other for them to be able ever to truly see me as one of them. Not because they want me to feel bad or rejected, but because, like Eugene said, 'we all identify with certain kinds of people more than with others'. You cannot demand people identify with you just because you want them to or just because you identify with them. It doesn't really work that way. I don't blame any Nigerian for looking at me and not exactly seeing themselves reflected in the mirror.

Of course, not identifying with someone is one thing, hurling racist abuse at them quite another. Eugene's experiences navigating black and white in Liverpool show how mixed people of his generation faced malicious othering and discrimination from both sides of the racial divide. The white kids called him 'Gene the nigga' while the 'Liverpool blacks' called him a 'half-breed'.

While there is usually no shortage of people willing to discuss the prejudices of white Britain past and present, and rightly so, there does, however, seem to be a shortage of those willing to discuss in any depth the prejudices of black or brown Britons. But the truth is that white people do not have a monopoly on racial prejudice and discriminatory thinking. No skin colour can render you immune from the temptation to make others feel less than or to make them feel outsiders.

In the competition for who has done the most racist things to the most people in history, white people have no equals. But that does not mean black prejudices should be shrugged off as inconsequential, with arguments about black people having no power so their prejudices having no consequences. They certainly had consequences for Eugene, and for countless other Eugenes in twentieth-century Britain called 'half-breeds' and other demeaning names by both black and white people. Yet because of a desire to focus solely on what is perceived as the more important big picture of racism from the white majority, only half the pain of people such as Eugene has ever truly been acknowledged. We seem to forget that from the point of view of the individual, the small picture *is* the big picture.

Skin-colour wise, Eugene seems to have felt most at home in Morocco where, for the first time in his life, he 'felt like the majority'. Most Moroccans are brown-skinned so this time he didn't contrast at all with the majority population the way he does in Britain and Europe or would in any black African country. As he rightly pointed out, when you look like everyone else no one is interested in how you look. Things beyond our control, such as exact skin shade, play a huge role in determining where mixed-race people can blend in as one of many or where we stand out as someone decisively other-looking.

Eugene's response to his life experiences has been to embrace an individualism that is strongly averse to groupthink and not bound by any particular group affiliations. I think his advice to mixed-race people today to avoid his mistake of spending a lifetime chasing group acceptance is important. We are born as individuals and we die as individuals. We may as well live as individuals. This, of course, is not as easy to do as to write. 'The bravest thing to be is an individual,' said Eugene. Indeed. We are all so keen for a sense of belonging to a larger community that asserting our individuality is a challenge in any circumstance, mixed race or not. 'The individual has always had to struggle to keep from being overwhelmed by the tribe,' the German philosopher Friedrich Nietzsche observed.

This struggle is especially difficult if the tribe knows you are particularly keen for its approval, as we mixed-race people can often be in our complicated quest for community, belonging and identity. It is also particularly difficult to be an individual when you are mixed race because you can often feel caught between two or more worlds, each tugging strongly in the direction of their own ways of doing and seeing things.

Like Eugene, we float between various cultural universes – in his case white, black and Muslim among others – searching for that safe space where we feel comfortable and accepted. If we do find such a space around a particular group, it can seem a small sacrifice to close our eyes to this or that group wisdom with which we may strongly disagree. But a sense of belonging, like all pleasurable experiences, can be addictive. It may not be long before our belonging fix lulls us into the insular 'groupthink' Eugene warns about.

While Eugene has adopted a more individualist approach to identity in recent years, he does however acknowledge it was a collective black cultural identity that helped mould him into the individual he is happy to be today. 'It was immersing myself in the traditions of the African diaspora, black spirituality, black music, black dance and black poetry that led me to my current state of mental awareness,' he said.

Arguing for a more individualist approach to identity should not be based on simplistic caricaturist depictions of collectives as inherently stifling producers of groupthink and nothing more. They can often be that, but there is also a great beauty and wisdom in the collective fusion of individualities that make up a community. And it is ultimately only in community that we can learn from others. 'A person is a person through other persons. I am human because I belong, I participate and I share,' is how Desmond Tutu, the legendary anti-apartheid activist cleric, summed up the southern African Ubuntu philosophy that drives his thinking.

It is usually in community that we experience our humanity most profoundly and it is certainly only in community that we can learn from others. Most importantly, it is only in community that we can ultimately survive as individuals, a lesson the terrible but eye-opening experience of Covid-19 has relentlessly driven home.

I think what is important is for us to maintain an individual core that does not wither under the stern gaze of group opinion, but always retains that essence of who we know we truly want to be.

Eugene complained about West Africans acting 'tribalistic' here in Britain. On the one hand, I completely agree with him that carrying on a conversation with a select few in a language you know half the table won't understand is an unpleasant form of othering. Language is powerful because it can include as well as exclude, evoke commonality or draw boundaries. In Eugene's experience with some West Africans, the latter was the case. While he rightly pointed out slavery had caused an 'identity confusion' among black people, it is also worth remembering that it is only because of slavery that 'black people' exist in the first place. Slavery created blackness.

The Africans transported to America, Britain and other parts of the western hemisphere as slaves arrived as members of diverse collectives who spoke different languages, believed in different things, had different customs and considered themselves very different from each other. Slavery turned them all into 'black people'. Since race organised everyday life in these societies, their blackness overwhelmed all the diverse identities the enslaved Africans had brought with them. Cultural genocide by redefinition.

Blackness has really only ever existed where there have been many white people, and black unity where there has been systematic white oppression. This is why Africa has been a massively polarised continent ever since the uniting enemy – European colonialists – left thousands of previously autonomous communities forced together into a few dozen 'nation-states'. I think some black and mixed-black Britons such as Eugene often have rather unrealistic expectations of the Africans who come here, believing that they see themselves simply as 'black people' and feel a sense of camaraderie with anyone who identifies as black here in Britain. It doesn't really work that way. People who come here from Africa come with their own distinct ethnic identities, languages and cultures, and don't see themselves as simply 'black people'. It is only in the eyes of others that they are seen that way.

## Chapter 3

# There is a pecking order everywhere

Justin (not his real name) works in London's financial City where he is quite well known, hence his preference for telling his story anonymously. He was born to a Nigerian father and white English mother in 1961. Unlike Rita and Eugene, Justin grew up with both his biological parents.

My father came to Britain in 1958 after touring Europe for a few months where he visited France, Germany, Holland and the Nordic countries. He had a guardian who was sponsoring his education at the time. It was this guardian who suggested (and paid for) my dad's travels because he wanted him to experience different cultures. When I think of a black man travelling across Europe on his own in the 1950s, I am struck by how brave and adventurous my father was. He eventually made his way to Britain where he intended to become a barrister.

He met my mum at a party in London in 1959. They started a relationship and I was born in 1961. Unfortunately, in the meantime, my dad's guardian passed away. This meant there was no one to finance his law studies, take him on for barrister pupillage or anything of the sort. Now a father and a husband, he had to ditch his dreams and look for a job to support his family.

This was 1960s England – the days of 'No Irish, no blacks, no dogs' – so finding work was a challenge for an African man. We stayed with my grand-mum in Surrey while my dad tried to find work and save up enough money so we could move into our own place. A white girl in a relationship with a black man was rare in those days. A white middle-class girl from the Home Counties married to a black man was extremely rare. Back then, people in the Home Counties only saw black people on TV, so my dad walking the streets of Surrey was a big novelty. I wouldn't say my mum was ostracised by her family for marrying my dad, but they certainly weren't thrilled with the relationship.

We lived in Surrey till I was about three. When I look at photos from my kindergarten, I was, unsurprisingly, the only child of colour in the class. But I have no memories from that period. My dad eventually got a semi-administrative job in the NHS and once he'd saved up enough money, we moved to north London. Most of my childhood was spent in Finsbury Park. Back then, the area was predominantly white working-class English, Irish, West Indian, Greek and Turkish. There were not many Africans. My dad was a minority within a minority, as was I, being mixed race.

Most people in the area worked for the rail, the Underground, the bus service or the NHS. It was a racial melting pot and we all generally got along. We shared the experience of economic struggle whatever skin colour we were. Our family lived in a Victorian house with six other families. They say you pay a price for everything in life. The price my mum paid for marrying my dad was giving up her comfortable English middle-class existence to live how the working classes lived. Money was a constant problem for us. But my mum really loved my dad, so as a child I never once got the impression she had regretted her decision, something I know sometimes happened in interracial marriages back then. The good side of the experience of growing up with lack was it provided me and my younger sister a great sense of value and a habit of never taking anything for granted.

What was really important was that we were a functioning family. Nowadays, there's so many kids from broken homes growing up without father-figures. Ours was a tight family unit with my father as our clear leader. He was the biggest influence in my life growing up. My dad didn't like his job or earn the kind of money a man of his intellectual capabilities should have been earning. But he did it without complaining.

He believed very much in personal responsibility and abandoned his dreams to make sure me and my younger sister had better opportunities than he did. 'You've got a roof over your head. You've got food on the table. You've got clothes on your back. All you have to do is study hard, that's your way out,' he'd tell me. My dad was from the Igbo ethnic group in Nigeria. The Igbos are famous across Africa for being particularly hard-working, aspirational and self-sufficient. My dad was stereotypically Igbo in this sense and made sure to imbue these values in me.

I enjoyed my inner-city urban primary school in Finsbury Park. There were perhaps three hundred to three hundred and fifty kids there. The only grief I got being mixed race was from some Caribbean girls in school who took it upon themselves to regularly call me all sorts of nasty names. Most often they'd call me a 'half-breed'. At the time, 'half-caste' was a pretty common term, but even back then, everyone knew 'half-breed' was a terrible thing to call someone. But they'd just go on and on at me. The worst thing was that they were girls.

Growing up in Finsbury Park those days, you learned to be rugged pretty early. When us boys had issues with each other, we settled them with our fists. I would say a more defining factor of my childhood than my skin colour was the fact I was always quite physically strong and good at fighting. None of the Caribbean boys in my school would have tried calling me a 'half-breed' because they'd know they'd get stomped.

But we had a code back then which involved never touching girls. So I couldn't do anything about those girls calling me names, I just had to take it. That was very difficult for me, and it was the major racial issue I remember having in primary school. I don't know whether those Caribbean girls had a chip on their shoulder because of the history of the places they came from, but whatever was the case, it was very annoying to have to listen to them calling me a 'half-breed'.

Anyway, back then, there was this eleven-plus exam, which you did in your last year of primary school, that was supposed to sift out kids with academic capabilities from the rest. If you did very well, you could theoretically get into a grammar school. However, despite the fact I did well in the test, I was screened out and sent to Holloway Comprehensive, which was an all-boys school near Holloway Prison. Those days you could get screened out based on postcode or race, so perhaps those worked against me, I don't know. This was 1972.

Holloway had been a grammar school in the past and so there were still some vestiges of discipline there plus a few good teachers. But generally speaking, it was a very rough place. Imagine roughly 1200 boys from different areas of London thrown in together into one school. The first six months were all about establishing a pecking order. It was very Darwinian, all about survival and your place in the pecking order. In those first six months, you had to set a lot of boundaries because the other boys would look to see how far they could push you. I got into quite a few scrapes, but after a while people recognise you for what you are, and you find your own friendship groups.

The pecking order was not determined by race, but other factors. Sport was very important, football especially. If you couldn't play football, you were marginalised. It was important to be generally popular and respected. You had to know how to banter and how to berate others effectively. The last thing you wanted was to be the kid always getting laughed at. If you were small, meek or in any way weak, you were picked on and marginalised. It was really all very rough and tumble.

But truth is, go to Eton, Harrow, Wellington, Marlborough or any of those other fancy schools and there'll be pecking orders there, too. There'll be kids who get bullied and there'll be kids who bully. There'll be kids who make people laugh and there'll be kids who get laughed at. There'll be kids in between. There is a pecking order everywhere you go. The only difference between us and the kids in those schools was that they had money and we didn't. They travelled and experienced different cultures, but we were stuck in our own small world, which was the only one we knew. But I learnt a lot of valuable lessons from Holloway that help me navigate the world of finance I now function in, a world not that different from a jungle either. Here too, you need to be able to assess people in an instant, size them up and sense what they are capable of.

I made some lifelong friends in Holloway. Back then, none of us kids did drugs or even smoked. Sport was what we did in our free time. I didn't drink alcohol until I was twenty-two. Don't get me wrong, I had friends who went on wayward paths, friends who died young. But within the school premises itself, there was a semblance of discipline we all respected.

Outside the school, racism was definitely manifesting itself. You had the British National Party, you had the National Front and various other groups espousing racist views all over the place. But in school, we all got along when it came to race. Sure, if a white kid was fighting a black kid, he might call him a 'black cunt' as they were exchanging blows, but it was all one-on-one stuff in the heat of the moment. The school was roughly 60 per cent white kids and

40 per cent black kids so there was no chance of any kind of racial domination. There were a few Asian kids as well. Another thing that helped race relations then was that you didn't have large influxes of ethnic minority kids who couldn't speak English. Everyone spoke English and we all spoke it similarly because we were all from similar London working-class backgrounds. That brought a commonality that doesn't exist in many British schools today.

When we fractured into friendship groups, it wasn't along racial lines. One of my best friends from back then – who is my son's godfather today – is Italian. I had Greek friends, Cypriot friends, Asian friends, white English friends and black friends. The racism in the outside world didn't cause a racial divide in our school. I don't know whether it was because we were all working-class kids or because black and white were evenly matched in terms of numbers, but that racial divide wasn't there.

I don't recall ever going through an identity crisis. Sometimes kids would say things like, 'But Justin, you're mixed. You're not black, you're not white, you're not one or the other.' To this, I'd usually respond that if the National Front were to get their way and black people were being repatriated back to Africa, they wouldn't say, 'Justin, you're mixed, so you can stay.' I'd be on a plane back to Nigeria in no time. Whether I was mixed race or not, I was a person with visible African ancestry. So I was in the same boat as those who had two black parents and that basically determined how I thought of myself.

Mixed-race kids today often talk about having problems knowing where they fit in, wondering whether they should hang around black people or white people. I say hang out with people who care for you, people who love you and respect you. Like I said, growing up, I had friends of all races. Paradoxically, it seems back then mixed-race boys and black boys were better at moving between different groups than they are today. Nowadays, young black males especially seem to have problems moving fluidly between groups the way my black friends used to. They only feel comfortable around black people. There's more diversity now, but also more segregation.

There are too many young black men from broken homes today. They have no role models, no one to teach them how to move easily between groups. These are vital skills you need to succeed in life. It is only by interacting with various types of people that you can get to where the opportunities are. You won't learn about opportunities hanging around with the kids from your neighbourhood, especially if you're from the kind of deprived neighbourhood I was from. You have to move around, you have to mix.

The worst thing about my Holloway secondary school was that it was not there to make the best of us, but to get us through the system and into a trade. When we were halfway through our fourth year, we started getting advice about the kind of trade we could go into. We were told we should think about whether we wanted to become carpenters, mechanics or builders because other ambitions were not 'practical'.

There's nothing wrong with those jobs, but this was not what my father intended for me. When I told him these were the options we were being presented with, he went ballistic. Like a typical Nigerian father, he went to the school and had it out with the teachers. Told them this was not what he expected his son to be hearing. Growing up, I definitely had a driver behind me. Someone who always made sure I was moving forward.

My father was a man who never reached his potential in life. But he lived vicariously through me and my sister, doing everything to make sure he gave us the direction and tools to be able create a better life for ourselves. One of my greatest regrets is that he didn't live to see me graduate from university (I went to what was a polytechnic back then) because he died in 1984, when I was twenty-three. I did business studies, which was how I started my journey in finance.

THERE IS A PECKING ORDER EVERYWHERE

When you are brought up without money, it becomes your norm until you are taken out of your world and see how other people live. It was only when we'd go to the Home Counties to visit my mum's family that we experienced a different world. But despite our financial situation, I'd say I had a happy childhood. I didn't face any direct racism as a young boy. I think this was largely due to my physical presence and fighting skills.

The other boys knew I could hold my own and be aggressive when I needed to be. We didn't have the gang culture kids have today. People hung out with particular groups of friends, but when it came to settling our differences, we did it one-on-one with fists, no knives or other weapons.

Before you decided to call anyone a name that might upset them, you knew you had to be ready for a fight. If the white kids around me had any prejudices against black or mixed-race people, they didn't share them with me. In my environment, your skin colour was less important than whether you could handle yourself. The white boys who couldn't fight were bullied as mercilessly as the black boys who couldn't.

One clear memory I do have of race was to do with my father and emigration. In the early 1970s, lots of English people started emigrating to various parts of the world, Australia being a particularly popular destination. When I first heard the word 'emigration', I asked my mum what that meant. I was ten or so at the time. 'It's when people leave their country to go work somewhere else in the world,' she replied. 'Like to Australia?' I asked. She said yes. 'Why do they move? Are the jobs better there or what?' I asked. She said yes. 'Then why doesn't Daddy take us all to Australia?' I asked. 'No, they wouldn't allow your daddy to come work there,' she said. I asked why not. 'Because he's a black man and they don't allow black people to come work there,' my mum replied.

I struggled to wrap my head round this. 'But there are aborigines there, aren't there? Why wouldn't they allow Dad to come work?' I wondered. 'Yes, there are aborigines there, but that's the Australian government's policy,' my mum concluded. Everybody talks about apartheid South Africa today, but many seem to have forgotten what kind of racist immigration policies Australia used to have back then, their own form of apartheid.

'A family that eats together stays together,' my dad used to say. On weekends, we'd always have dinner together. My mum would make a curry or something and my dad would tell stories about the colonial era in Nigeria or about the Nigerian civil war. Despite living in what is now considered a very racist era in British history, my father never focused on racism in our family discussions.

Don't get me wrong, he told me and my sister we should be ready to come across people who would try to pull the rug out from under us. But he always emphasised we shouldn't take it personally or focus on those people. Rather, we should focus on becoming excellent at whatever we did. He encouraged us to be better at sports, better in school and more articulate than other kids.

My dad did more than tell me I *should* be better. When I was a young boy, he'd say to me that I was like no other child, that I was better. 'What do you mean better?' I'd ask him. 'You're just better,' he'd say. 'Better how?' I'd press. 'In every aspect, you are just better, always remember that,' he'd say. There was a bit of Nigerian arrogance in that, but when times were tough at the beginning of my career in finance and people weren't treating me the way they should, I drew on those words to get through those times. I definitely had an arrogance about me and I'm happy I had it. I don't think I would be where I am now if I hadn't had it.

One bad thing I've noticed in my professional life connected to race these days is that whenever a mixed-race or even a black person starts progressing significantly in their field, especially in the corporate world, he or she is often labelled a 'coconut' by some other people of colour. This is childish. The reality is that in every profession, there are certain rules and ways of doing things. Whether you're a barrister, an accountant or a hedge-fund manager, your professional world will have certain rules.

The fact some people of colour – way too few, unfortunately – have learnt how to navigate the professional world doesn't mean they are coconuts. What it means is they have realised that if you want to progress in life, if you want to get a good job, earn reasonable money and do things for your family, it will require certain things from you.

For one, it requires you to have the ability to move easily between different worlds and different kinds of people. It's not about changing yourself, it's about getting ahead. The problem in the corporate world is that there are so few black people in positions of responsibility the young ones don't have many role models to follow. So the few that have made it can easily be labelled with derogatory terms like 'coconut'. That's why, where I work, I always try to make sure there is a black professionals network, so the younger ones can learn from those who have made it what exactly it takes.

Things have changed in Britain since I went to school in the 1970s, but I still think the education system is unfair and most schools are not preparing young black people to navigate the professional world at higher levels. There are lots of diversity and inclusion programmes at the moment and they're good, but they're not hitting the mark yet. The gang culture popular among some young black males isn't helping either, nor are absurd ideas about being too bookish somehow not being black.

I'm almost sixty now so it's hard for me to tell young black boys that I know what they're going through at the moment. I don't have all the answers. But I have come from a difficult background, I have faced a lot of challenges and I have somehow overcome them. My dad always told me you have to differentiate yourself. People like us get one crack at most. There are no second chances, no nepotism for us. No one to open the door and say, 'Oh, you're Johnny's son, aren't you? Come work here. I know you. You're like me.' We haven't got the 'people like us' factor going for us yet because there are too few of us in high places.

This is changing, slowly. In the finance world, there is a smattering of black people in good positions. It's not unusual these days to walk into a hedge fund and see a black person working there, typically someone of West African heritage, most often of Nigerian heritage specifically. Things are changing, but it's happening too slowly.

However, we must play our own part too. We can't be walking round with chips on our shoulders. We have to be asking ourselves questions. Have we got the skills? Are we making sure we are presenting them in the best way possible? Are we making sure we are looking out for all the opportunities out there? If it's not happening for you in company X or Y, then make the change, do something about it. It's like back in school: there is a pecking order and you need to make sure you do everything to go up that pecking order. Use all the legitimate skills you have and if you need a bit of aggression, cunning and guile to move up the order, you use those too. No one is going to give it to you: you have to take it.

I found Justin's story particularly intriguing because he is not the typical personality type you come across in stories about race and identity. We usually hear about these issues from those who have found it particularly challenging dealing with them, people of an often more sensitive and self-conscious nature. It is not every day we hear how an alpha male has navigated identity. Powerfully built and clearly very fit at fifty-eight, with a penetrating gaze I felt could see right into my soul, I wouldn't like to be stuck in a room with Justin if there was just one piece of bread between us.

Justin started out negotiating his place with his fists, but now does it with his wits. Even though he grew up in an era when racist movements such as the National Front were at the height of their popularity, he never seems to have doubted his ability to find a worthy place for himself in Britain. His father's hand was clearly at work in this aspect, infecting him with the Nigerian sense of exceptionalism I mentioned earlier. Justin himself even described it as an 'arrogance'. However you name it, it shielded him from the weakening forces of self-doubt that have consumed many an ethnic minority in Britain and the West, and continue to do so today. His physical prowess spared him the experience of racial humiliation, at least from his male peers. I believed him when he said he never experienced an identity crisis. Some people seem to go through life virtually untouchable. The rest of us can only envy them.

Although some people suggested to Justin he was neither black nor white, 'not one or the other', the ubiquitous presence of send-them-back movements such as the National Front fostered in him a feeling he was in the 'same boat' as black people. This was a strong perception among all the mixed black and white people I spoke to who grew up during that era.

They identified black based on a shared fate of discrimination. Even a strong-willed individual such as Justin did not have much of a realistic choice in how he could identify considering the circumstances around him. Sometimes we develop our identity in a certain direction on purpose, but sometimes our environment takes charge.

Aside the individual qualities that helped him cope rather well with his situation, racial demographics played a role, too. Unlike in the cases of Rita and Eugene, white kids did not have the numbers to dominate Justin's immediate environment. His secondary school was 60:40 in terms of white–black ratio while his Finsbury Park neighbourhood was multiracial.

When no group has the numbers to dominate an environment, power falls into the hands of dominant individuals irrespective of their group connections. If Justin's all-male school had been, say, 90 per cent white, it would have been a very different story. But with the gap in numbers between black and white being so small, individuals had to fend for themselves, allowing him to thrive thanks to his physical strength and forceful personality.

When he spoke about the 'pecking order' in his Holloway school, it reminded me of my secondary-school years in Nigeria. We may not like to hear things such as this because they offend our equalitarian sensibilities, but Justin was absolutely right when he said, 'There is a pecking order everywhere.' In line with our instinctive need for hierarchies, the only things that vary from environment to environment are the criteria determining who is positioned where.

In my middle-class Lagos secondary school, just like in Holloway, how adept you were with your fists and mouth were definitely important in determining your place in the (male) pecking order. But more important than that was how much money your parents had. In a country where 70 per cent of the population is poor, money is the main thing on the mind of most Nigerians most of the time.

The majority are wondering how to survive, the rest how to make sure they never become poor, always possible in a country with no social security system. Most Nigerian behaviour is driven by economic calculations. Growing up in Lagos, I learnt very quickly that my assigned spot in the economic hierarchy determined whether I would be treated deferentially, dismissively or somewhere in between. It's nothing personal, just the way a society conditioned by scarcity works.

In my case, my mixed-race features conjured up associations with whiteness in the minds of Nigerians. Everyone knows white people are rich, so the default instinct was to treat me well based on that association. In reality, my family was in the very middle of the economic range, by no means rich and not even upper-middle class, which is the minimum most Nigerians would expect from anyone associated with the wealthy world of whiteness. This general overestimation of my economic status meant I had to engage in significant verbal acrobatics to keep people believing we had more than we actually did. Putting it simply, I lied we had stuff we didn't and grossly exaggerated how well my dad's small architectural firm was doing.

In an honour culture where your value is not derived automatically from your status as a human being, but from the esteem in which others hold you, the last thing you want to do is disappoint people's expectations. In honour cultures, esteem is subject to constant review. If my family had become poor overnight, my light skin would not have saved me from the contempt Nigeria's middle and upper classes show the country's poor. In Nigeria, race only matters in the context of class.

Speaking of class, I was intrigued by Justin's fond memories of a multiracial class solidarity back in his day, one where 'Everyone spoke English and we all spoke it similarly because we were from similar London working-class backgrounds.' He said that with a nostalgia I found telling. People seek sameness in all sorts of spheres, including accent. In our focus on skin colour, the power of accents in creating a sense of sameness or difference is vastly underestimated. Accent differentiates me from Britons of my skin shade. They think I'm them until I open my mouth. After that, I sometimes sense a distance like they're not sure what to make of me, because while I look like them they know I haven't lived like them. I'm from a there, not here.

I also found interesting Justin's comments about there being more diversity in Britain now, but also more 'segregation'. Again, I think this boils down to numbers. If I lived in London today, I could, if I wanted, inhabit a more or less Nigerian world cut off from significant contact with wider society. I'd live in Peckham where I'd be surrounded by Nigerians. I'd cut my hair in Nigerian barber shops, eat in Nigerian restaurants, go to Nigerian churches and party at Nigerian weddings. If I worked from home or ran a business in the area, I wouldn't even have to leave Peckham often.

I know Nigerians who live this way here, de facto separated from the rest of society. I also know Poles in Britain who rarely venture outside Polish circles. It's not a racial thing, it's an immigrant thing. Putting it simply, people often feel most comfortable among their own, especially in a foreign land.

This kind of lifestyle was not really feasible for ethnic minorities when Justin was growing up because there were far fewer of us here than there are now. You had to mix with others just to go about your daily life. Today, you don't. That is one of the paradoxes of globalisation. We now live among each other but not necessarily with each other. Whichever way you look at it, I agree with Justin that only feeling comfortable around your own is a serious limitation in terms of what you can achieve in a society. A limitation from which mixed-race people are usually free. Not really having our own fixed tribe, we are often instinctive minglers.

In Justin's case, this has definitely helped him in his impressive career. That a mixed-race working-class boy born in 1961 who never went to any posh schools could succeed in the exclusivist world of London's City speaks for itself. We often talk about race as if people are prisoners of their skin colour, predetermined to react in the same way to the same circumstances. In real life, some people thrive in environments in which others like them struggle.

Of course, not everyone gets to be a confident alpha male, and I don't think we should judge a society by how the strongest cope in it. But I think it is important to acknowledge the role of personal psychology in how people deal with issues of race, identity and belonging. We shouldn't pretend individual personality doesn't make a difference and that all that matters are the wider structures of society, the so-called 'system'. The internal can be every bit as important as the external. I say this as someone who has struggled more often than thrived while trying to navigate my own way in this world. I realise today, however, that my story was never predetermined, but shaped as much by what was going on inside my head as what was going on outside it.

## Chapter 4

# We can't bring an English girl to Mugabe's birthday party

Sophia's late father was Zimbabwean while her mother is mixed English-German. She grew up in Crouch Hill, north London, not far from where Justin spent his childhood, except she was born two decades later, in 1982. Sophia is an actress and a teacher.

My German grandmother fled her Nazi-sympathising family after the Second World War, eventually marrying an English man and settling down in Britain. She was involved in civil rights activism and socialist politics, which was how she met my father, who was also a socialist activist. They became good friends and it was my nan who introduced my dad to my mum, her daughter. They became romantically involved and had me and my brother, who was born two years later than me.

However, my parents split up when I was around three so I grew up with my mum in Crouch Hill. My dad lived just five minutes away from us, though, and I saw him on most weekends. Sometimes, he'd come over for dinner. He remained very good friends with my nan and, growing up, it felt like I had a family. But since we were ultimately raised by my mum, there was nothing in the way of Zimbabwean culture in our home.

We knew we were from Zimbabwe through our dad, but we didn't know anything about the country. My dad himself was more interested in politics than culture, so he never talked to us about everyday life in Zimbabwe or how things were done there when he was around. Growing up, we definitely didn't feel Zimbabwean. We felt black.

While I didn't know much about Zimbabwe, I wasn't like some of the other mixed-race kids who didn't know anything about black culture in general. When Nelson Mandela was freed in 1990, I remember us going to marches and rallies in London. I knew black history. I knew what was happening in South Africa. I was raised to be very aware of my blackness and of racism from a young age.

My mum told us we were 'black kids' and would have to work twice as hard as white kids. She said people would be racist to us. This was the 1980s when the National Front and other racist groups were still very active. I was aware I was mixed race, but I felt black. When I was around five, I did go through a phase where I wanted to be white. I wanted to have white hair and wondered why I didn't have white skin. But my mum nipped that in the bud early on and quickly talked me out of it.

I went to a primary school near Finsbury Park with mostly white working-class kids. I don't recall any issues with race there. Secondary school was a different experience, though. The catchment area for my school was quite wide so while there were white middle-class kids from Crouch End, there were also many black kids from Tottenham. Most of the school friends I ended up with were black and seemed to have been raised very differently from me. They all thought I was spoilt, and said it was because I had a white mum who didn't beat me.

They also let me know that they saw my situation as different from theirs. When I once mentioned my mum told me I'd have to work twice as hard, one of them laughed and said, 'If you have to work twice as hard, that means I have to work three times as hard.' This forced me to start thinking about colourism and light-skin privilege, which I couldn't really comprehend at that age.

I felt quite a bit of bitchiness towards me from some of the black girls in school. I don't want to say it was jealousy but there was something there. One time, a group of black girls surrounded me in a club and threatened to put a lighter to my hair. 'You think you got nice hair, yeah? We gonna burn it,' they said. I was really scared. Another time, someone came up to me at a party and said there were some girls outside who wanted to speak to me. Quite naive at the time, I was about to go out, but a guy stopped me, 'Where you going? Don't you know those girls want to beat you up?' he said. 'Why would they want to beat me up?' I asked. 'Because they just don't like you,' he replied.

These incidents really shook me, especially as someone who'd been brought up being told I was black. On my way back home the day those girls had wanted to beat me up, I was so stressed I had an asthma attack. When I got home, I cried and told my mum what had happened. She narrated a story about going to a party in the 1970s where she was the only white girl, and how she'd danced with a black guy whose black girlfriend had wanted to beat her up as well. *This has nothing to do with my story. I wasn't dancing with anyone's boyfriend and I wasn't a white girl in a black party*, I remember thinking.

My mum was trying her best, but it was at moments like this I realised she'd never really be able to prepare me for the experiences I would have. She could theorise about race and tell me I would face racism as a black person, but now it turned out that I wasn't black, I was mixed race. Her expectations of what I would face applied to black people, not to mixed-race teenagers. She couldn't prepare me for that.

I understand the negative feelings those black girls had towards me. When you are brought up to believe you are not beautiful or desirable, anger and resentment can easily follow. And it's not just how white men view them, the way dark-skinned women are often treated by black men is pretty terrible too, so I get their anger. Women with light-skinned privilege need to have empathy for dark-skinned women being treated worse. However, while I understood their feelings, I couldn't really think of how I could change the situation, and the hostility I felt from some of them was really hard for me to take.

I responded by immersing myself even deeper in black culture. I got into Malcolm X. I started learning about the Nation of Islam and Black Panthers. I was really into black culture, especially black American culture, as a teenager. I made a conscious effort to identify with my black roots. I wouldn't say I ever wished I was fully black, though. I was aware there was a value in being mixed race. I did get a lot of male attention and to be honest I enjoyed my pretty privilege. I wouldn't have traded that. I know this all sounds contradictory, but I'm just trying to be real. I grew to like being mixed race.

My mum wasn't the only white person who raised me. My nan was always around, and my aunt lived with us for ages. They both helped look after me and my brother when we were little. Our cousins would come over too. My mum's family were mainly from Chesterfield, but my grandparents had a cottage in Cornwall where we went on holidays. I felt comfortable around my white family. But in Cornwall itself, which is very white, me and my brother did not usually feel that comfortable. We knew we didn't quite fit in there.

We were very much London kids. We felt comfortable in London, we liked our music and our culture. We were always reluctant to go to Cornwall because we didn't like the thought of being in that virtually all-white environment. But we'd always go eventually, and we'd always end up having a good time. When I was around thirteen, we met some other mixed-race kids from London, and they said they were moving to Cornwall. I remember thinking, *What? Moving here?* I've often wondered how those kids' lives turned out in Cornwall.

My first visit to Zimbabwe was in the early 1990s. But I was around nine at the time and don't really have strong memories from that trip. I just remember meeting lots of my dad's family and generally having a great time. However, I went back to Zimbabwe in 2015 and, this time, everything was different. Many of my dad's family members who we'd met when we came in the early 1990s had died of AIDS.

I went to Zimbabwe because my dad had had a stroke and was very ill. It happened while he'd returned to attend his mum's funeral. Meanwhile, there was a fire and his personal documents were all lost. Even though he'd lived in Britain since the 1970s and worked as a teacher, the Home Office did not acknowledge my dad was British and said the onus of proof was on him.

I went to Zimbabwe to try to sort things out because he was in really bad shape and needed to get here for medical treatment. 'I am British now, I just want to come home,' he told me. He was yearning for London. It was really sad. Jeremy Corbyn was our MP and he was amazing in trying to help get my dad back here. But it didn't work out. My dad wasn't able to return from Zimbabwe.

During the period I was there, I spent a lot of time with my Zimbabwean family and started coming to some realisations about how different I was from them. They were very religious, I was not. I believed in feminism, they did not. The patriarchy there was very overt. Also, Zimbabweans viewed me differently from how I viewed myself. I once went with a cousin to pick up my nephew from school. When the kids saw me, they started running out of the classrooms to come and see me they were so fascinated. They wanted to touch my hair, they wanted to hear me speak. I said, 'Hello, how are you?' They started mimicking my accent, repeating what I said. 'Hello, how are you? Hello, how are you?' As we walked back home, there was a trail of kids following us. I'd never felt so white in my life.

One day I was told it was President Mugabe's birthday and a big party was being organised for him. One of my uncles worked for the government, so my family had some invitations. I wasn't particularly keen to go as I wasn't a Mugabe fan. But I said, 'Fine, let's go to the party.' We were told to buy new clothes, dress nice and all that. So, I got all dressed up and we went to my cousin's place from where we were meant to leave for the party. When my cousin saw me, he said, 'What? Are you all crazy? We can't bring an English girl to Mugabe's birthday party.' I was like, 'Wow, I grew up around black activism. I was immersed in the anti-apartheid movement as a child, but here I'm told I'm an English girl, not one of us Africans.'

In Britain, I am mainly a black woman. I've always felt black because that is how white people have treated me. But in Zimbabwe, even my family saw me as 'white'. It's weird when you grow up thinking of yourself as black only for people in Africa to see you as white. As not one of them. It's difficult to reconcile this in your head.

Here in Britain, I feel like the other, but it's a kind of other I'm used to being. It's become so normal for me I know how to navigate that otherness, I know how to articulate it. That's what black Britishness is all about. But I didn't know how to navigate the kind of otherness I was associated with in Zimbabwe. It felt uncomfortable and unfamiliar. I didn't know how to deal with it. It's a good thing that trip didn't happen when I was in my teenage years, at the height of my Malcolm X fascination. I think it would have really confused and upset me then. Luckily, I was in my thirties and had a more rounded view of who I was.

Truth is, I did feel incredibly British in Zimbabwe. I felt alien there. People expected things I wasn't used to people expecting from me. They thought I had a lot of money and were constantly asking me to buy things for them. They wanted to know how much I earned. Obviously, I knew my life was much easier than theirs, so I did buy some stuff. But I was never sure how much I should be doing and whether I was being taken advantage of or not. Or whether I wasn't doing enough. I just wasn't sure.

Also, I remember thinking, 'There's an AIDS crisis here. People are dying every day from the disease, but there doesn't seem to be any major health campaign going on, no sense of urgency.' I mentioned this to my cousin. 'People don't talk about these things here,' she told me. *Well, they should*, I thought to myself. But I felt a hostility anytime I tried to raise the issue. One of my aunties once said to me, 'People say we have AIDS here. You have it there too, but you people just call it cancer.'

*Oh my God, this is a forty-year-old woman, who is supposed to be educated, exhibiting this level of ignorance. This is so sad, so awful*, I thought to myself. But I was coming at the AIDS issue with my English brain, and since I wasn't getting a friendly response, I started keeping my thoughts to myself.

I saw a lot of poverty in Zimbabwe, the kind I'd never seen before. Kids walking for miles to school with no shoes on. Abandoned children left on the streets to fend for themselves. When I arrived back in London, I felt an overwhelming sense of relief from the moment we landed at the airport. I'd never returned from a holiday happy to be back to Britain, but this time I was. I remember looking at people's clothes in the airport and thinking about all the stuff we just take for granted here.

For the first time in my life, I felt lucky I was born in Britain even though I was raised by a single mum who didn't have much money. Of course, I was very disappointed I hadn't been able to come back with my dad, who passed away a few years later. I feel like this country failed my father. It's these kinds of experiences that make me feel incredibly conflicted about Britain. I don't feel like it embraces people like me and my father. On the other hand, this is my home, my city, my country. And especially after what I saw in

Zimbabwe, I do feel incredibly fortunate to live in a place with social protection and proper infrastructure.

What the Zimbabwe trip taught me about mixed-race identity was that you can't let other people define who you are because, if you do, you'll never fit in anywhere. It will always be others deciding your identity. You have to take ownership of it. In Zimbabwe, I was made aware I was not considered a black woman there. But that doesn't make me white either. You've got to have a strong sense of who you are, take the bits you value from both your heritages and enhance, develop and nurture those particular bits in your life.

Personally, while I feel mixed race, I know I often slip into referring to myself as a 'black' woman. I realise this comes from feeling that is how the white majority defines me. But I feel comfortable referring to myself as 'black' and will never repel that label because there is already too much self-hate among black people. White society has tried to make us hate our blackness, hate our features.

I want to fight against that self-hate, but at the same time I realise I am claiming blackness because society has viewed me as black even though I am as much black as white. This is the contradiction of being mixed race in Britain. Every mixed-race individual has to find their own way of navigating that contradiction.

You also have to find the strength to defy expectations. When I was in secondary school, we'd have these special days where everyone was supposed to bring food that reflected their culture. I knew nothing about Zimbabwean food. My mum made the stuff other British mums make, so I decided I'd take crisps. 'You can't bring crisps, you need to bring something Zimbabwean,' a friend told me.

I remember feeling very irritated by that. I understand why some mixed-race people get annoyed when people assume they must identify with a particular race or culture based on their appearance.

One major lesson I learnt from my Zimbabwean experience was how others can see you very differently from how you see yourself. In this case, it was people seeing me as white when I felt (mostly) black. However, I can imagine it being a problem the other way around: society seeing a mixed-race person as black when they feel white, perhaps because they grew up in an all-white environment.

Ultimately, mixed-raceness is interesting because it can be such a rich experience. I like having a strong insight into my mother's white world while simultaneously knowing a different personal experience. My grandmother's life story, how she came here from Germany – that whole side of my life is incredibly interesting. I wouldn't like not to have that. I like the fact I got to experience my African heritage, however uncomfortable an experience that was.

I have black friends who are incredibly uncomfortable in white spaces. I'm not. I can operate fine in both black and white spaces. This is definitely helpful. As mixed-race people, we can choose bits of our identity rather than be one or the other. We can choose what feels right. But we have to be active in developing our identities, otherwise society will do it for us.

As mixed-race women, we also have to guard against others wanting to decide who it is proper for us to date. Apart from often treating dark-skinned girls badly, many black men still hold very conservative and misogynistic views. They date white girls but get upset when mixed-race girls date white guys. That's all about men wanting to own women.

I was in a play recently called *#Hashtag Lightie*. I played a mixed-race woman engaged to a black guy while her sister was in a relationship with a white guy. It explored the nonsensical idea that when you choose a partner, you choose a racial side. That is complete rubbish. Mixed-race women should be able date whoever they want. Personally, I've only really dated black guys because I feel closer to my black identity.

There was a time I tried dating white guys because I was frustrated black men didn't seem to get the fact women of colour were facing the double oppression of racism and misogynism. Problem was the white guys couldn't get me. Race is a big part of my identity, but it wasn't a big part of theirs. So that didn't work out and I went back to dating black men. I posted about this experience on Instagram and got so much hate from so many men. Black men were furious I said they didn't get black women, white guys were offended I said they couldn't understand what people of colour go through. Everyone was so angry. Men really like to tell women who they should be dating, especially mixed-race women. It's bizarre.

Though I know I myself have expressed some very contradictory thoughts on being mixed race, I find the stereotype of us being perpetually confused and in a permanent identity crisis quite annoying. Some mixed-race people are that way, but others aren't. Ultimately, it is less we who are confused about being mixed race than it is society being confused about how to deal with us. Britain is still coming to grips with the idea of someone belonging to two or more cultures because it doesn't know how to place such a person.

Things are improving on this front, though. Society is getting more used to mixed-raceness because there are so many more of us around than there used to be. When I was a teenager, Neneh Cherry was the only mixed-race woman I'd see on TV apart from dancers in rap videos. There are lots of online spaces for various people of colour these days.

That doesn't mean everything is changing for the better. Today, mixed-race girls often get called 'lightie'. This derogatory term didn't exist when I was growing up. Back then, some people used the term 'half-caste', but I'd call them out whenever they did. As someone who teaches teenagers in secondary school, I've observed this younger generation seems to think 'lightie' is an all-right term. To them, everything is banter. It's all about memes, everything is a laugh.

I don't think they fully understand the weight behind terms like 'lightie'. A lot of the mixed-race girls even embrace the term. They say, 'Yeah, they're saying I'm light-skinned. Probably means they're saying I'm pretty. I'm going to own that.' I find that really disturbing because 'lightie' has undertones of colourism and light-skinned privilege. It's saying the closer to European you are, the better you are. But young mixed-race girls don't seem to see it as a big deal.

What would I change if I could do my teenage years all over again? In retrospect, I see now that, back then, I was really trying to fit in with a set of people, specifically black people. There's nothing wrong with that, and I'm still interested in black culture. But if I were to do my youth again, I would be a bit more relaxed and just try to enjoy my life without feeling the need to force any allegiances. I know it's easy to say this to a teenager who's just trying to fit in. But ultimately, there is a confidence that comes with being yourself. If you can accept that who you are is just fine, you will find yourself feeling more relaxed about everything. Your tribe are those who like you for who you are. Those who don't like you as you are, those are not your people. It really is as simple as that.

It is often a jarring experience for mixed-race Britons of African heritage to visit the continent and discover they are often seen as white there, including by their own African families. Several people I spoke to related similar experiences to Sophia. Phillip, the twenty-four-year-old son of a Kenyan father and white English mother, told me: 'Growing up in Manchester I usually thought of myself as black or mixed race. When I first visited Kenya at the age of twelve and people called me "*mzungu*", which generally means white person, I was quite shocked. Nobody had ever seen me as a white child before. This left me feeling quite confused over there.'

Danielle, the twenty-two-year-old daughter of a white English father and Ugandan mother who grew up in south London, was particularly frustrated. 'My father being a white man made me white in the eyes of my Ugandan cousins. This made me angry. I'd tell them I could communicate in my mother's language, I could cook Ugandan food, I grew up listening to Ugandan music, and most importantly, my white father had never even been a part of my life because he left when I was a baby. But because Uganda is such a patriarchal society, to them I was what my father was, period,' she said.

This is a dynamic to being mixed race that is absent here in Britain but affects mixed-race Britons when they are elsewhere. Not just in Africa, but in many parts of the world, society assigns you an identity according to a patriarchal logic. Put simply, you are primarily what your father is. Mixed-race Britons such as Danielle can thus often be denied a claim to their mother's identity based on this logic.

Sophia described her experience in Zimbabwe as a kind of otherness she 'wasn't used to', in contrast to the otherness she is familiar with in Britain. This is what the mixed-race experience often entails: learning how to navigate the particular kind of otherness you represent in the particular society you live in.

The kind of otherness Sophia and other mixed-race Britons who grew up here weren't used to was precisely the kind I grew up dealing with. While the fact it was my father who was Nigerian and I was growing up there meant I was seen as having a legitimate claim to Nigerianness by those who knew my background, to most casual observers I looked like an *oyinbo*, period. Interestingly, there are some full-blooded Nigerians who are lighter-skinned than me. But no one calls them *oyinbo*.

Every society develops a keen eye for spotting physical features outside its norms. South Africa aside, sub-Saharan Africa is virtually all black, so Africans are quick to notice anyone with Europeanish features because we are so far outside the everyday norm. Over here we are 'exotic' for being darker-skinned than the norm, over there for being lighter-skinned than the norm. That I understood why Nigerians saw me that way, however, does not mean I ever liked being called *oyinbo*. It always made feel like an other despite the fact I had lived in Nigeria all my life.

Another word that was often used to describe people such as me was 'half-caste', the term Sophia told people off for using when she was growing up in London. Up until today, very few people use the term 'mixed race' in everyday Nigerian speak. When I was growing up, no one used it. We were 'half-castes'. My mum would get furious anytime she heard that term.

'It's a very offensive word with terrible historical connotations going back to the times of the horrible Indian caste-system. People should not be using it,' she would fume.

But on this front, I couldn't see what she was banging on about. I didn't like being called *oyinbo*, but I didn't mind being called half-caste at all.

'Mum, people don't mean it in a negative way here. No one has any idea about this Indian caste-system stuff you're talking about. If you hadn't told me about it, I wouldn't have known either. The word has no negative connotation here, absolutely none. It is neutral. As long as the intentions behind it are not negative and no one is deliberately trying to insult me, what's the big deal?' I'd ask her.

'But didn't you understand the historical context I just explained to you, Junior? It's an offensive word.'

'But I don't feel offended, Mum, neither do I know any other ha... mixed-race kids here who feel offended at that term. It is an offensive word in your mind, but not in the minds of people here and that's what matters.'

'Well, you all should feel offended.'

'But we don't, Mum, that's the point.'

I know my mum was trying to defend my dignity. But my dignity never felt under attack by the term 'half-caste'. Up until today, it is not a label I can bring myself to get worked up about when it is used by Nigerians because I know there are no bad intentions behind it. Besides, unlike *oyinbo*, 'half-caste' at least acknowledges my part-Nigerianness. I use the term myself in conversations with Nigerians. My Nigerian wife calls me 'half-caste' at home, though she would never use the word publicly as it's a big no-no here in Britain.

I brought this up in my conversation with Sophia. I could see she disapproved of how relaxed I was about Nigerians using the term. She said the kids who called her 'half-caste' in London didn't know the history of the word either but that didn't mean they should get a pass for using it. Because then it never stops. I would probably feel the same way if I were in her shoes. It is much easier to be relaxed about things such as that when you live in a society where there is no history of people like you having been systematically demeaned and discriminated against.

The difference between me and Sophia was that I didn't grow up expecting to be treated worse because of my skin colour. It is the expectation of attack that hones our defensive instincts. Teaches us how to be on guard. Unlike Sophia, I didn't grow up in a defensive crouch. I always knew that the Nigerians who called me *oyinbo* never considered me a worse kind of human being because of my *oyinbo*-ness.

They saw me as a different kind of human being, but not a worse kind. And that is a big difference. So while being othered in Nigeria didn't feel nice, it never felt humiliating. That is a very different psychological position to be in from a mixed-race kid growing up in a society such as Britain that has a long history of racism towards black and mixed-race people. It was not until I moved to Poland

and began receiving regular racial abuse that I started developing defensive instincts of my own.

Sophia says she will never 'repel' the label of black in Britain so as not to further black self-hate. But on the other hand, she acknowledges she is claiming blackness mainly because she knows (white) Britain views her as black even though she is 'as much black as white'. This is the catch-22 situation many mixed black and white Britons find themselves in today. Their freedom to be individuals is limited by history and by the white majority's perceptions of who is 'black'. Perceptions that still generally boil down to a 'if you're not white, you're black' attitude.

For understandable historical and socio-psychological reasons, Sophia does not want to reject the 'black' label, but she is well aware that label does not explain many of her individual experiences and was more or less imposed on her by white Britain. It is, as she says, the 'contradiction' with which mixed black and white people such as her have had to learn to live.

I really liked her line at the end about there being 'a confidence that comes with being yourself'. I've noticed whenever I leave a party or some other social gathering where I know I was myself, that knowledge fills me with a confidence and sense of strength I really enjoy. But anytime I replay scenes in my head from a gathering where I know I wasn't being me, where I was just trying to act a part or come across a certain way, it always makes me feel weak and angry with myself. Because even if nobody around knew I wasn't being me, I knew. We all know when we are pretending to be someone we're not.

I found interesting Sophia's point about her mum trying to prepare her for life in Britain as a black woman without realising the mixed-race experience can be very different from the black experience in many situations. 'Her expectations of what I would face applied to black people, not to mixed-race teenagers,' she recalled, in relation to the incident in which some black girls had wanted to burn her hair.

Parents who are not mixed race can never know, by mere instinct, how to prepare a child for the experience. It's just too different from the monoracial journey. That's why I think it's important for them to learn as much about the mixed-race experience as they can from whatever sources are available: books, YouTube videos of mixed-race kids talking about their lives, other parents talking about raising such children.

The tensions Sophia sometimes experienced with black girls were another common theme in stories I heard from mixed-race females of black and white heritage. Kayla, the twenty-six-year-old daughter of a Jamaican father and Scottish mother who grew up in Luton, recalled her experience from secondary school: 'From when I was around fourteen, I started noticing none of the black girls in my year wanted to speak to me. They'd pass me on the corridor like I wasn't there. I wondered what was going on. I later learnt they thought I was stuck-up, that I felt I was better than them because I was mixed race. They were also upset black guys they liked seemed interested in me. One time, I was standing in the playground talking to a friend from my drama class and this group of black girls encircled us. They didn't say anything, they just kept walking round both of us. "What are you guys doing?" my friend asked them. They didn't respond at first, but after a minute or so, one of them said to the rest, "See, I told you she *wasn't* pretty," and they all walked off.'

Sophia hinted at the psychology behind these kinds of tensions between black girls and mixed-race girls: 'When you are brought up to believe you are not beautiful or desirable, anger and resentment can easily follow.' This displaced anger can then be projected onto mixed-race girls who are seen as getting too much attention from black males. Ralph, the son of a Nigerian mother who appears in a later chapter, explained this dynamic so eloquently I will leave it to him to sum up. Finally, I think Sophia was spot on describing the phenomenon of black men getting upset with mixed-race girls for dating white guys – another common theme in the stories I heard – as yet another manifestation of men trying to exert control over women, in this case mixed-race women.

# Chapter 5

# That extra factor

Isaac is the son of a white English father and Jamaican mother. He is twenty years old, grew up in Cardiff and currently studies mathematics.

My mother was born in Jamaica but moved to Nottingham when she was three. Both her parents were very Jamaican. They brought her up with Jamaican values, respect probably being the most important for them. My father also grew up in Nottingham. In fact, both sets of my grandparents lived on the same street there.

My parents met in secondary school and got married in their twenties. From their stories, it's clear interracial relationships were still controversial in 1990s Nottingham. A waiter once refused to serve them in a restaurant. Though it was one particular waiter and not the entire restaurant that refused to serve them, I still find it hard imagining something like that being even possible today. I guess that shows how much things have changed since then.

I was born in Nottingham but for the first three years of my life we lived in Anguilla, a British territory in the eastern Caribbean, where my dad worked as a flood-risk expert. After that, we moved to Cardiff, which is where we've lived ever since.

My primary school in Cardiff was predominantly white. There

was just one Asian kid and two black kids in my year. They were the ones I hung out with. It's interesting how I got lumped into that social group. Looking back, I realise it wasn't my decision to hang out with them or even an instinctive preference.

I remember sensing that the white Welsh kids simply assumed I would hang out with the minority kids. Whenever they'd be looking for me, they always instinctively glanced at the corner where the minority kids where. This got me feeling I probably *should* be hanging out with the minority kids. I'm not saying I didn't enjoy their company, I just find it interesting how that friendship was socially imposed on me rather than something I chose.

When I was a young boy, I'd ask my mum why my skin was light brown. 'I don't look like you, I don't look like Dad. What's happening, Mum?' She'd tell me I was 'special'. It wasn't that I didn't like my skin colour, but it confused me. When my friends from primary school started coming to my house, they were shocked to find out my dad was white. They thought I was adopted.

I had never thought it strange my dad was white. To me, he was just Dad, and this was how Dad looked. But the other kids couldn't wrap their heads round it. And not just the kids. I used to play football and my dad would come watch my games. He'd be cheering me on from the sidelines and the other parents would be looking at him bemused, like, 'Why on earth is he cheering that kid?' They never seemed to make the connection.

For a while, I didn't know what to make of these situations and the questions about whether I was adopted. I remember speaking to my younger brother about it and us thinking perhaps we were adopted. We asked my dad about it and he had to bring out our baby photos to prove we weren't. Only then did we feel reassured. Of course, when we were with my mum, everyone knew she was our mum. I have a sister as well.

By the time I was ten and had started thinking in terms of

race, I identified as a mixed-race kid. I didn't know it was normal to call a mixed-race boy 'black'. I always thought it strange when people called me that. My parents brought me up telling me I had two sets of grandparents who were very different from each other, both racially and culturally. They said I should be myself around my grandparents but should expect them to be different from each other. So I grew up assuming I was basically fifty–fifty. That is what I am really.

However, when I was thirteen, my mum had a long talk with me about what I should expect from Welsh and British society as I came of age. That conversation is one of my clearest memories from childhood. She told me stories about how life had been for her and her brothers growing up black in Nottingham. She said I should expect similar experiences in Cardiff. That my experiences would essentially be the same as that of black boys. That things would happen to me I wouldn't be able to discuss with my white friends because they wouldn't understand. That a time would likely come when I'd feel more in common with black boys than with white boys.

She said when I started going to job interviews I would have to learn how to impress my interviewees by acting as white as I could. I would have to speak formally, in as posh an accent as I could muster, none of that slang I used with my black friends. 'You will get a lot further in this country speaking the way white people speak than speaking the way you normally speak,' she told me. I found this all difficult to take in. It felt like my mum was telling me I would have to hide my real self to succeed in Britain. She also told me the police were way more likely to target me than my white friends.

That conversation left me feeling very worried about my future. The things my mum said scared me. But looking back now, I'm glad we had that talk. When I did eventually experience the kind of things she had told me would happen – white people looking at me weird in some places or treating me differently from my white peers – I was psychologically prepared for them. They didn't destabilise me the way they would have if I had not been expecting them. As she predicted, I've been stopped and searched by Welsh police on several occasions. So have all my black friends. But none of my white friends has ever been stopped and searched.

These police checks have never ultimately amounted to anything serious. They'll usually just say I matched the description of someone they were looking for, check my details and let me go. Still, to have experienced this, and know my black friends have as well while my white friends haven't, creates in me a feeling me and my black friends are in the same boat in a way me and the white friends aren't. Also, while Cardiff itself is quite diverse and you don't get stared at here for being brown, whenever we'd visit the Welsh countryside on holidays, people would often look at us funny. No one ever said anything, but a look is enough to make you feel out of place. This too helped create in me a distinct feeling of difference from my white peers.

My secondary school was more diverse than my primary school – roughly 70 per cent white. My mum's predictions proved right. The older I got, the more I started hanging out with black friends rather than white friends. It just kind of happened. We listened to the same music, we were interested in the same stuff. I realised my outlook was more black than white. Most of my friends were the kids of Nigerian immigrants. It always struck me how Nigerian they felt even though most of them were born here or came at a very young age. Their parents told them they were Nigerian no matter what their British passports said.

Sometimes, they made jokes about which 'side' of me I was showing in a given situation. I've always liked maths and been quite good at it. They'd see me doing my maths homework and say, 'Oh, that's the white side of him there.' When I'd listen to rap music, they'd say, 'Oh, that's his black side.' Stuff like that. Sometimes, I wondered why they considered liking maths a 'white thing', but there you go. I don't get offended at that sort of talk, but it does feel a bit strange. I've always thought of myself as a whole rather than these two halves that clash. But for them, if I did one thing, it was because of this part of my heritage, if I did another, it was because of that part.

I found visiting my black friends more interesting than visiting my white friends. There always seemed to be more going on in their homes. And they were more similar to mine. I'd be in a white friend's house, their mum would give them a plate of food and they'd say, 'No, I don't want lasagne today.' And she'd take the plate away and make them something else. The first time I saw that, I was like, 'What? So you can actually do that?'

That would be impossible with my mum. In my home, you ate what was given to you, period. And you finished what was on your plate. It was the same in the homes of all my Nigerian friends. It was little things like that which made me realise I had a more similar upbringing to my black friends than my white friends. I could relate to the family dynamics in the black homes easily; the dynamics in the white homes always left me feeling a bit bewildered.

I think our family dynamics were more 'black' because my dad worked nine-hour shifts, so it was my mum who decided what we ate, allocated our household chores and generally ran the home. She was very no-nonsense with us. It's funny, though, when my dad came home in the evenings, my mum would change. She'd become more lenient, almost sweet. Whenever I wanted a biscuit, I'd always wait till my dad got back before asking. I knew if I asked before he got back, my mum would say no. We ate a lot of Jamaican food. My dad liked it, but I don't think he wanted it as often as my mum did!

My parents had different tastes and perspectives, but they were good at compromising. For our Christmas meal, my mum always wanted rice and peas, my dad always wanted turkey stuffing. They both wanted the Christmas meals of their childhood. So on Christmas Eve we'd have one dish and on Christmas Day the other. They were good at resolving issues that way so there were really no tensions at home because of their different backgrounds.

In recent years, I've started discussing race with my dad and he is always very supportive. But when I was a teenager I only discussed such issues with my mum because I felt she'd be able to relate to what I was going through in a way he wouldn't. Surprisingly, I've now found out my dad is easier to talk to about race than my mum. My mum has always maintained this hard exterior.

She never wants to appear weak or show that anything can get to her. Apart from that conversation we had when I was thirteen, she has generally always maintained an 'I was fine, you'll be fine too' message with me when it comes to race. It is easier to discuss feelings of vulnerability with my dad. I think my mum got her attitude from her parents. They are the kind of people who brush things off and move on like every day is a new day and you need to focus on what's ahead of you.

Out of curiosity, I once asked my mum why she'd chosen to marry a white man. Knowing her parents, I could guess they would have much preferred she married a black man. 'Because your dad was the man I loved. I don't really care about colour,' she told me. That made sense to me. In my mind, race is no barrier to the kind of person I can be with. But I'm not sure how much sense it made to my grandparents.

I never saw both sets of my grandparents in the same room. Not once. Even though they lived on the same street in Nottingham, we always visited them separately. When they came to Cardiff, they came separately and never on the same day. I think my parents deliberately planned things this way. Whenever we'd visit

Nottingham, we'd stay at my mum's parents' place and then go spend the day with my dad's parents. At the time, I didn't think much of it. It was just what our family did. But now I think about it, that is more than odd and probably no coincidence. My mum's parents are both dead now so that means I'll never get to see all my grandparents together in one room.

Visiting my dad's parents was always a very different experience from visiting my mum's parents. The food was very different, even the questions they asked me were very different. My white grandparents always wanted to know my future career plans, what path I wanted to take and how things were coming along with that. My Jamaican grandparents were very now-focused; they never looked more than two weeks ahead. I always found that difference quite interesting.

I spoke differently to my different grandparents. My Jamaican grandparents spoke patois to me and expected me to reply in patois. When I was younger, I didn't understand it. It sounded like a foreign language to me and when they'd ask me something, I'd look at my mum to translate. By the time I was around eight, I noticed them giving my mum looks like, 'Why haven't you taught your son patois yet? This is a crucial part of his heritage.' I felt like I was letting them down, so I asked my mum to teach me basic patois. I did it to impress my grandparents and they were duly impressed and happy when they saw I now understood what they were saying to me.

I adjusted my tone and accent depending on which grandparents I was around. While my dad's parents weren't posh, they were definitely traditionally English. They spoke properly and expected me to speak properly too. They took table manners very seriously. Making sure your fork was on the right side of the table was a big deal for them. My Jamaican grandparents didn't care about things like that.

Even the way I greeted my grandparents was different. My dad's parents would shake my hand and say something formal like, 'Hi, how are you?' My mum's parents would never greet me that formally. Me, my brother and my younger sister used to joke about these differences between our grandparents. On our way to my mum's parents' house, we'd say to each other, 'OK, bring out your Jamaican masks now. Let's pretend to be Jamaican.' On our way to my dad's parents, we'd say, 'Remember, make sure you act posh.' In both cases, I was pretending to be someone I wasn't. Only at home could I really be myself. My parents were both very laid-back. They knew we were mixed, so neither expected us to be like one or the other.

On job applications, I tick the 'white and black Caribbean' option. But when people ask where I'm from, I usually say I was born in Nottingham, live in Cardiff and have a Jamaican mum and English dad. I give that whole background info because I don't know which aspect of my story people want to know. Sometimes, I just say I'm half-Jamaican, half-British.

I don't feel full-British because society doesn't see me that way. When the average (white) Briton sees me, they don't think, *Oh, there's a British man*. If there's a picture of a British man in computer games, it will be of a white guy wearing a hat, dressed in khaki shorts or some other type of clothes I'd never wear. When you're not white, people here know someone in your ancestry wasn't born and raised in Britain, so you're not 100 per cent British in their eyes. Also, my mum told me that whatever happens, I will never be fully British. That there is a chunk of my heritage from elsewhere that will always be a part of me. I know it would mean a lot to her if I took a bigger interest in my Jamaican heritage and I intend to do that in the future.

I see my identity as a circle. If you're 100 per cent British, there is no room for anything else. So if I have a slice of Jamaicanness then I can't be 100 per cent British, can I? Or is that being too mathematical about it? Sometimes, I really don't know. I'm still trying to figure it out. I have friends who are not white but identify full-British.

When I'm around them, I'm like, 'Hmm . . . maybe I am more British than I think?' I definitely feel more British than Jamaican. I grew up here, I know the culture. If I moved to Jamaica today, I'd have to learn society from scratch. All in all, though, I like having a distinct Jamaican heritage. It's always a talking point and gets people interested in me. I quite like that. If I was just British, I wouldn't have that extra factor.

Welshness doesn't mean anything to me. I've never really taken an interest in the culture or seen myself as Welsh at all even though I've lived here virtually all my life. I guess if my dad was Welsh, it would have been different. I would have visited Welsh grandparents and there would have been a connection. It's hard to feel connected to a place where you have no family roots, even if you grew up there.

I think Britain has become more racially tolerant in my lifetime. I used to see my colour as a potential obstacle to achieving my ambition, which is to work in the financial world. I no longer think that. There's a massive push for the inclusion of ethnic minorities and women in financial institutions these days. I see it when filling out job applications. So I think I'm treated pretty fairly now.

If I could change anything about the way society approaches mixed-raceness, it would be for there to be some more education on the topic. There are all sorts of mixes these days in terms of racial heritage. People just assume being mixed race means having one white parent. But in my generation, it's becoming increasingly common to see mixed-race people with no white parent. I don't think this has really sunk into society's imaginations of mixed-raceness yet. Apart from that, I wouldn't change too much, to be honest. I'm always happy when people show an interest in my heritage and ask me questions about it. I don't get asked enough in my opinion.

I found it quite disheartening that the predictions by Isaac's mother that he would have negative experiences his white friends wouldn't

– such as being harassed by the police – proved right. That tells a story in itself, and hardly a positive one. The more often such pessimistic predictions prove right, the less likely it is black and mixed-race boys such as Isaac will grow up feeling they are in the 'same boat' as their white peers.

As Isaac stated explicitly, his experiences with the police created 'a feeling me and my black friends are in the same boat in a way me and the white friends aren't'. Justin spoke about this 'same boat' feeling in the 1970s when he knew the send-them-back movements that wanted black people out of Britain wanted his kind out as well. It is sad Isaac speaks of having a similar 'same boat' feeling four decades on.

The problem is not in young mixed-race men feeling they are in the same boat as young black men, the problem is in that boat too often still being an unfortunate one to be in. One which unites black and mixed-race people by the negative emotion of shared persecutions. That is not how a country wants to be uniting members of its society.

That in twenty-first-century Britain a black mother felt she needed to tell her thirteen-year-old mixed-race son to 'speak the way white people speak' and act 'as white' as he can at job interviews is also disheartening. We've all had to engage in some level of acting at job interviews, whatever our skin colour, but surely that should not mean ethnic minorities feeling pressured to mimic white Britons?

To create an atmosphere in which ethnic minorities feel under that kind of pressure is to encourage a colonial mentality among your own citizens. The very essence of colonialism was, after all, to get black and brown people to start talking and acting as white as possible. Many ethnic minorities in the West have become so used to this expectation they often put on an act automatically whenever white people are around. I have caught myself doing this here in Britain.

I do not try to affect a British accent. That would doubtless produce comical results. But I do know I speak differently to white Britons than I do to my Nigerian wife and Nigerian friends. With them, I just open my mouth and say the words however they come out. But outside my home and comfort zones, I am way more careful and controlled not just with what I say, but with how I say it. I modulate my voice and my words, consciously softening my Nigerian accent.

What is this? A colonial mentality? An adaptive tactic of trying to blend in with my environment? A bit of both? It's difficult for me to say to be honest. But I do know it's a thing. And I do know a British person in Nigeria would *not* adjust their way of speaking to adapt to their Nigerian environment. They would not feel the need. I guess it comes down to a power thing. Who needs who to get ahead in this world? As of today, the white world is much richer than the black world. So the reality is that we need them more than they need us to get ahead. Hence, we adapt to their ways rather than them adapting to our ways. I'm fine with having to do this as an immigrant in Britain. I came here of my own free will and will adapt as best I can without making a fool of myself.

But I don't think ethnic minority Britons such as Isaac should feel a pressure to conform to *white British* norms of speech and behaviour in order to get ahead in Britain. That just doesn't seem right. I'm not suggesting Isaac be able to burst into patois at a job interview, but he should not feel the need to mirror his (probably white) interviewer either. He should be allowed to be British in his own way within some broadly accepted norms, I would think.

As Isaac's stories about putting on 'different masks' with his different grandparents suggests, the mixed-race experience often involves performing roles determined by the racial composition of the audience. If you are full-black or white, you don't have to act it to be seen as it. If you are mixed black and white, you often do. Or at

83

least feel like you do. Which in effect means the same thing.

Isaac said by the time he became a teenager, he realised his 'outlook was more black than white'. This self-perception was driven not just by him noticing he seemed to have more shared interests with his black friends, but also because the dynamics in black homes were more relatable to him than those in white homes. Is there such a thing as a 'black' outlook and a 'white' outlook?

I don't know if I would categorise 'outlooks' in strictly racial terms, but it is clear cultural sensibilities can vary vastly from place to place and people to people. The dynamics in Isaac's home were largely shaped by his Jamaican mum and, interestingly enough, chimed with the dynamics in the homes of his Nigerian friends.

While it would be absurd to suggest the dynamics in black homes everywhere are similar, I certainly know of no African or other black culture where children are allowed the kind of latitude they are allowed in white Western homes. White children often boss their parents. That simply does not happen in African cultures, which place a high premium on obedience from children. Virtually all the mixed-race Britons of African heritage to whom I spoke emphasised they could never speak to their African parent the way white kids speak to their parents here. Personally, I think black African cultures can often be too authoritarian in the way they raise children while Western cultures can be way too laissez-faire. So in this sphere, I am really somewhere in between both worlds.

While there may be many similarities in the way black people do certain things, that does not mean we can speak of a 'black outlook' per se, but neither can we speak of a 'white outlook' or 'white way' of doing things. Poland and Britain are both white-majority countries, but they are very different cultural planets. Poland is a significantly more conservative society than Britain, and a greater premium is also placed on obedience to authority. Most Polish mums would also tell their kids to eat what was put in front of them the way Isaac's

Jamaican mum did. But we have come to think of race in such essentialist terms that how the white people of one nation do things is often seen as the way white people all over the world do things. Ditto for black people. This is, of course, absolute nonsense.

At just twenty years old, Isaac is clearly still trying to figure out where he fits in Britain's big picture. On the one hand, he doesn't believe he will be seen as 'full-British' by white Britain because of his Jamaican roots, but on the other, he is not sure he even wants to be seen that way because he likes having a 'distinct Jamaican heritage'. It gives him that 'extra factor', makes him interesting to people. I can relate to this. I always enjoy telling people here in Britain that I'm Polish-Nigerian. The response is inevitably something along the lines of, 'Huh? Polish-Nigerian? How did *that* happen?' Whichever way you look at it, it's always better to be considered interesting than not.

# Chapter 6

# Here I am Latina, there I'm the *gringa*

I was really excited about meeting Daniela. I'd never met someone like her before, much less been able to discuss race and identity with them. Her father is a white Englishman and her mother a black Colombian. She is a twenty-six-year-old DJ and artiste who was raised in the seaside town of Great Yarmouth in Norfolk. But we met in Bristol, which is where she currently lives.

My parents met in the early 1990s when my father was a sea captain. A confirmed bachelor at the time, he was the kind of guy who had a woman at every port. My mum went to a party on his ship in Ecuador and that was how they first hooked up. She was twenty-four, he was much older. My dad is in his eighties now. She got pregnant shortly afterwards and I was born in England.

My mum had a difficult life before she met my dad. She ran away from her home in Colombia at the age of thirteen, stowing away on a boat to Ecuador. There she took what work she could find to survive. She had my brother when she was nineteen. His father was Afro-Ecuadorian, so he is fully black. Taking care of him mostly fell on my mum.

Her beginnings in England weren't easy either. After I was born, my dad had to return to sea. My mum was left with me and my brother in the small town of Great Yarmouth – a black woman from South America who couldn't speak English. At first we were a sensation in town, people would stare at us everywhere we went. But being such a small place, after a while, everyone knew who we were, so we attracted less attention.

I missed my dad. He would send me letters from sea with pictures of dolphins and turtles. Those letters are some of my most treasured possessions today. He retired when I was around six and was home with us from that point on. We often visited my mum's big family in Colombia. There, even your fifth cousin is considered close family. My mum spoilt me rotten. She grew up very poor, so she wanted me to have all the things she'd never had.

When she was a little girl, she used to get a doll on Christmas Day. She could play with it for a few hours and then back it went on the shelf until the next Christmas when she'd get the same doll. So she showered me with lots of nice clothes and fancy toys. Whenever I'd outgrown my clothes, we'd pass them on to my Colombian cousins, so I grew up aware there were people who had much less than I did.

My childhood memories from Colombia are generally happy ones. I remember dancing in the rain. In England, rain is never warm, it's something you hide from. In Colombia, when it rains, that's when all the children come out to play because the water is so warm it feels lovely on your skin.

But I can't remember a time I didn't feel different from everyone around me, including in Colombia. No one had my kind of racial heritage. My brother was full-black. So was my mum's family. I couldn't explain my feelings to anyone, even my mum. Because of the colourism in Latin America and the fact I'm so light-skinned, as far as she and her family are concerned, I basically won life's lottery, so what could I possibly have to complain about? They can't understand the turmoil of being a mixed-race person. To make matters worse, they used to say my mum treated me better than my brother because I look white. This made me feel even more isolated. I am not even white-passing in Britain, but in the eyes of my Colombian family I am basically white.

I think these comments about my mum treating me better got to my brother, too. I remember once we were in a taxi alone and I fell asleep on the way. He took my favourite teddy bear from under my arms and flung it out the window. A child's favourite teddy bear is a big deal! When we got home and I woke up, I was devastated. My brother told my mum a cat had eaten my teddy. She knew straight away he was lying. He never told me outright he felt Mum treated me better, but I believe he acted out his frustrations in ways like that.

If I was the favoured child, it was not because I was lighter-skinned but because he was very badly behaved. I was a studious goody-two-shoes while my brother was literally Dennis the Menace, who always gave my mum a hard time. But when family start putting ideas like that in your head, it's difficult not to be affected by them.

I felt very different from the English kids at school. I remember us lining up in the sun before going to class and me always looking at our shadows. You could see all the white girls had neat hair while mine was always sticking out. I hated that. Other girls could re-brush their hair into a nice ponytail in a few minutes. You can't re-brush black hair that quick and that smoothly because it gets very dry.

We often played a game in class which involved making masks of our faces. The white kids would be given white and pink paint while me and the half-Mauritian kid, who was the only other ethnic minority, would be given tea and coffee, like there was no paint available for our skin colour. This made me feel abnormal. At swimming lessons, my teacher would make me take my cap off to show other teachers my hair.

For a long time, I felt too self-conscious to eat the sandwiches my mum packed in my lunchbox. They were different from the sandwiches the other kids had because she used colourful South American spreads and all sorts of prawns. Not wanting to draw attention to myself, I wouldn't bring out the sandwiches at lunchtime but would sit there and watch the other kids eating. My class teacher noticed what was going on so one day she asked if she could try one. She took a bite and went, 'Mm . . . this is so delicious,' loudly so everyone could hear. 'You should be happy you don't have boring sandwiches like the other kids,' she said. Only then did I feel OK eating them. I was six or seven at the time. Even though I never spoke to my mum about my self-consciousness around the white kids, she must have noticed it because she once asked me if I was ashamed she was black. That really threw me.

One of the starkest moments of racism I witnessed growing up in Great Yarmouth was at a supermarket car park. I was eight. My mum had taken a white man's parking space by accident. He rolled down his window and screamed at her, calling her a monkey, saying she should go back to where she came from. I remember feeling so scared for her. Another bad one was when one of my classmates had snot coming out of his nose. I pointed it out to him so he could wipe it off with tissue. 'Yeah, well, at least I'm not black,' he snarled in response. I didn't know what to say.

When I was around eleven, my mum said something to me that shook me. She was chairperson of the Race Equality Council in Norfolk and wanted someone to do a reading of Agra Gra's famous 'And you call me coloured' poem. I wanted to do it. But my mum said I couldn't. I asked why. 'Because you are not black,' she replied. 'You're too white to read that poem.'

I remember feeling incredibly sad when she said that. I didn't understand her explanation that, because of my proximity to whiteness, I couldn't claim certain expressions of pain. Today I get what she meant. I do have a lot of privilege because of my proximity to whiteness. While I have faced racism, it's a less overt one than dark-skinned people experience. If I have a light-skinned daughter who wanted to read that poem in public, I'd tell her exactly what my mum told me. That this poem is about the pain of someone who is very dark-skinned. Reading it in public should be an opportunity for a dark-skinned person to express that pain. It's all about passing the mic.

I've been othered not just by white people but also by people of colour. In England, I am Latina. But in Latin America, I am the foreign *gringa*. Even though I speak perfect Spanish with the Colombian accent I learnt from my mum, Colombian taxi-drivers still overcharge me. They can smell my foreignness. The blatant overcharging is always a reminder of my outsider status in Colombia.

But the othering is not just from strangers. Music is a big deal in Colombia. If you are Latina, you grew up dancing salsa, merengue, bachata. I love those sounds. In fact, I DJ Latin music here in England. I recently did what we DJs call a Boiler Room. It's a live-streaming session of a DJ playing a set. At any moment, there could be hundreds of thousands of people watching you online around the world. It's a pretty big deal for us.

Somehow my mum found the video of my Boiler Room session and sent it to my Colombian family. Their reaction? They laughed their heads off and said the way I moved while playing the music was all wrong. That I don't know how to dance Latin music. Here I am, sharing our music, including songs about slavery and suffering, with thousands of people, yet all my family can do is laugh at me for not moving right? This reminded me of another time in Colombia when

I went out with my cousins to a club and they burst out laughing when I started dancing.

Unlike English humour, Colombian humour is not subtle, it is very direct. People will mock you to your face, not caring how that might make you feel. I am very Latina in some ways, but my sensitivities are definitely British. I need people to be tactful with me. Colombians aren't tactful. I feel like telling my cousins, 'You know what? I'm a new type of person. So what if I can't dance the way you guys dance? I would love to, but I can't. But so what? I've got my own rhythm and I still dance better than all the English people!'

It's in situations like that I feel most in limbo, someone who is othered by everyone. When I was younger, I usually cried after such incidents. But what can I do now I'm an adult? All I can do is tell myself DJing and dancing make me happy so I will continue doing them, irrespective of what anyone thinks.

My last trip to Colombia was a real eye-opener for me. I spent two-and-a-half months travelling round the country on my own. I wanted to see it for myself. The experience made me realise how wrong my imaginations about Colombia were. I remember calling my boyfriend in tears, telling him I'd believed Colombia was such an open culture while it is actually anything but.

One the one hand, Colombia is definitely a more fun place than England. But it is also a monolithic closed culture where anything remotely different is frowned upon and singled out as abnormal. For example, as a feminist, I don't shave my armpits. I don't believe it's a question of hygiene because if it were, men should shave theirs too. But they don't. However, while nobody makes comments about my unshaved armpits in Britain, Colombians can't stomach a woman with armpit hair. And they show you that by giving you disgusted looks.

My cousins couldn't understand it either. 'Daniela, you've

forgotten something,' they'd say to me in embarrassed tones. I told them it wasn't an accident but a choice and tried to explain why. They couldn't get it and authentically thought me disgusting. 'How does your boyfriend feel about it?' they asked. I said he was fine with it and many English girls don't shave their armpits either. 'Those English girls are disgusting too,' they said.

British people are more open to change. Colombians don't like anyone veering from the established norm. I had built it up in my head that Colombia was where I could be me. But that trip actually taught me a lot about Britain and about myself; how open Britain is, how inquisitive, how tolerant. I realised these really are British attitudes. And that I myself am very British in my attitudes.

Another thing that bugs me about Colombia is how men are tacitly given a right to cheat on women. 'All men cheat,' my cousins always say. When I tell them I know my boyfriend would never cheat on me, they burst out laughing. 'How exactly do you know this?' they ask, looking at me like I am the most naive woman in the world. They didn't believe it for a minute.

This general acceptance men are going to cheat and there's really nothing women can do about it reminds me of what my mum used to say about Latin men. 'Don't be with a Latin man. They are sexist. They will expect you to cook and clean for them non-stop. And they will cheat on you. They are also often violent. I don't want that for you,' she would tell me. Growing up, I thought she was exaggerating, but the more I learnt about Colombia the more I started to see her point. I feel bad generalising about my culture, and I know I'm airing our dirty laundry here, but the truth is, Latin men *are* quite sexist. There *is* a lot of cheating there and they *do* have huge expectations of women. And all this is accepted by society.

I also don't like how my Colombian family always assume I have loads of money even though I work minimum-wage jobs to support my DJing career. They believe everyone here has money. They are constantly demanding money from my mum. She can't even afford to help me out, why should she help them? It's not like they're ever there for her when she has problems. And whatever she gives, it's never enough. They always think it should be more.

I once thought Colombia was the place I would want to live. I know now I could never live there. Perhaps I might change my mind in the future, but for now I can't imagine it. This is a difficult thing to accept for anyone who is mixed race and has tried to go back. Britain is not perfect, but I now understand no country is. You have to take the good with the bad wherever you are. You can't over-glamorise any culture in your head. So I take the beautiful parts of both cultures. That is the best thing about being mixed race; you get to choose which cultural norms work best for you.

Despite being from very different cultures and generations, my parents have a similar worldview. They are both quite traditional people. Don't embarrass us in public. Honour thy father and thy mother. Always be respectful, especially towards those older than you. I once yawned in the middle of a family dinner. My dad, who is generally a very calm man, completely lost it. I had the audacity to yawn at the dinner table? How disrespectful! I got sent straight to bed with no dinner and my mum supported the decision.

My parents both believed children need to have some fear of their parents and know their place in the household. British kids swear at their parents. My mum would never tolerate that from me. And because my dad is from a generation when British kids were not allowed to disrespect their parents, he and my mum were very much on the same page here. Today, I'm happy I was brought up this way. I think one of the reasons many of my British peers find it hard to hold down a job is because they struggle with authority. Sometimes, you just have to shut up and eat your food, as my mum used to say.

This doesn't mean there were no cultural disagreements in my home. My dad is very much into the British politeness thing, as am I. But at the dinner table, my mum would say to me, 'Pass me the salt.' I'd ask her to add 'please'. She never wanted to. 'I've asked you to pass me the salt. You know you're going to pass me the salt. You know I am grateful you are passing it to me. Why do you expect me to say please and thank you every time you pass me something? Those words don't mean anything, Daniela,' she'd say. To me and my dad, saying 'please' and 'thank you' was very important. To my mum, British politeness is worthless fakery. Also, based on her cultural mindset, I think there was also an element of her wanting to demonstrate her position of power over me as my mother by not using words like 'please' and 'thank you' when addressing me.

She always encouraged me to have a strong relationship with my father, and I do. We share many passions; we both like P. G. Wodehouse, classical music and opera. But when he inevitably passes away – he's in his eighties now – I know my mum will go back to Colombia. She misses her culture. Her Colombian heritage has always been about culture rather than race; the food she cooks, the way she raised me, how she communicates. All she ever wanted was for me not to be too culturally English, to never turn my back on Latin culture.

People of my generation often discuss being a person of colour in Britain in the context of race and specifically in relation to whiteness. We talk a lot about our oppression; it's how we bond. I get this, but it can sometimes feel a bit limiting. People of colour should bond not just around negative experiences with white people, but also around positive experiences connected to their various cultures.

I have to admit I face some struggles in twenty-first-century Britain connected to how my mother raised me. When I was a young girl, she taught me the typical things Latina mums teach their daughters; how to cook, take care of a man, and generally be wifey. She taught me well. My boyfriend is white English, so to be honest he doesn't expect any of this. He actually complains I fuss over him too much. But cooking him meals and fussing over him makes me feel happy. This causes conflict in my head. I am a strident feminist, so why am I acting this way? Worse, why do I feel happy acting this way?

I've also recently come to the realisation I can't put up blinds. Each time I try, I end up breaking them. Again, I feel bad because a feminist should be able to do such 'practical' things. But I can't. Feminists don't consider cooking something you should be able to do because of its gendered context. But it is actually what I do well and enjoy doing. So there is this battle in me between my Western feminism and the things my Latina mother taught me to do that I enjoy.

Considering my current boyfriend is white, I try to imagine myself with kids who look white. I know this sounds bad, but I don't know how I would relate to children with so much privilege. I feel an instinctive bond with other women of colour; it would feel strange having a daughter I could not share that bond with. If my kids are just a quarter Latina, the culture would be diluted in them. And if they got married to a white person, my grandchildren probably wouldn't feel Latin at all. They would no longer be part of the African diaspora. The thought of that makes me sad. But then again, I'm not willing to leave the man I love just because I don't want to have white kids. It can all be very confusing.

Today, I identify as British Afro-Colombian. But I'd like people to respect that, being mixed race, I am not one thing or the other. Society should stop expecting mixed-race people to represent a specific community. We are non-binary individuals like transgender citizens. We need our individual autonomy.

It's a funny thing, though, identity. My brother, who is fully South American by birth, has never been very interested in Latin culture. He's never made the effort to learn more about it. But because I am mixed race, I have always felt I have to make the effort to connect

95

with the culture. My identity has always been really important to me while my brother couldn't care less. I guess that's how it is when you're fully something. You don't need to think about your identity. It's just there.

It was interesting to hear it's not just in Africa mixed-race people can be seen as 'basically white' by black people, but apparently in South America too. Daniela's Colombian family think she 'won life's lottery' with her light skin colour and so has nothing to complain about in the sphere of race or identity. This attitude sounded familiar. It is the painfully pragmatic approach to colourism in the poorer global south where people focus on surviving the world as it is rather than trying to rewrite the rules of its current racial hierarchy.

What is more intriguing and almost never talked about is that the existing hierarchy seems to *make instinctive sense* to many people in the global south, including black and brown people. Of course, I'm not talking about academics or intellectuals, but the regular folk who make up the overwhelming majority. The African intellectual is outraged at the idea of white people sitting atop a global racial hierarchy, the average African not so much. I've often wondered what exactly, in the twenty-first century, sustains a racial hierarchy that places white people at the top, black people at the bottom and everyone else somewhere in between? 'White supremacist propaganda,' many will readily respond.

Western movies, TV shows and media are full of covert and overt messages propagating the idea white people are better than everyone else. In this way, the ideology of white supremacy is kept alive and internalised by black and brown people worldwide. So goes the argument. While this could all have been technically plausible in the twentieth century when we all dieted on Hollywood movies and got our news from CNN and the BBC, it does not explain why the hierarchy still endures in people's minds today.

It does not explain why it endures in an internet age where people have access to many sources of information and decide what news they consume. It does not explain why it endures today where the average Indian watches more Bollywood movies than Hollywood movies, and the average Nigerian is more familiar with Nollywood celebrities than American stars. In today's world, people can follow whoever they want on social media and internalise whichever worldview suits them. The days when everything we read and watched was produced by white people are well and truly over.

Yet despite this, we know much of the world still instinctively positions white people atop the human hierarchy and black people at the bottom. Whiteness is still something to which much of the world aspires. White people are welcomed with open arms on every continent, black people aren't. Why? The Poles have a saying, 'When you don't know what it's about, it's about money.' The belief whites are above was created by ideology, but it is sustained by economics.

We live in a capitalist world, so people's values are shaped by capitalism's values. We are *Homo capitalismus*. What does capitalism value above all? Wealth and success. So these are what impress *Homo capitalismus*, be it on a conscious or subconscious level. It is why even intellectuals who love bashing capitalism make sure to emphasise they are 'best-selling' authors on their social-media profiles. It is why most people adopt an instinctively respectful tone in the presence of the significantly successful. They listen to them attentively, their expressions suggesting they expect to hear something insightful, something worth knowing. Because, like it or not, the whole world has bought into the idea of success being an indicator of specialness.

As it works on an individual level, so too does it work on a group level. White and predominantly white nations remain the richest and most successful nations in the world while black nations remain the poorest and least successful. The rest of the world is somewhere in between. It is no coincidence that the world's informal racial hierarchy faithfully reflects its formal economic hierarchy. The current economic hierarchy was arrived at brutally and unfairly. Slavery, colonialism, overt exploitation. But recalling the history of how today's economic hierarchy came about does nothing to change the existing realities on the ground. The GDP of 1.2 billion-strong Africa, where 90 per cent of the world's black population lives, is smaller than that of Britain, a country of 66 million people. It is this unsentimental reality which guides *Homo Capitalismus* in mentally positioning who is who on the racial hierarchy today. It is also no coincidence that not all white people are considered equal in the hierarchy.

A friend of mine recently spent some time working at a university in Dubai. He said irrespective of academic achievements, both Emirati staff and students treated white lecturers from rich Western nations such as France or Britain far more respectfully than those from poorer white nations such as Serbia or Bulgaria. The latter were often treated particularly dismissively by their Emirati employers who instinctively placed them lower down the human hierarchy because the UAE today is richer and better developed than the likes of Serbia or Bulgaria. Years of living in Poland made it clear to me Poles instinctively placed themselves lower on the global hierarchy than their richer white cousins in the West and higher than their poorer cousins to the east in Ukraine, Belarus and the other less successful post-communist states.

Growing up in Lagos, Nigerians would sometimes take digs at me because my mum was from Poland. 'Isn't that one of those poor communist countries behind the West in everything?' they would ask mockingly. I would furiously insist Poland was not 'poor', God forbid. The basis of the respect my Nigerian peers felt for the West was not in the white skin colour of its inhabitants, but in the wealth and development they associated with it. Thirty years ago, the world didn't have much respect for the Chinese. The proverbial poor Chinaman in the rice fields was the butt of global jokes. No one is laughing today. The Chinese have risen rapidly up the hierarchy because China has become richer and more successful.

Colourism will not be eliminated by well-meaning intellectuals telling people it is a bad thing; it will be eliminated when the white world stops being so much richer and more successful than everyone else. Then regular black and brown folk will stop looking up to it so much and start admiring their own kind. But this will only happen if their own nations become rich and successful. I do not like that this is the way it is, but this is the way it is. Wealth and success are what impresses the world today. The road to the end of white supremacy lies in economics, not sociology, history or semantics.

Another part I found really interesting in Daniela's story was when she talked about her Colombian family mocking her for the way she danced to Latin music. Mixed-race people often face authenticity tests. Can you really be like *us* with all that *other* blood in you? Daniela's experience reminded me of a scene from my own childhood. Dancing competitions are usually organised at Nigerian children's parties. The DJ will play a series of songs, kids dance to each song and after each round a winner is proclaimed by popular acclaim. At the end of the series, an overall winner is proclaimed by the same method.

I remember taking part in such a competition when I was nine or ten. I can't remember how many rounds of dancing there were, but I do remember I was leading by the time we got to the final round. But when the DJ switched on the last song, I froze. It was jùjú music, a traditional style of music from south-western Nigeria derived mostly from drumbeats. I had no idea how to move to it. No one had ever taught me. We never listened to that kind of music at home.

My dad wasn't interested in music at all, so he never listened to anything really. My mum listened to pop music, Dolly Parton and

99

some reggae. I listened to rap and hip-hop. Aware all eyes were on me as I was the only one who had frozen, I tried moving to the music. But I must have been so awkward because a few dozen kids and adults burst into uncontrollable laughter at my attempts. 'The *oyinbo* can't dance jùjú,' they guffawed. My confidence vanished in an instant. All I could do was pray for the song to finish as quickly as possible to end my torture. Finally, it ended and, indeed, because I had been the worst in the last round, I was pronounced second overall. My mum was furious. I remember her ranting on the way home.

'You were the best overall. You would have won the competition if not for that damn jùjú music,' she fumed. 'Don't worry, Junior, nobody listens to that music anywhere else.'

Who cared what people listened to elsewhere? This was the kind of thing my mum never seemed to get. I didn't live anywhere else, I lived in Nigeria. And that was where I needed to be recognised. I couldn't care less what happened in the rest of the world. I was distraught. I had come so close to winning my first competition in anything ever, but then I had failed an authenticity test woefully.

It didn't matter that my dad couldn't dance to jùjú music any better than I could. He was 100 per cent, so no one could ever call into question his 'authentic' Nigerianness. I was the one expected to keep proving mine. I never had the courage to take part in a Nigerian dancing competition after that. I was always afraid the DJ would play jùjú or some other traditional Nigerian music at some point in time. Nothing stifles self-expression as badly as self-consciousness.

While Daniela said the best thing about being mixed race is that 'you get to choose which cultural norms work best for you', this choice clearly comes with its own challenges. In her case, these are manifested in the internal conflict she experiences as a result of enjoying some things she learnt from her Colombian mum, such as cooking and 'fussing' over her man, and her Western feminist beliefs, which are at odds with such behaviour. Likewise there is the clash between her love for a Colombian culture that is warm and 'fun' and yet she also knows is significantly more judgemental and controlling than laissez-faire British culture.

Her disappointment with Colombia once she got to see it up close was a theme with which I became familiar while gathering stories. Like Daniela, many other mixed-race Britons to whom I spoke had built up the homeland of their 'ethnic' parent in their heads only to visit there and feel somewhat let down by reality. Daniela said the experience taught her not to 'over-glamorise' any culture. Indeed.

While interviewing people, I tried to imagine how differently I would see the world if I had been brought up in Britain, surrounded by the descendants of those who conquered and humiliated my ancestors – knowing these descendants still often look down on people such as me, as conquerors always look down on those they have conquered. Yet at the same time also knowing there isn't much I can realistically do about all this considering my minority status. Despite the obvious diversity of cities such as London or Birmingham, at the end of the day out of every 100 people who live in Britain, only 15 are not white. I can easily imagine entertaining fantasies of a wonderful and welcoming homeland, a place where I would be the dominant majority, where I would never need to prove I belonged or was worthy of belonging.

Unfortunately, as Daniela discovered, the reality can often be that you 'go back' and it turns out the homeland is not as welcoming or easy a place to live in as you had imagined. What's more, you might actually end up discovering the last thing you expected to discover there of all places: your own acute Britishness. You have become that about which you grew up sceptical. This is not an easy thing with which to deal.

As the legendary African-American writer Maya Angelou put it: 'The ache for home lives in all of us, the safe place where we can go as we are and not be questioned.' Most of the mixed-race Britons I spoke to visited ancestral homelands only to find they were questioned there as well. The realisation there really isn't anywhere you will never be questioned is a painful one. It is the tragedy of the diasporan, especially the mixed-race diasporan. To be questioned. Everywhere.

# Chapter 7

# Black, white or what?

Ralph is the son of a white English father and Nigerian mother. He grew up in Nigeria, Ethiopia and Britain. He is twenty-three and currently lives in Reading, which is where we sat down to chat about his experiences.

My father met my mother while he was working for the Foreign Service in Nigeria. She was a TV host. Although I was born in England, I spent my earliest years in Nigeria. I remember Nollywood celebrities coming to our home, which is where my mum recorded her show. I also remember that whenever I'd go to the market with her, there'd be kids running after us shouting *oyinbo* at me. It was in no way malicious, but of course such things make one conscious of being different from the norm. I don't remember much else from those early years in Nigeria, though. It would be afterwards when I returned there that I would really get a feel of the place.

We moved to Ethiopia when I was seven, which is when my vivid memories start. The Ethiopian kids at school would ask me whether I was black or white. I would say I was black because that was the safer answer. If I said I was white, it would probably have struck them as a bit odd because I do look more black than white. But aside from that, even as a young boy I instinctively sensed I needed to emphasise I felt black because, if I didn't, I could be seen as self-hating or trying to distance myself from blackness.

Historically, most mixed black and white kids have felt an affinity with black people, especially in the days when there was more racism and such kids were openly excluded or denigrated by their white family members. I also instinctively felt that affinity, though I wasn't sure why. However, while most mixed-race kids today would answer that question the same way I did – that they identify black – I think for some it might be an almost forced declaration of affinity. They feel they *have to* say they identify black rather than white because doing otherwise could open them up to ridicule or hostility.

While I told the Ethiopian kids I was black, I was unsure enough to speak to my mum about it. 'Mum, what am I really, black, white or what?' I asked her. I also asked her what it meant to be 'black'. I understood why some people were described as 'black' because of their skin shade, but I was always fascinated by what it really meant to be black. Was there a special way black people behaved that was different from the way white people behaved? 'You are your own person. You must develop your own sense of self. Don't just follow others or try to behave like they behave because you think they look authentic. You don't have to fit into any box,' my mum told me. She was very relaxed about it and this in turn made me feel less stressed about the whole black or white thing. I took to heart what she said, and it helped with my uncertainties.

Nowadays when people ask what I am, I say I'm a human being first and foremost. An individual as multifaceted as anyone else. I won't conform to anybody's idea of what an 'authentic' black person is supposed to be like, what kind of music I'm supposed to listen to and what not. We all need to be given the space and freedom to develop our own sense of self. I'm grateful my mum gave me that.

Because my dad worked a lot and my mum was the black parent, I instinctively went to her anytime I had questions about my identity. She knew the black experience and always emphasised I should never let people bring me down because of my skin colour. We moved back to Britain when I was eleven, specifically to Reading, which is where I've lived ever since.

My dad's family is much smaller than my mum's family. My grandma lives in Chichester while his other close relatives are scattered around London and Surrey. We would often gather in Grandma's home for Christmas and I would be the only kid there who wasn't white, so I did sometimes feel like I stuck out in my dad's family. But apart from the self-conscious feeling, I don't remember any negative experiences from those family gatherings.

My secondary school reflected the demographics of Reading – predominantly white, but with significant numbers of black and Asian kids. I never felt I was being oppressed by the white kids. White girls were often fascinated by my Afro, but not in any way I would describe as racist or fetishist. People would sometimes say I looked like Jermaine Pennant, the footballer. But I didn't see that as anything to get offended at either. Most of my friends were black or mixed race. But I also had white friends. I never felt any hard borders between us and the white kids.

Race did sometimes enter the conversation, though. I was fifteen when the 2011 London riots happened, and me and my friends talked about that a lot. The riots made a big impression on me. Even though my middle-class Reading world was far removed from the world of inner-city London, and even though I'd never felt oppressed because of my skin colour, the riots did make me become more interested in race and race relations in Britain.

By the way, I am not saying there was no racism at all in Reading. I am saying I don't remember ever personally experiencing it and I don't remember my close friends saying they had either. Sometimes we might try to get into a club, five or six of us at the same time, and the bouncer might say, 'Sorry, guys, already full tonight.' Walking away, we'd joke they were afraid of letting six black guys into a club. But we didn't seriously believe it was because of our skin colour we weren't let in. These weren't incidents that traumatised us or affected the way we viewed our status in Britain.

Nevertheless, after the London riots, I started reading books about the history of the British police, its relationship with young black males and British inner-city racial conflicts. I started actively thinking about race and racism. I read books by Frantz Fanon and radical Black Panther thinkers. I became more politically conscious. My teenage years were pretty turbulent times in the world. Around the period of the London riots, the Arab Spring was also going on. In America, the Occupy Wall Street movement was in full swing following the effects of the 2009 financial crisis. Then there were race-based events like the Michael Brown shooting in Ferguson, which I remember discussing a lot with my mum in the context of racism in America.

My conclusion to all that was happening was that racism was alive and well in the West, including at institutional levels. The solution lay in radical left-wing policies. We needed to rid the world of capitalism and revolutionise society. This was the only way to defeat racism and classism. Of course, as you get older, you rethink some of the views you held as a teenager. I am still left-wing, and I still believe racism and class oppression exist, but I don't think the identity politics that is currently fashionable on the left is the way to deal with it.

I'm against racism and the far right, but that doesn't mean I'm for identity politics. They both share the same thought patterns. They both seek to essentialise human beings, to put us in racial boxes. Just because racism exists doesn't mean your analysis of it is correct. People should always be suspicious of tribalist and communalist rhetoric. Some people love invoking a 'black community' when in reality a black community does not exist: there are countless black communities all over Britain.

I am always suspicious of would-be thought leaders who want to dictate how you should think about race. Ultimately, the most identity politics can offer you is the potential freedom to be a black man. But we need a far more radical freedom than that. We need the freedom that allows you to become the best man you can be, not the best black man you can be. The politics of today complicate the lives of mixed-race people. Some see this as a crunch moment where you have to pick a side, especially since the emergence of Trump and his form of identity politics. Things are often framed in 'Are you with us or with them?' tones these days. There is pressure to declare which tribe you are loyal to. These pressures can be very difficult to resist if you are a mixed-race person who wants to belong somewhere.

One thing I do remember from school connected with race was that mixed-race girls often had issues with black girls. The core of these issues revolved around black girls being jealous mixed-race girls got a lot of attention from black guys. The black girls would get angry because they saw the mixed-race girls as stepping on their turf. I think what really drives this is a perception among black women that they are at the bottom of the sexual hierarchy. They feel the only guys they can count on being interested in them are black guys, so when they see mixed-race girls 'taking' potential suitors, they worry there'll be no men left for them.

Black women have historically been misrepresented as either masculine and ugly or as ultra-sexual Jezebel-types you'd best stay away from. They do have problems attracting male attention and there is definitely a perception white and light-skinned women are more beautiful and desirable than dark-skinned women. Hence the us-versus-them feelings in the latter. These feelings are reflected in sayings like 'he's gone to the other side' whenever a black or mixed-race guy starts dating a white girl. I really have no idea how to resolve this for now.

My mum has always been into Nigerian literature and music, and she imbued that in me. I grew up listening to Nigerian Afrobeats, to artistes like P-Square. An increasing number of Brits in my generation now listen to Nigerian music. It's a cool feeling when someone tells me they've just discovered a Nigerian artiste and it's someone I've been listening to for years, back when no one here knew who they were.

Thanks to my mum, I also grew up reading novels by the likes of Nigerian writers Chinua Achebe and Wole Soyinka. I connected to those stories despite their distance from the realities I was living in. I liked their focus on the conflict between tradition and modernity, and between the individual and the group in Nigeria. I've never liked the ethnic identity politics that dominate Nigeria and have already led to one civil war.

Tribal loyalties are very strong there. This has never sat well with me. Pressure is applied in various ways to try and keep you loyal to the group. My Nigerian uncle is always joking about how I must marry an Edo woman like my mother, someone from her ethnic group. Though my mum would never say this directly, I know she too would be delighted if I married a woman from her group.

My mum herself is quite liberal, but whenever we visit Nigeria, it always strikes me how conservative the society is. The religiosity of Nigerians is incredible. I am an atheist, but there everyone is either a Christian or a Muslim and regularly attends church or mosque. When we're in Nigeria, I usually tag along with my family to church on Sunday because that is simply what everybody does. But it's not just Christianity and Islam Nigerians believe in, there are also all sorts of superstitions about witches and black magic. These are popular not just among uneducated people. I've met very well-educated Nigerians, including in my own family, who believe in what I see as pure bullshit.

In my view, superstitious thinking is one of the major things holding back Nigeria. And it's not harmless superstition either. People offer human sacrifices to perform rituals they believe will make them rich. Children are tortured because it is believed they possess demons which need to be exorcised. People join all sorts of 'secret societies' where rituals are performed to appease ancestral gods and all sorts of supernatural entities. The superstitious thinking encourages conspiratorial thinking.

Many Nigerians will tell you the West is trying to 'export' homosexuality to Africa. All part of a plan for Western culture to dominate the world. Another thing that gets me is how unabashedly patriarchal Nigeria is. Even if a woman works twelve-hour days, the man is still automatically regarded as the boss of the house. Parents consider sons to be more important than daughters. 'Tradition' is used to justify all sorts of conveniences for men. My uncle says tradition is what entitles him to the two wives he has.

The society is also very hierarchical. My mum usually spends most of the plane journey there reminding me to act deferentially towards my uncles and aunties. I must always say, 'Good morning, sir' and 'Good morning, ma.' If not, they would be very offended. For someone brought up in Britain, things like this make me feel very different in Nigeria, like this is not my world, I don't belong here.

The things we take for granted here in Britain don't work there, like non-stop electricity. Most of the time there is no power from the state grid, so people have to use generators for light. In other words, to have light twenty-four hours a day in Nigeria, you have to be quite rich considering all the fuel you'll have to consume.

As someone whose mum is Nigerian, I've always been disturbed by how many issues the country has. I've always wanted things to get better there. When I was younger, I'd get outraged at all the corruption in government and things like that. But then I started sensing that the middle- and upper-class people I came into contact with don't really care about what is going on in the country as a whole. All they care about is making money. They are like parasites sucking the blood out of the country in their own attempt to survive.

What I do like about Nigeria is the way people work hard and party hard. I also like the close attention Nigerians pay to how they dress. Sometimes they can be a bit too flashy and over the top, but I generally like that attitude of always trying to look your best, always dressing to impress.

Even though I spent some of my childhood in Africa, I am very culturally British. I might support the Nigerian football team at the World Cup, but that doesn't change this fact. Like most people, I went through a period in my youth when I was trying to find myself. Race was an element of this search. Looking back, I realise I became interested in black radical thinkers to try and resolve the contradictions I was feeling inside. But I've moved on from my fascination with race. I'm now more interested in developing my individual self, as my mum always encouraged me to do.

There is this absurd idea of 'acting black', which originated in America. If you speak a certain way, you are either acting black or acting white. If you are too bookish, you are 'acting white'. If you're too 'posh', you're not 'acting black'. Unfortunately, this kind of gangster mentality is becoming increasingly popular among some young black Britons, especially males. What is bizarre is that this kind of thinking is often pushed by relatively well-educated black intellectuals here, people with authoritarian personalities who want to decide what other people do and think. They want you to believe there is only one way of being black and others must conform to this or risk being outed as 'coconuts'.

I once watched a close mixed-race friend of mine change before my very eyes under such pressure because he wanted to conform to demands he 'act black'. His metamorphosis was a weird thing to observe because I knew he wasn't being himself. It was all so forced.

I want to live in a society where people are seen as complicated individuals, a society where no one is put in a box because of their skin colour by anyone of any skin colour.

I really think we need to transcend the restrictive definitions racial categories impose on us and adopt a much more humanistic approach to issues. There is no doubt there are problems in the way British society functions with regards to race, but no mixed-race person should allow that to make you doubt your own individuality. Be yourself. There is no reason you have to conform in order to confirm that you are this or that.

But I know many people do conform because they want to feel accepted by a group. As human beings, we all want to connect. Paradoxically, I think things were better in the twentieth century in some aspects. At least we had social movements with universalistic aspirations, like Marxism. People of all skin colours were able to connect to such ideals. But the identitarian movements of today are much more narrow-minded and exclusivist.

There is some truth in claims of the existence of white privilege and white-passing privilege for very light-skinned people. But compared to the totality of experiences you will have in your time here on earth, these privileges will not define your life. Will things be easier for you in some contexts and situations? Perhaps. But there are so many other factors that play a role in how our lives unfold, that focusing on skin colour as the key is absurd and often blown out of all proportion. Yes, wide disparities do exist between whites and other racial groups in this country, but they exist for various reasons, only one of which is or might be race.

Ultimately, I think a lot about how you view race has to do with your general attitude to people and the world. Some ethnic minorities complain a lot about being asked questions like, 'Where are you from?' It is often described as this traumatising experience, the worst question you can ever be asked as a black or brown person.

I know what people are really asking when they pose that question. They are asking about my ethnic origins because I clearly don't look like the standard white Brit. So they are curious about how I came to be. I don't feel offended by this question or consider it a traumatising experience. I say my mother is from Nigeria and my father is white British. Simple. That's usually the end of it unless it happens to be someone particularly interested in Nigeria. I really don't see the big deal in this.

One of the popular perceptions about mixed-race people that I don't like is the idea we are these vulnerable, traumatised individuals in a perpetual identity crisis. Some of us are. But I also know a lot of mixed-race people who are very confident human beings just wanting to live their lives and not be defined by race. They don't want to dance to the tune of identity politics and victimhood. They have no patience for this climate of fatalism and pessimism about Britain simply being a racist nation and there's pretty much nothing we can do about it. This is simply not how we see the reality of Britain today.

Ralph was so eloquent in describing his individualist stance to identity, there really doesn't seem much I could add to that. One thing I thought about when listening to him, however, was how, aside bewilderment at being seen as white in Africa, another common trope in the stories of mixed-race Britons of African heritage who visited there was just how culturally British the place made them feel. Just like Daniela in Colombia. Sometimes we learn more about ourselves in a foreign land than we do at home. Most importantly, we learn who we are not.

The conservatism, religiosity and often far-reaching patriarchy of African societies were something Britons like Ralph and others found difficult to accept. It is hard to understand the logic of a culture if you have never been immersed in it. Having an African parent does not make you an African because the essence of Africanness is culture, not blackness. Blackness may be meaningful in Britain where most people are white, but it is meaningless in an African society where everyone is black. What is meaningful in African societies are the cultures through which people make sense of the world.

When I say having an African parent does not make you an African, I am not trying to deny anybody Africanness (as if I could). I am simply stating the reality of how Africans tend to view mixed-race people brought up in Western cultures, and understandably so. Even though I grew up in Nigeria, I am but an amateur African in terms of cultural knowledge and how I live my everyday life. I do, however, understand enough to see the logic of many African values that baffle the European mind.

Listening to Ralph's take on Nigerian religiosity, conservatism, ethnocentrism, corruption and patriarchy reminded me a bit of listening to my mum. You know that story where a person gets married to someone from a different culture, moves to their spouse's country, is put off by the way things are done there at first, but then slowly comes to understand and appreciate the place? That was not my mum's story. In fact, it pretty much happened the other way round.

When my mum first arrived in Nigeria in 1970, she was fascinated by the country. Everything was so new for her, so different, she gobbled it all up. She read books about Nigerian history and its diverse cultures. She wanted to know everything about the place. She wanted to understand. She wanted to belong. But Nigeria was not impressed. By that I mean the middle-class, often intellectual, Nigerian world into which she was thrust. She sensed a certain hostility from some Nigerian women who were unhappy seeing so many eligible Nigerian men come back from their studies abroad with white wives.

In some intellectual circles, it was felt interracial marriages, especially those involving a white spouse, were sending the wrong message to post-colonial Nigerian society. The 1970s ushered in a wave of cultural nationalism that swept Nigeria and much of post-colonial Africa. Brilliant authors such as Wole Soyinka and Chinua Achebe, who Ralph mentioned, were writing about how Africans needed to shed their colonial mentality and rediscover themselves. Rediscover their Africanness.

Coupled with the black cultural wave from across the ocean in America, the sentiments behind slogans such as 'Black is beautiful' were very much the vogue in 1970s Nigerian intellectual circles. Some of the more zealous supporters of this wave suggested the Nigerian men marrying white women were doing so out of a racial complex or an illogical love of whiteness. Suffice to say, this was not the kind of example the educated elements of the country needed to be giving at this point in history. My mum was caught in the middle of all this.

My father's family, too, showed my mum their displeasure at him having married her. In their case, the reasons were purely cultural, not racial or ideological. My dad hails from the Yoruba 'ethnic group' in Nigeria. I use the term in quotation marks because I have always found it odd that the three million Welsh and five million Scottish are 'nations' while forty million Yorubas are an 'ethnic group'. This semantic absurdity is the result of a neat trick of mislabelling that took place during the colonial era.

Somewhere along the line of the colonial project, Britain decided the territory inhabited by hundreds of diverse collectives which it had dubbed 'Nigeria' was now to become a 'nation-state'. Its pre-colonial communities, no matter their size, were proclaimed 'tribes' or 'ethnic groups'. The logic behind this was for Yorubas *et al.* not to think of themselves as nations because, if they did, that would create complications for the Nigerian nation-building project. It is difficult to imagine a multinational nation.

So, anyway, my dad is a Yoruba. The Yorubas are very proud of their culture and history. They prefer their sons and daughters to marry fellow Yorubas because that means their marriages will be shaped by Yoruba culture and, very importantly, their children will be raised with Yoruba cultural values, speaking the language and respecting the traditions. Through these children, Yorubaness will be passed on to the next generation. Mortality transformed into continuity is the genius of identity.

A Yoruba family member marrying a white person brings a whole load of unwanted complications to the picture. Think about it from the point of view of the family. In our son's home, Yorubaness will now have to compete with *oyinbo* culture, which we know is very different from ours and thinks it knows everything better than we do. Worst of all, our son's children will be raised by a white woman who will obviously raise them in her ways rather than our ways.

Our son's children may never even learn how to speak our language, the foundation of our identity. How can children who do not speak Yoruba be taught Yoruba proverbs and schooled in our traditions? These children will be Yoruba in name only, essentially lost to the group. Worse, they might be lost to the family itself. We all know white people don't care about their extended families. For them, the immediate nuclear family is what counts.

What if the white mother tells our son's children we are not important? They will grow up feeling no sense of obligation towards us. We won't be able to count on their loyalty. The children will likely leave Nigeria for their mother's homeland after they finish secondary school or university here because life is easier over there. And that could be the last we ever see of them. Best-case scenario, once in a few years they will come here on vacation for a few weeks, complain about the heat, the corruption and the mosquitos, and go back to the white lands in which they live.

If I were in my father's family's shoes, I too would have been unhappy at him marrying a white woman. And truth is, in my case, their cultural anxieties were absolutely warranted. I understand some Yoruba, but I can't really speak the language at anything more than a very basic level. I definitely don't understand it well enough to get the proverbs, the main route by which Yoruba wisdoms are shared. My knowledge of Yoruba tradition and culture is limited to say the least. It would be disingenuous of me to say Yorubaness means much to me. Neither do I feel the kind of obligation towards my extended family that a full-blooded Yoruba would feel. I am their loss.

My mum would tell me how, at family gatherings, my dad's people would speak Yoruba to each other while she was around, purposely excluding her from the conversation. This happened in other social situations as well. Worse thing for her was that at Nigerian social events, the general rule was for the men to sit on one side of the room and talk men stuff while the women sat together and talked women stuff.

So she'd usually be separated from my dad and essentially often spend the evening ignored while the women spoke in their 'ethnic' language. This would not sit well with anybody; it particularly did not sit well with my mum who loved to be at the centre of a conversation. She was denied that in Nigeria. Of course, not all the time and not by everybody. But over the years it happened often enough for her to start feeling the kind of resentment that comes when we feel ignored. That 'you don't like me, well I don't like you too' attitude.

She generally stopped going to Nigerian gatherings with my dad unless she knew for sure there would be people to whom she'd be able to chat. Her close circle of friends became mostly white women who were also married to Nigerian men. These German, Scottish, Polish, Finnish and Irish women all bonded in their shared otherness in Nigerian society. I do not recall my mum having a single close Nigerian female friend. I remember some black American and Caribbean friends who used to come round when I was little before they left Nigeria, but no Nigerian friends. 'Maybe they didn't think they had anything in common with me. I guess they were right. I've never really been able to find common ground with them either,' she said to me when I asked her one day.

The 1970s, when my parents moved to Nigeria, was also a very optimistic decade. The country was still relishing its recently won independence. There were plentiful economic opportunities for the relatively few university-educated Nigerians such as my father who, as I said earlier, was an architect. He found work easily and was soon making good money. But there wasn't much work available for a female Polish journalist in 1970s Nigeria. My mum did a few jobs completely unrelated to her profession but none of them really worked out, so my dad eventually told her to stay at home and focus on trying to get pregnant.

My mum eventually had me in 1978 and I became the centre of her life. Our relationship was one of mutual adoration and we were inseparable when I was growing up. I'd come back from school and tell her every little detail about what happened in my day. I was a real mummy's boy. This meant my mum's opinions of the world shaped my thinking more than anybody else's when I was a young kid. Certainly more than my father's. And her opinions of Nigeria grew increasingly negative as I grew older.

By the late 1980s, when I was in my formative years, the heady optimism of the 1970s was long gone. Nigeria's oil boom was over, and the country was in a state of perpetual economic crisis, ruled by one group of corrupt generals or the other. The generals took out loans from the IMF that were conditional on Nigeria implementing draconian austerity measures. The local currency became virtually worthless overnight. Inflation skyrocketed. Most Nigerians are very poor, so my family was still better off than most of the country. But with only my dad working, money became tight. My dad would design houses for clients and sometimes wait years to get paid or not get paid at all. We could no longer afford to eat the posh stuff such as ham and cheese, which were imported and expensive. My dad frowned at me having more than one egg for breakfast. Before, families such as ours could vacation abroad regularly. That stopped overnight. I don't think a middle class has ever gone broke as fast as it did in late 1980s Nigeria.

Ever since I can remember, there had always been regular power cuts in Lagos. Now they became even more regular. Before it used to be the case we had power cuts in between having light, now we had light in between having power cuts. Water stopped coming out of the public pipes. So if you wanted running water in your home, you needed to build your own private well, get a pumping machine and essentially supply yourself with water. It was messed up. And in the midst of all this, the newspaper headlines every day screamed about the billions going missing from state coffers. To add insult to injury, in the midst of a society growing poorer by the day, the Nigerians in government looting the country didn't even bother to hide the fact they were stealing. They flaunted their stolen wealth in your face, confident there was nothing you could do except envy them.

By the time I was in my early teens, my mum complained about Nigeria every single day. 'Why does everyone have to be so corrupt here? Why is this country such a mess? Why can't anything work properly here? Why can't things be organised better? When is this country ever going to become a normal country?'

My father's reactions to her criticisms gave me my first lesson in race psychology. When he discussed Nigeria with his Nigerian friends, they complained about all the problems my mum complained about and more. They talked about how the generals had ruined the country, how nothing worked, how badly things were organised, how values such as honesty and hard work were no longer respected but corrupt people were because they had money, how the society had lost its way. But when my mum would say these same things, my dad would immediately assume a defensive stance.

'Well, what do you expect of a country that was still a British colony not so long ago?'

'Not so long ago? It's been over thirty years! How long are you going to be talking about colonialism?'

'You don't understand.'

'What don't I understand?'

'Anything. Do you think it's easy to build a country from scratch? Rome wasn't built in a day, you know.'

'What does Rome have to do with Nigeria?'

'You keep on criticising Nigeria. How much better is Poland than Nigeria anyway? You were a communist country until just recently. After all, it's not as if you can compare Poland to developed countries in western Europe. Poland is way behind the likes of England or Germany.'

'Yes it is. But even during communism we had twenty-four-hour electricity and running water. You people can't even get that right here.'

'What do you mean by "you people"?'

'What do you mean "what do I mean"? You know exactly what I mean. You Nigerians.'

'Well, nobody is forcing you to stay here.'

My dad's radically different response when my mum criticised Nigeria and when his Nigerian friends did taught me a really valuable lesson. Nigerians and Africans generally know perfectly well that post-colonial Africa has so far been a failure, but they can't bear white people pointing that out. However innocently ventured, it will always be perceived as a rehash of the humiliating argument Europeans deployed to justify colonialism in the first place: 'You people aren't up to it.'

119

After an initial period of accepting this claim in the early colonial era, the African intellectual response evolved into one of defiant indignation: 'Rubbish. Of course we are. That is just your excuse to stay here and continue plundering our resources.' Educated Nigerians such as my father who personally experienced colonialism firmly believed Nigerians were up to it. But decades into independence, everything seemed to be going horribly wrong.

This was very frustrating for people such as him who just wanted to work hard and help build their country. Yet, it was almost as if successive Nigerian governments were *trying* to prove the white man had been right after all. 'What the hell is going on? We know we can do much better than this,' people such as my father screamed. But those in power seemed more interested in becoming as rich as possible than in building a successful country.

So to have my mother asking what could be interpreted as 'perhaps you people *aren't* up to it' questions infuriated my dad. Especially as he had no hard evidence he could cite to prove Africans were capable of building successful modern states. There was no indisputable success story on the continent. That time between when you are assumed worse and when you have indisputably disproved that assumption is a psychologically fraught one. A period when your guard is up.

You know you are better than they say you are, but you don't have the hard evidence to shut your doubters into silence and make them look stupid for having made those assumptions in the first place. If Africa was doing well today, with at least a few indisputably successful states, those white claims of black inferiority would now be recalled with much amusement and mockery by African intellectuals. But no matter how we try to spin it, the reality is that Africa is *not* doing well.

The wealth and power imbalance between the black world and the white world is no smaller today than it was at independence. On the contrary, it has grown even bigger. In 1960 when the independence wave began, GDP per capita in sub-Saharan Africa stood at $987 compared to $6825 for western Europe, according to OECD figures. Half a century later, in 2010, the figures stood at $1481 compared to $20,841. In those fifty years the GDP per capita gap between western Europe and black Africa doubled from sevenfold to fourteenfold! This depressing reality makes the humiliations of the past still sting in the present. It also makes Africans and black people in general acutely aware that white people still look down on them. As a result, the default emotional stance of black towards white is an instinctive defensiveness. Self-criticism is reserved for black ears only.

As the African-American writer W. E. B. Du Bois once put it: 'Our worst side has been so shamelessly emphasised that we are denying we have or ever had a worst side. In all sorts of ways we are hemmed in.' Black people will continue to feel 'hemmed in' as long as Africa, the only continent run by black folk, remains significantly behind the rest of the world in terms of economic development and effective self-organisation. For as long as this remains the case, there will continue to be a group of white people sniggering gleefully in the corner, 'See? We said so all along. They ain't up to it.'

It is the knowledge that that kind of white people are still very much around that causes the African to self-censor in the presence of whites. Many white people such as my mum have never really understood how deeply and strongly these feelings run, especially as black people are often loath to admit them. For to do so is to acknowledge vulnerability. Perhaps even an element of self-doubt. And we can never show self-doubt again. Because if we do, the white man will exploit it as mercilessly as he did when we showed it before.

He will have us return to our previous position as his inferiors. So no matter how hard our eyes sting, we must not blink. This is the psychological dynamic that governs the relationship between black and white today. I learnt early on not to expect a black person to speak honestly about black shortcomings in the presence of a white person, even if that person is his wife.

Another thing that frustrated my mum in Nigeria, as my dad's family had rightly predicted, was the extended family culture. The way she saw it, his family members were constantly coming to him for financial help while he never got anything from them in return. Although things became quite difficult for us as well by the early 1990s, my dad was still financially better-off than the rest of his family. To my mum, the relationship was one of exploitation, plain and simple. Thing is, she didn't get the logic of the culture.

My dad *was* receiving something from his family in return, something highly valued and carefully rationed in his cultural universe: respect. In return for helping out financially, he got to play the emotionally rewarding role of family patriarch. If his family members had a dispute, they came to him to resolve it. When my dad spoke at family meetings, everyone listened. They laughed at his jokes, no matter how unfunny. His opinions were never contradicted except in a very roundabout deferential fashion.

At the start of family meetings, he would be thanked profusely for any recent help he'd provided, reminding everyone of his benefactor status within the fold. In an honour culture, respect and esteem mean everything.

As a young boy fighting for esteem among my Nigerian peers, I understood exactly why my dad was generous with his family when he could be. It was not out of the naive kindness of his heart. Every society lives in its own moral matrix. Outsiders see it for the matrix it is, insiders simply live it. I was in the unique position of living both inside and outside the matrix.

Because I could see Nigeria through my mum's critical eyes, I felt different from the kids around me. To them, the way Nigeria worked was basically 'the way things are'. But because my mum had told me how things worked in Poland and gave me a lot of novels to read set in different countries and continents, I knew this was not how the world worked, this was how Nigeria worked. On the other hand, I also saw certain things through Nigerian eyes rather than my mother's eyes. I never liked her criticism of Nigerian religiosity, for instance.

There are definitely downsides to the popular Nigerian belief that virtually everything that happens here on earth is orchestrated by God. This breeds a fatalistic worldview in which you generally accept things as they are because that is obviously how God wishes them to be. This allows Nigeria's rulers to get away with nauseating levels of corruption and oppression. People genuinely believe they have been placed in their high stations by God – how else could they have got so high? – and should thus not be questioned too rigorously. After all, God knows best. This kind of stance does not encourage critical thinking, something every society needs to develop its potential.

Nevertheless, while I would never claim to be the holiest of Christians myself, I have always strongly disliked the anti-religious bent of which secular Western societies are so proud. The constant sniggering at Christian beliefs and the arrogant assumption we are the highest form of existence in the universe. I like the fact the Nigerian believes life itself is a gift, and that anything we get from it during our time here on earth, no matter how small, is worth being grateful for. The Westerner is rarely grateful for anything but feels entitled to everything.

That presumptuous sense of entitlement, that lack of existential humility and seeming unawareness of how utterly inconsequential we all are, is something I find very grating in the Western world. If anything positive can come out of our terrible collective experience with Covid-19, I am hoping it will be in the form of a greater sense of humility and gratitude in the West. Humility at the reality we are not the masters of the universe and gratitude for the privilege of life itself. While on an individual basis, Nigerians can be quite proud, even sometimes arrogant, there is a palpable collective humility they demonstrate in the belief we are not in control. That as humans we are but tiny insignificant specks of dust in a universe ultimately beyond our understanding.

I am happy to have a Nigerian wife with whom I can say a prayer of thanks before each meal. I am happy to have a Nigerian wife who constantly reminds me we should be grateful for the things we have, grateful for life itself, and that we should never take anything for granted. I am happy to have a Nigerian wife who reads the Bible every day and does her best to live like a good Christian. My wife is my moral compass. Of all the things I am grateful to Nigeria and God for, she is definitely number one. Without her, I would be just another lost soul wandering the Western wilderness.

# Chapter 8

# Time to end the one-drop rule

Blaise's father is Irish while her mother is Guyanese. She spent her childhood shuttling between Ireland and England. She is twenty-seven and currently lives in London.

My parents met in the early 1990s at a London squat rave. At the time, my dad was around twenty-six and had run away from Ireland while my mum was twenty-nine. They hooked up, but they were never a couple nor planned to be. I was conceived entirely by accident. When my father found out my mum was pregnant, he said he wasn't ready to have a child. But she wanted to keep me and told him he wouldn't have to be involved in raising me if he preferred it that way. My dad gladly took the not-involved option. He is from a place in southern Ireland that is amazingly beautiful but has scarcely any racial diversity. I think the idea of having a child terrified him at the time; the idea of having a mixed-race child was simply too much.

Though he did want to start seeing me about a year after I was born, he wasn't really active in my life during my earliest years. My mum raised me in London with the help of her amazing community of friends. We lived in Hampstead. My dad moved back to Ireland when I was four, so from the age of five or so I would go visit him there on holidays. By then, he'd gotten used to the fact he had a daughter like me. I would spend half my summers in Ireland with him and the other half in London with my mum.

One thing I learnt early on in life is how love and friendship can render race irrelevant. I wasn't just raised by my mum. I was raised by her diverse group of friends as well, some white English, some Irish, some African, and a couple of them mixed race. I had so many godmothers I was spoilt rotten. They came round ours all the time. They picked me up from school when my mum couldn't make it because of work. They were always there for both of us.

My godmothers were all very different people, but they had one thing in common: they loved my mum, and because they loved her, they loved me. She met most of them while growing up in the care system in Bedfordshire. There is a special bond between kids who grew up together in care. My mum was a social worker, as were most of her friends. Thanks to them, I can honestly say, hand on heart, I never missed having a dad at home.

By the time I was old enough to hop on a plane all by myself and go visit him in Ireland, I actually kind of liked my family situation. I had my London life with my mum and my godmothers, but I could be transported into the lush green world of southern Ireland in a mere couple of hours. I didn't have that much contact with my extended Guyanese family growing up. They are spread all over the world, so we usually only met at funerals and major family events.

I never thought being mixed race was an issue until school age. Like with many other mixed-race girls I know, hair was a major thing. All the girls I saw on TV and most of the girls at school were white and had straight hair. In my head I was Buffy the Vampire Slayer, but I couldn't be that in real life because I didn't have the hair to be Buffy. I wanted straight hair, too. I couldn't understand why my hair couldn't be straight.

I have typical mixed-race-girl hair; half curly, half straight. I struggled to maintain it and my mum could see I didn't like the styles she was doing for me. I had to have my hair conditioned and straightened, but even when it was down, it still didn't look the same as the white girls' hair. All this was a big deal for me as a young girl.

The feeling of difference intensified when we got to year six and kids started fancying other kids. I noticed I was never really fancied by any of the boys. We'd play husbands and wives and the group would immediately pair me with Habib, the only other dark-skinned child around. It all felt a bit weird but I wasn't sure why this was happening. There wasn't much diversity in my Hampstead primary school and all the boys I fancied were white blondes. I didn't understand why I couldn't be with them and why they always seemed to fancy the blonde girls. It was really annoying and quite disheartening. At the time, I thought I simply wasn't fanciable, but I didn't connect it to race in any way.

When I was ten, I finally summoned up the courage to ask this boy I really liked why he didn't fancy me. 'Er . . . because I like white blonde girls,' he mumbled in response. I was dumbfounded. It was one of those moments that stick with you for the rest of your life. You remember what you were wearing, what kind of room you were in and exactly how you felt. You might experience worse cases of othering or racism, but that kind of moment when someone tells you something like that to your face matter-of-factly, those moments you remember. After my initial shock, I remember just feeling sad about the whole thing.

In my teens, I listened to a lot of metal and often felt quite depressed. I didn't like the way I looked (I was also a bit chubby) and that made me feel insecure. At the time, I was an only child living on a well-to-do street where kids didn't come out to play outside. My mum worked long hours and usually came home late. So I'd sit in my room on my own for hours, playing with imaginary friends. I created all sorts of dialogues and scenarios in my head. I think that's what got me interested in acting, which I did for some years and would potentially like to go back to sometime in the future. Right now, I work for London Zoo.

When I'd visit my dad in Ireland, there were never any hair products available for my kind of hair. My dad himself was clueless about this sort of thing. So whenever I'd get back from Ireland, my mum would always scream in horror at the state of my hair. A lot of mixed-race girls relax their hair. But my mum never let me do that. She said I had beautiful hair and didn't need to relax it. She never straightened her own hair either, but always wore it natural. At the time her stance annoyed me because all the mixed-race girls I knew were allowed to relax their hair. But looking back now, I am grateful she never let me do that. She never gave in to society's unspoken rule that said only straight hair is beautiful. She let me know curly Afro hair was beautiful too.

I've experienced some racist incidents in Ireland, the kind I can't imagine happening in London. An Irish boy once called me a 'nigger' because I didn't want to make out with him. First he fancied me and wanted us to kiss, but once I rejected him, I became a 'nigger'. Just a few years ago, I was walking down the street in my dad's village. A group of boys passed me and one of them slapped my bum. I'm a massive feminist so I find that kind of behaviour completely unacceptable. I ran up to them and we had an argument. When it got really heated, one of the boys called me a 'cotton-picking nigger'. I was shocked. People still saying that kind of stuff in this century?!

My dad is from a small Irish village, the kind of place where there are no black people. When I'd visit him, the other villagers would often stare when I passed by. Even driving, they'd be staring at me from their cars. But I could sense it was mostly out of curiosity rather than anything malicious. I love Ireland. A few negative experiences haven't changed this. I consider it my home just as much as England. I am incredibly proud of being Irish. There is something mystical about the country, something so beautiful about the landscape and Celtic culture. I love how hilarious Irish people can be. The Irish used to face discrimination in the days of 'No Irish, no dogs, no coloureds.' Of course, they never faced the kind of racism black people faced, but they do know what it's like to have been systematically discriminated against as a group. English people have never known that feeling.

I love London, but I would move to Ireland in a heartbeat. This despite the fact anytime I tell Irish people I'm Irish, they seem quite puzzled. 'How?' is their most common response. I have to explain that my dad is Irish. That's the difference between England and Ireland. If someone who looks like me says they are British or even English, few people in England would ask 'How?' with a puzzled expression on their face. But many Irish still haven't quite internalised the idea someone of visibly black heritage like me can be Irish.

My mum went out of her way to teach me about both my heritages. She'd tell me stories about Guyana and the black people who lived there. She made sure I kept in touch with black culture and history. She talked about America and slavery, told me how black people used to be treated there. She educated me on how the apartheid system had worked in South Africa. She let me know there were white people who were racists, white people who simply hated black people.

But she also taught me about Irish culture and history, which I think was pretty amazing considering she was no longer in a relationship with my father. She'd tell me about Irish artistes like Van Morrison and Christy Moore. She talked about the potato famine of the 1800s and how that affected Irish society and culture. She made Irish dishes and told me about St Patrick's Day. These were little things, but for a black woman with no Irish roots, I think this was pretty incredible stuff. My mum always emphasised I was both Guyanese and Irish. My dad barely taught me anything about Ireland, much less about Guyana!

I think the way my mum brought me up is a major reason I firmly identify as mixed race, not as black or white. When people call me black, I correct them. 'I am not black, I am mixed race,' I tell them. When you're mixed race, people often try to place you in the identity category they think is appropriate. I refuse to accept this.

I know some people will say I am trying to distance myself from blackness. They will say I think I am better than black people or that I am ashamed of my black roots and consumed by self-hate. They will say people like me are helping to entrench colourism in our society. For me to act like colourism isn't a thing would be wrong. It is. There definitely seems to be this general belief that the lighter-skinned you are, the more beautiful you are. And it exists in many different cultures, not just Britain or the West.

I've had guys say to me they would date a mixed-race girl, but they'd never date a black girl. I don't get this. My mother is a beautiful black woman and I see stunning black women all over the place. Yet black women continue to be massively undervalued when it comes to notions of attractiveness. So I understand where black people are coming from when they react negatively to mixed-race people like myself differentiating ourselves from them. But the fact of the matter is that I have a white father and a black mother, so to say I am black or white is simply inaccurate. And it certainly doesn't accurately describe how I feel. My mother is black. I am not black, I am mixed race.

To say I am black is to bow down to the one-drop rule invented by white racists, which says that if you're not 100 per cent white, then you are black. Why should a bunch of racists long dead still be deciding who is what today? It seems quite ironic that a rule imposed by white racists centuries ago is still being adhered to by some in the black community today. It's not that I am ashamed of my black roots, but I am descended from two amazing peoples and cultures and I am proud of both of them. I am not going to apologise to anyone for that. And no one is going to pressure me into claiming to be something I don't feel I am on the inside.

I am very happy my mum always allowed me to be mixed race. I know it's not easy raising a child like myself. But it's all about opening the minds of future generations. Only now are we starting to have open discussions about what it feels like to be mixed race. Only recently have mixed-race people started feeling confident enough about their status to say the kinds of things I am saying without being afraid of what one or the other community might say about them. I love both sides of me and I should never have to pick.

These days it is unfashionable to say you don't see colour. But I don't. I see people, not colours. If you are horrible, you are not a horrible white man or a horrible Asian, you are a horrible person. I'm not saying I don't see the lack of diversity in certain environments in Britain. I see it in my current workplace, for instance, and I believe there needs to be a push for way more diversity in places where it is lacking. But that doesn't mean I view the people I work with as white people, I simply view them as people. One should be proud of one's heritage, but I do not believe that means you should mentally divide people according to race.

There is some truth to the idea it is easier for white people to relate to mixed-race people than to black people. If one is black and three is white, we are two. Likewise, black people will instinctively feel more of a cultural affinity with someone like me than with white people. This is an opportunity for us to be bridges from one to the other.

The mixed-race friends I have navigate their mixed heritages in various ways. Some constantly joke about it. If they are late for a meeting, they'll say that's their 'black side' coming out or stuff like that. But many of them feel they are often being forced to pick a side, however subtly, and they don't like feeling pressured to do that. However, many are still not ready to 'come out' on this issue. They are wary of what others might say if they speak more honestly about how they view their identities. But there is no doubt it is already much easier for my generation to talk about these things openly than it was for those before us. It will be even easier for future generations.

Considering my current boyfriend is white, I know if we were to have kids sometime in the future there is a high probability they would look white-passing or maybe even simply white. I would definitely want them to know black history, but I would not want them to feel pressured to fit into any kind of box either. I would teach them about their multiple heritages and leave the rest up to them. I'm sure attitudes towards mixed-race people will be more nuanced and understanding by then.

Racism definitely still exists in Britain. But it's not just from white people. There are loads of black and Asian racists around too. Racism is a mindset, not a physical attribute. We mostly hear about it in the context of white people. But I've also been around black people who are proud to say they would never date a white person or would never want mixed-race children because they don't believe races should mix.

If a white person said this, you can imagine the uproar. I myself would be outraged. The reaction should be no different when a black person says things like this. But it is different. There is usually no outrage. It's more like, 'Well, if that's how you feel, fair enough then.' This is wrong. Everyone should be held to the same standards, irrespective of their skin colour.

I've been called a 'half-breed' and 'lightie' by black people. That is actively using my skin colour against me. Some argue racism is prejudice plus power, so black prejudice doesn't harm anyone because black people don't have power. I get this argument. I am strongly into Black Lives Matter and similar movements. White privilege exists. I couldn't date a white guy who doesn't understand the privilege he has as a result of his skin colour. And yes, white people do have way more power than black people. But considering they are the vast majority of Britain's population, that's hardly surprising.

I don't want to downplay anyone's pain. I know I haven't experienced the kind of racism some black people have experienced in Britain. But I think you can be racist no matter your skin colour. Racism is a human problem, not a white problem. We live in a white-majority society so naturally we focus on the problem in white people. And I agree it seems to be more of a problem in white people than in other people. But if an Asian or a black person is making racist comments or openly discriminating against people from other groups, why on earth can we not just accept that is racism, too?

As Blaise rightly points out, in the twentieth century, perceptions of mixed black and white people were dominated by the idea behind the racist one-drop rule developed in America, which stated that even a minuscule amount of black ancestry meant you were black. While that rule is no longer legally in effect, it is still very much psychologically in effect in a place as far away from America as Britain, as some of the stories we have heard indicate.

But Blaise represents a new kind of mixed black and white person: one significantly more assertive than her predecessors. Due to the historical contexts of racism and colourism, people of black and white heritage who have emphasised they consider themselves mixed race, not black, have often faced bruising accusations from some in the black community.

As Blaise clearly realises, taking a position like hers often leads to talk of trying to distance yourself from blackness, of internalised self-hate, or of a combination of both. In the first case, it is suggested you are one of those mixed-race people who think you're better than black folk because you have some white in you. You have a superiority complex towards black people and, for this reason, don't want to be associated with blackness. Or you are attributed mercenary motives. You are an opportunist who wants to use your 'proximity to whiteness' for personal advantage and think distancing yourself from blackness is simply the beneficial thing to do since everyone knows white people are where the money is at. So that's where you want to be – screw black people.

Or you are pronounced to have an inferiority complex. You have come to internalise the ideology of white supremacy so deeply that you are ashamed of your blackness and want to do everything to escape it. You are a mixed-race Michael Jackson, terrified of the world seeing you as black. Perhaps you suffer from a combination of all these issues. Whatever is the case, you are, at best inadvertently, helping propagate colourism because your distancing yourself from blackness sends a message to the world that blackness is something negative, something to be ashamed of, something to avoid. It is undeniable that in various societies at various times in history, there have been 'mulattoes' who have had all these complexes and opportunistic behaviours. It would be unrealistic to claim these issues are all dead and buried now. Colourism is very much still 'a thing', as Blaise points out and as I discussed in an earlier chapter.

But that does not give anyone the right to suggest every mixed-race person who says they don't identify as black is suffering from some kind of complex or is an immoral opportunist. Just as the fact some black men may marry white women out of a racial complex or desire to improve their societal status hardly means all black men who marry white women do so for the same reasons.

However historically understandable the misgivings about mixed-race people consciously not identifying as black may be, psychological pressure on them to do so or be accused of self-hate and worse amounts to nothing less than emotional blackmail. Toe the line or we'll paint you as someone worthy of contempt or pity. It's time to move past such tactics.

I think Blaise's assertive, unapologetic mixed-raceness is a sign of things to come among younger generations, many of whom no longer want to be prisoners of the ideas of centuries ago, ideas such as the one-drop rule. I think this is a good thing. First of all, it is a good thing because it means more mixed-race people of black and white heritage today feel they have a choice in how they can identify rather than society and history making that choice for them. It is also a good thing because surely everyone will agree the mixed-race experience should no longer be dominated by fear of rejection or reprisal, as it was for a long time. Mixed-race people of all heritages should be able to feel confident to declare boldly and loudly how exactly they see themselves, history or no history.

# Chapter 9

# People see me as white, but . . .

There is now an increasing number of Britons who have a black heritage but not one that might be visible to all. 'White-passing' or 'racially ambiguous' are terms often used to describe such individuals. We pass them on the streets every day, sometimes never even imagining for a moment that we just passed someone who has black roots. I've always wondered how folk like that deal with navigating the no-man's-land between black and white. Is it a very different experience from being of 'visible' black ancestry? If yes, how so? How do they identify and what decides that? Bea is the daughter of a British mother with Armenian roots and a mixed-race British father. She is twenty-four and grew up in the countryside around Brighton.

My father is mixed Nigerian and white English while my mother is British with Armenian roots. My great-grandma on my mum's side came here to escape the Armenian genocide of the early twentieth century. Her daughter – my grandmother – grew up in Britain and felt British. As for my mum, she grew up all over the world because her father was a British Army officer, though she spent most of her childhood in Singapore and Cyprus. On my dad's side, his Nigerian grandfather married an English lady. My dad was born and raised in London. I was also born in London twenty-four years ago, but we only lived there until I was about five years old.

After that, we moved to the countryside of Brighton, which is where I grew up. My parents wanted me, my sister and my brother to grow up in the countryside where we'd have lots of space and green. My dad grew up rather poor, so he always worked hard for us to have a more comfortable childhood than he'd had.

Brighton is a very liberal-minded, green-oriented kind of place, but it was definitely not diverse. We lived in a small village in the countryside and my dad would sometimes joke he was the only black man for miles and miles. There were sixty-nine kids in my primary school, and me and my siblings were the only children of colour. We were all very light-skinned. My older sister was the darkest, but my brother has always just looked like a white guy. I too definitely have white-passing privilege.

Obviously, when you're six or seven, you're not really thinking about race, but I remember one incident from that period really upsetting me. My dad dropped me off at primary school and when one of the kids saw him, he asked me if I was adopted. This kid clearly saw my dad as black and me as white, hence the question. I felt very confused and upset. I remember thinking to myself, *What if I am adopted?*

It's a powerful thing for a kid to start doubting their parent is their real parent. I was very aware my dad was black. Though technically mixed black and white, he's quite dark-skinned and people generally view him as a black man. But to me he was just dad; it never occurred to me that we didn't look the same to other people. I started thinking perhaps that kid was right and, when I got home, I asked my dad if indeed I was adopted. He got very upset and told me I wasn't. But I think there might have been some doubt in my mind for a while. I can't remember how long.

It was a very unsettling experience for me, being taken out of my innocent childhood bubble and shoved before the judging eyes of the outside world. After this, I started becoming very self-aware. Other little things intensified this feeling. The kids were always fascinated with my hair, which was a soft Afro. I've always had a complex about my hair. Everyone wanted to touch it. But I got mixed signals that confused me.

The girls would say they loved my curly hair, but then when their hair would get curly in the rain, they'd get really upset. Why would they get upset their hair was turning into mine if they considered it 'lovely'? I wondered. I was always trying to wet my hair and keep it as straight and unfrizzy as possible. Teachers would tell me I needed to 'control' my hair more, that it wasn't 'neat enough'. Our dinner lady was this old white lady from the countryside. She'd always go around the class saying, 'Kids, eat your crusts, it'll help your hair grow stronger,' which is one of those old wives' tales. When she got to me, she'd say, 'Well, you obviously love your crusts.' I don't think she had any bad intentions, but little otherings like that always made me feel very self-conscious.

It's these kinds of little othering experiences that my white friends can't understand. They can understand outright racism having a negative effect on someone, but they don't understand how little otherings like that could have had an eroding impact on my psyche. You can't understand it unless you experience it. My white friends say, 'Bea, you're not really black. Why are you always going on about racism? This doesn't really affect you.' It's exasperating people telling me I don't have a right to be passionate or angry about racism or exclusion because I look white to them.

I remember struggling to fit in at primary school. I got bullied a bit, though I wouldn't necessarily want to draw a link between that and race. Back then, I definitely wasn't thinking in terms of race or of being mixed race. We were not even aware of such concepts in our Brighton world at the time.

This does not mean there were no incidents that made me realise our family was different to others around us. Once we were with my dad in Brighton city and the British National Party was organising a march through the centre that day. I must have been around eleven or twelve. I can clearly remember a policeman telling my dad, 'You might want to get out of here, there's many of them coming,' and us leaving that area. I remember thinking, *Wow, my dad is black and there are people who hate him because of that.* We then joined the anti-BNP march, which was being organised by Brighton residents, chanting anti-racist slogans and all. That was a moment that stuck with me.

Another memory I have connected to race from around the same period was an incident on a bus. Me, my dad and my sister were on the bus. There was a group of white girls and a black boy was with them. They were talking about something and one of the white girls just casually said to the black boy, 'Oh, shut up nigger!' My dad turned around and said to her, 'You shouldn't use that word.' My sister was like, 'Shh dad, don't make a scene.' This is a vivid memory from my childhood.

There were also occasional comments from kids like, 'Oh, your dad is so cool.' I'd ask why and they'd say, 'Coz he's black.' Those, of course, weren't vicious, but they also served to remind me of a difference between us and the other families in our world. I thought my dad was cool, too, but I thought he was cool because he was incredibly knowledgeable and funny, not because he was black.

In general, we didn't really discuss race at home. It is only recently, as we've gotten older, that my dad has started to divulge some of his experiences growing up in 1960s Britain. I guess this was partly because we lived in such a predominantly white area and also partly because my parents wanted to raise us to be colour blind, to see people's soul rather than their body.

I would describe our home as a fusion of various cultures, some not even connected to my parents' ancestral roots. Because my parents came from different backgrounds, they each brought what they'd learnt in life to create their own unique way of raising us, based more on personal values and experiences than on a single group culture or set of values.

For instance, because my mum spent many years growing up in Singapore, she knew how to cook many dishes from that part of the world. So, while neither of my parents was actually from the region, our diet was heavily South-east Asian. Our mum also told us a lot about her experiences growing up there and so we learnt about South-east Asian cultures. Then there was my dad's very strong emphasis on personal achievement, which I think came from what his Nigerian father passed on to him. My dad said his dad always pushed him to be better, to achieve more. He did the same with us, be it in education or sports. He always told us we could do absolutely anything we wanted in life if we set out minds to it and worked hard.

One thing in my home that clearly differentiated me from my white peers at school was the kind of music my parents, especially my dad, listened to. While he listened to all kinds of music, it was mostly black music: jazz, funk, hip-hop and Afrobeat. The kids in my Brighton schools listened to the Beatles and Fleetwood Mac at home. They knew the words to those songs. I didn't know the words to those songs. I knew the words to songs like Public Enemy's 'Fight the Power'. This too created a sense of difference in me.

Things took a turn for the worse in my life from the age of twelve. I went to a comprehensive secondary school which had about 1500 pupils, of which there were perhaps 30 or so children of colour. I started constantly comparing myself to how the girls around me looked. They were all proverbial petite, skinny, straight-haired English roses. I wasn't that. I was naturally curvy with thicker thighs. I didn't feel beautiful.

I'd trained in swimming from when I was very young and was always told I looked 'strong'. I hated hearing that just like I hated my thicker thighs, no doubt inherited from my father's side. I hated the Nigerian element of my physique. I didn't want to look strong, I wanted to look fragile and delicate like the English roses around me. Maybe it's harder for females in general because we are judged more on our looks than anything else, but this was how I felt. It was especially difficult not having another me around me, not seeing another mixed-race girl in my class. I started becoming obsessed with female bodies, looking at them, then looking at myself and comparing a lot.

My obsession centred around my weight and general physique. With regards to weight, what paradoxically really started me on a downward spiral was . . . praise. I was a bit chubby when I was eleven or twelve, but by the time I was thirteen, I had shed my puppy fat and become quite skinny. Girls started complimenting how I looked, saying I looked striking and could probably become a model. Having previously felt very insecure about how I looked, I became addicted to those compliments and got it into my head that I really did want to become a model. All the models in Western fashion then were skinny white women, so I believed I needed to make sure I looked like them to become a model. I basically stopped eating and developed anorexia.

My aspiration was for white thinness and so I told myself I had to train my body to become that way because I wasn't born like that. I don't want to attribute all my problems with anorexia to my racial background. There were definitely some other personal issues going on in my head as well, other reasons behind it. But I do think the racial aspect was an important factor, especially with regards to the white Western beauty standards I was constantly being bombarded with on TV and in magazines.

Up until my late teens, I was very much consumed by this

141

shadow inside me, but I didn't really think of it in terms of race or identity. This started when I went to university in Bristol. It was university and the books and ideas I came into contact with there that equipped me with the words to describe my emotions and feelings about race and racial inequality.

Bristol as a city is very culturally and ethnically diverse. There is a vibrant Somali and Jamaican music scene and people of all shades of skin colour live in the city. But Bristol University is extremely white, privately educated and middle or upper-middle class. I made good friends there and everyone was really wonderful to me. But the demographics around me were very narrow. There was no single person of colour in my history faculty. No one really who could give me expert guidance and supervision when I was writing my dissertation, as I was specialising in black history. All the history academics in my faculty were very focused on the British Empire, from a very white British point of view.

I am very aware of how white and middle class my education has been and because most of my friends today are from the schools I went to, it is becoming increasingly apparent to me that we view things differently, especially with regards to race. Like I mentioned earlier, they can't understand why I get so worked up about racism because they basically see me as a white person. This is my conflict. People usually see me as white, but I don't *feel* white.

I think if I only had contact with a white middle-class demographic all my life, I probably would not have become as passionate as I am about racial inequalities. I would probably identify more with being white than with being black. But even though we grew up in very white Brighton, my dad was always a big advocate of black literature and art, so that consciousness was always there somewhere. But it was only reading all the literature on black history in my university years that really brought that consciousness to the fore.

However, the fact I know many people do see me as white means I worry if ethnic minorities think I am culturally appropriating from them. I don't want to come across as a white saviour. I know I am very light-skinned, and it would be incredibly arrogant of me to think me and my dark-skinned friends have shared the same experiences just because we may both have Nigerian roots. When I meet Nigerians, they almost never believe me when I say my dad is half-Nigerian. They say I'm lying, and I have to bring out pictures of him to 'prove' to them that I am mixed race.

Though I've never had the aggressive 'you're not really black' accusations some other light-skinned mixed-race people experience, it always kills me a little when people don't believe I am mixed race. It affects me negatively, having to 'prove' it. Maybe it's just me, because I care, because it's important for me that people know where I came from. My brother, for instance, couldn't care less whether black people believe he has black roots or not. He doesn't care what they think. He's always been one of those guys who's just successful and popular at everything he does, starting from sports when we were younger to his business today. If he told someone he was mixed race and they didn't believe him, he'd just laugh and move on. He knows who he is and that's all that matters to him. But I'm not like him.

I've always been more self-conscious about my identity. For instance, the way I dance is very much influenced by the way I saw my father dancing when I was a kid. But knowing people perceive me as white, I've always been self-conscious about black people seeing me on the dancefloor and wondering, 'Who's this white chick dancing like a black girl?' I've always been anxious for the black community not to see me as one of those white girls who want to be black, who just think being black is 'so cool'. I don't want them thinking I'm some white chick appropriating their culture, I just want them to know – I am here for you and I hope you are here for me. Just that bit of acceptance.

143

Like I said, my white privately educated middle- and upper-middle-class friends do not get what I am on about when I bring up race inequalities. It makes them feel uncomfortable and they often get defensive. To them, I look like them and we have a similar upbringing, so what's my problem? They don't get that I view things differently because of my blood and because of my surname. I have a long Nigerian surname, one people have always had problems pronouncing. Even during my graduation ceremony, my surname was pronounced completely wrong, in front of my parents. These are experiences 'Alice Smith' will never have. But when I bring up race issues, my friends tell me to calm down and they act like I'm crazy or over the top. This creates a distance between me and them.

In my perfect world, there'd be no such thing as 'identity'. I don't find it useful. I know why we have it, but I don't think it reflects anywhere near all the emotions and feelings I am, like love and kindness. I don't think the categories society has given me with which to categorise myself – such as 'black', 'white' or even 'mixed race' – are useful, and they are definitely divisive. I believe we are all one human family. Yes, there are differences between us in behaviour, but those differences between us should not mean we treat each other differently. We are different, but we should treat each other the same.

However, considering these identity categories do exist and are commonly used, I would like to be seen as mixed race because that is what I am. That is a fact. As for the identity category of 'British', it means nothing to me at all. I feel no pride or any other strong emotion associated with that label.

One thing I would really like society to understand is that mixed-race people, like monoracial people, are not a homogenous group. Our experiences are different so just as we should always say 'some' black, 'some' white or 'some' Asian people feel so and so way about X, so we should always do when speaking about mixed-race people.

Lumping us all together the way monoracial people are lumped together doesn't make any sense in either case. We have very different views and you should never judge a book by its cover. Just because I look similar to you does not mean we've had the same life experience.

If I were to give advice to young mixed-race girls growing up today, I'd say, don't listen to the noise. Focus inward. Focus on what you feel deep down, not on what others tell you that you are feeling or should be feeling. Don't be a projection of other people's perceptions and expectations. Develop your inner self. Do what makes you passionate, what gets you excited. And listen carefully to what other people tell you about what they are feeling inside without projecting your perceptions and expectations upon them.

'What a beautiful soul!' was my first thought after my conversation with Bea. She just seemed such a good and well-intentioned person. I felt bad for all the pain and anxieties she has experienced related to her racial background, starting from the 'little otherings' in Brighton to having to prove she is mixed race with pictures of her dad, something which she says 'always kills me a little'.

I think Bea's story is very important because it emphasises strongly a theme that came up repeatedly in the stories of other mixed-race women I spoke to: the central role of 'looks' in their self-perceptions and identity trajectories. Bea thinks it's because women are 'judged more on our looks than anything else'. I think she's spot on. Decades of feminist activism have unfortunately not changed the fundamental reality that how society treats a female individual is still largely determined by how attractive she is deemed. Hence it is hardly surprising mixed-race female self-perceptions of identity often revolve around the issue of looks.

As you may have noticed, virtually all the women of mixed black and white heritage who have told us their stories brought up the subject of their hair causing them anxieties when they were younger because it wasn't like white girls' hair. Issues revolving around looks also come up in the stories of mixed-race women of other racial configurations in later chapters. I don't think we have yet truly realised the impact of society's focus on looks in the psychology of female mixed-race identities. I dare say that subject on its own deserves a book or two. I hope Bea's story and those of other women here at least help to draw some attention to this issue.

On another note, while it is laudable Bea recognises her experiences have been different from those of her dark-skinned friends and tries to be sensitive about this, I wish we didn't live in a world where someone as good-hearted as her has to fret so much about not coming across as a 'white saviour' or being seen as 'cultural appropriating' from black people because she dances 'black'. That someone as positively inclined as Bea has to be constantly second-guessing herself about these kinds of things is for me a clear sign there is something a bit over-the-top and paranoid in the atmosphere around race in Britain today. From what I heard, all she's ever wanted is 'just that bit of acceptance' from the black people around her and acknowledgement of her black heritage by the white people around her. Surely, that is not too much to ask?

It was the same message I got from Isabella, the twenty-one-year-old daughter of a Danish father and mixed black and white British mother who grew up in New York, Copenhagen and Brighton. Although she acknowledged in refreshingly frank fashion that as a teenager her identification with blackness 'definitely had something to do with me wanting to be edgy', it was nevertheless genuine because her mother had raised her to identify with blackness. 'Whenever we visited America, my mum would take me to black history museums. She bought me books about the civil rights movement. Add the fact my mixed-black mum was the only one raising me after she and my dad separated when I was six, and by the time I was in my teens, I had really started identifying with black people and seeing myself as a woman of colour,' said Isabella.

Because she went to an all-white boarding school in Brighton, however, 'One definitely unpleasant experience I had was often hearing from my white peers how *not* black I was in comparison to my mum. For these kids, you had to have dark skin to be black. I hated them telling me this. I knew I was light-skinned and had privileges because of that, but blackness is also about culture.'

A turning point for Isabella was in her first year at the university at Edinburgh when she was elected BAME students' officer responsible for liaising between BAME students and university authorities. 'It felt great when they announced the results. I thought, wow, finally, I've been accepted. People see me as BAME!' Which doesn't mean no one tried to spoil the moment for her. 'A few minutes after the announcement of my election, a student came up to me and said, "But I thought you had to not be white to get elected BAME students' officer?" I replied that I'm not white, thinking to myself, *Jeeze, I've just been elected BAME student officer and still someone is telling me this*! However, luckily for my psyche, this student was white, so I didn't really feel that bad about it. If a black student had said that, I would undoubtedly have felt much worse,' Isabella told me.

Fortunately for her, no one ever questioned her BAME credentials again, at least not to her face. She did sometimes feel people were 'thinking about it' when she walked into a room, and often wondered how she was being racialised. This feeling of not knowing if people perceive them as having an *authentically* black heritage or not was a common theme in many of the stories I heard from white-passing people of black heritage.

This sometimes created in them an uncertainty and insecurity about their identity, as much in the presence of white people as black people. Isabella said even as a BAME student officer, 'I continued to internally question my right to be in student spaces reserved for black people.' As in Bea's case, it is laudable Isabella tries to be conscious of racial and social realities, but I didn't envy either of them what sounded like an often pretty exhausting experience. There was, however, also a different kind of story I heard about being white-passing, one best exemplified by the experiences of Dion.

# Chapter 10

# Who is that girl in the mirror?

Dion is multiracial. Her father is equal parts Jamaican, Saint Lucian, Indian and Scottish. Her mother is mixed English, Irish, Spanish, Dutch and Latvian-Jewish. She was born in London but spent a significant part of her childhood in the rather insular village of Aylesham in Kent. She is twenty-five.

My mother grew up in south-east London where she was immersed in black culture from a young age despite being white. Most of her childhood friends were black. She used to sing in a black gospel choir where she was known as the 'honorary black girl'. My mum didn't like that term because she has never been one to see colour, but she was always aware there were others who felt differently. Her parents brought her up to be very conscious of racial discrimination in Britain. Her love of music was how she met my father, who owned a record store. They had me twenty-five years ago, but their relationship didn't last. He left not long after I was born, and I've never had a relationship with him.

The first time I had to think about race was when I was around six. We were discussing family trees in class and I was asked where mummy was from and where daddy was from. All I knew about my father was that he was black. I had no recollection of how he looked. I imagined him as this very black man from Africa – tall, ebony-skinned, strong accent, wearing glasses and brightly coloured shirts. Clearly, I must have gotten this image of an African from TV because I can't imagine from where else. It shook my core when I met my father soon after and he turned out to be much lighter-skinned than I'd imagined. But I did not identify with him in any way. He was my father, not my dad.

When I was eight, my mum married a white man who became my adopted father, so I grew up surrounded by middle-class white people. I didn't have anyone of colour to identify with as a child. My appearance can be described as white-passing. Growing up, I didn't think of myself as mixed race, I thought of myself as white, just slightly darker than other white people. Ironically, my white mother was way more familiar with black culture than I was as a child. She tried to teach me about it, but it sounded foreign to me. To be honest, I wasn't really interested. I didn't feel the need to delve into that aspect of my heritage.

The arrival of my blue-eyed, blonde-haired adopted dad further entrenched my white identity. They say you see yourself reflected in the people around you. When I looked in the mirror, I couldn't recognise the girl I saw looking back at me. Her eyes were darker, her hair was darker, and her skin was darker than I imagined mine was. I didn't quite identify with that child. It was a confusing and unsettling feeling I remember having for many years. When I started using make-up in my teenage years, I'd always buy them in shades too light. 'Surely I'm not this dark. I must have gotten a tan,' I'd think to myself when trying to make them match my colour at home.

When I was eleven, we moved to a small village called Aylesham in Kent. This was a huge change from multicultural London. In the 1940s, people moved to Aylesham from the north to work in Kent's coalmines. The place is so insular many of the villagers still have a northern accent. First day in school, one of the girls saw me and said, 'Oh, you the new people at the Paki shop?'

'What? First of all, what is a Paki? Second, what shop are you talking about?' I replied, bewildered. Turned out a new shop had been opened at the post office by an Indian family. That incident really shook me. In one sentence, that girl had casually obliterated my entire self-image. But that doesn't mean I stopped seeing myself as white. It was the only identity I knew.

When I imagined my future, I envisioned myself as this woman in V-neck cashmere sweaters and khaki pants with great hair and a degree from Oxbridge. That was my idea of what I wanted to be.

But as we entered the age of sexual awareness, I started getting more explicitly racialised comments from boys my age. 'Wow, you are so exotic, you've got this Brazilian look.' 'You've got a beautiful black bum.' 'You've got black-girl lips.' They didn't just objectify me, they objectified me through a racialised lens. They wouldn't say to a white girl, 'Wow, you've got beautiful white boobs.' They'd just say, 'You've got nice boobs.' Clearly, race was starting to play a part in how I was perceived by my peers.

People started asking questions about my heritage. But I had no answers. As far as I was concerned, I was British, period. When I was fourteen, I went back to London to visit a black friend from primary school. Through her, I met another mixed-race girl. Her dad was black and her mum was white. But she was a blue-eyed blonde, much lighter-skinned than I was. You'd never know she wasn't white if she didn't tell you. We were chatting about what kind of guys were attractive and all of a sudden she says, 'I hate white people, they're ugly and boring. Their music is trash, their fashion is trash.' I found this quite a strange thing to say.

'So do you hate your mum?' I asked her.

'Yes I do, coz she's white,' she replied.

'So do you hate yourself?' I asked.

'No, coz I'm black,' she stared back at me defiantly.

I'm looking at this fourteen-year-old blue-eyed blonde girl telling me she's black and I gently try to remind her she is at least half-white. But she refused to accept this. 'I'm black,' she insisted. This was the first time I realised mixed-race people can feel they have to consciously choose one side while rejecting the other. And that if you're mixed black and white, you should choose your black side. But for me, this was not a feasible option. During that same trip, I remember going to a very culturally black birthday party with my friend. There were people from Nigeria, Kenya and Jamaica. I remember feeling so out of place and uncomfortable, like this wasn't my world. I couldn't wait to leave.

When I was fifteen, my dad started catfishing me. Things got really unpleasant and, partly because of this, I changed my name from Dion – short for Dionyves – to Darcy. Darcy is a very white British name, so this distanced me even more from blackness. Did I purposely change my name to distance myself from blackness? Looking back, I don't think so, but I can't say for a hundred per cent that had nothing to do with it. Apart from my father catfishing me on my former name, I do think I felt back then 'Darcy' reflected who I was more than Dion, which is a popular black name. Being white-passing was my comfort zone. Association with other identities felt uncomfortable.

Up until my late teens, I identified white. All my boyfriends were blue-eyed blondes, which has been the case to date. I definitely had an ingrained Aryan preference. I mistrusted black men because I'd had bad experiences with them. Apart from my negative experiences with my father, it was almost always black guys who'd yell sexually explicit comments to me on the streets like 'Bring that big booty here' or something similar. This kind of catcalling always made me feel dirty, made my skin crawl. A black guy once held me at gunpoint for not getting on his bike. So, truth is, I had prejudices against black men which I've had to rid myself of over the years. It's a nasty feeling realising you are racist towards your own kind.

But I didn't start thinking of black people as 'my own kind' until I was nineteen. This was when I reconnected with cousins and aunties from my father's side. Even though I didn't have a relationship with him, they reached out to me and we all met for a family dinner. It was an awakening experience. I remember sitting at the dinner table with all these mixed-race women and for the first time in my life, when I looked at the people around me, I saw myself looking back.

It was then it really hit me that, throughout my life, I'd always been the only person of colour in family settings. But here all the women around me looked like me. They had similar curly hair, a similar nose and a similar skin colour. I experienced an overwhelming feeling of belonging. It was at that moment I understood why people really need that feeling. It was then I started imagining myself as a woman of colour.

By this time, I had moved back to London and was working in Top Shop. One day not long after, some of my work colleagues were having a conversation about their favourite retro R & B songs. 'I know my favourite song,' I volunteered. 'No, you don't, you're the whitest girl in here,' a Pakistani colleague sneered. This was the first time in my life someone was actually suggesting I wasn't allowed to identify with blackness – because I had gone to grammar school and did theatre and all these other things that were supposedly so white.

By now, I'd done some research on black history. I knew I was the direct descendant of slaves through my father. And yet a Pakistani guy felt he had a right to judge how not-black I was and exclude me from a conversation about black music! I calmly pointed out I was the only person of black heritage in the room and my social background didn't have anything to do with how I connected to music. They all agreed, so I learnt that day that there is a gift in being able to discuss race in a calm way rather than reacting defensively as I could have done.

Not long after, I had a conversation about identity with a mixed-race girl I also worked with. She was likewise of black and white heritage. One day she asked me point blank, 'Do you identify black or white?' I said I identify as mixed because I'm not black or white. She said I had to choose. 'Because it is an alliance, it is who you are. I choose black because I'm more socially black, I look more black, I act more black and I talk more black,' she said.

I told her I had problems understanding what it meant to 'act more black'. She couldn't understand how I couldn't see the difference between the way white people acted and the way black people acted. This was when the cultural black–white divide started interesting me; a divide I think is more toxic than the symbolic racial one, especially considering it is cultural norms attributed to certain races that have been the basis of dangerous stereotypes for centuries.

I don't think your everyday behaviour should be defined by the colour of your skin. I know the human need to identify with a collective is in our DNA. However, most mixed black and white people seem to believe that if they're choosing a side, it's only acceptable for them to identify black. I've often wondered why this is. I think it's because when you identify black, you are explicitly acknowledging the struggle your black ancestors waged and identifying with that struggle. There is an empowering feeling of unity in identifying with that struggle. If as a person of black heritage you are perceived as behaving in a manner associated with cultural whiteness, it's treated as if you're not recognising the struggles black culture has faced.

I recognise black unity is inherently tied to the struggle. I respect that. I also know I haven't personally experienced much struggle in my life. But I see no reason to bring struggle on myself when people have fought so hard to end it. I think we can sometimes bring struggle on ourselves by self-pigeonholing. I get where this comes from.

Historically, the divide started from whites evaluating others – including blacks – in their literature, art and other forms of expression. Black people had this divide thrust upon them. But some black people have now come to embrace that divide too dogmatically. In part, it's about a need to protect and preserve black culture. A fear that integrating with white cultural norms means relinquishing any other cultural identities you may have.

Black characters on TV are often portrayed as either rich and successful but lacking an authentic identity because they have been assimilated by white culture, or poor, but having retained their identity. It's almost implied you can't really have both. Personally, I don't think embracing my white roots disqualifies my black heritage. I also don't agree with the fashionable idea that identifying as a person of colour signals a rich experience while identifying with white heritage is inherently elitist.

I've noticed that whenever I talk about cultural experiences seen as prevalently white around my black or mixed-race friends, they'll often scoff 'that's white stuff' and let me know it isn't welcome with them. But when I talk about black or other non-white cultures around my white friends, they are usually curious and eager to learn something new about other people, other places and other ways of doing things. I definitely prefer the latter attitude. Irrespective of whether you're black, white or mixed race, I think it's enriching to be interested in more than one culture.

I mentioned that I started imagining myself as a woman of colour after reuniting with my mixed-race aunties and cousins when I was nineteen. However, it was not until my trip to Australia at the age of twenty-three that I truly began to feel a woman of colour. In Australia, I spent a few months backpacking around the country. Since most of the other backpackers I met in the hostels I stayed in were foreigners, it was normal for me to get asked where I was from seven or eight times a day. Each time I'd say 'England.' And each time, irrespective of whether the person asking was white, black, Asian or mixed race, they would inevitably say, 'No, but where are you really from?'

There was clearly a disconnect between how I saw myself and how others saw me. These were all travellers, people genuinely interested in learning about other people and cultures. I could see they were asking the question as a way to connect and learn, not to put me in a box as is often the case when people ask it in Britain. I think it is a beautiful thing being allowed to ask that question and it never meaning anything other than having a genuine interest in another person's life story.

It was in Australia it really hit me that there was much more potential to my identity than I'd realised. It was my experience there of meeting so many people from different places that got me interested in delving into the Jamaican, Jewish and Saint Lucian cultures I was descended from. Prior to that, I'd only explored British culture and general black history, mostly the slave trade and its effects.

Paradoxically, it was in Australia I first felt comfortable in a black cultural setting. There was a reggae club on the same street as a hostel I stayed in for a while. I decided to go in one day. It was the first time I stepped into a space that belonged to black culture and felt comfortable. I started realising the discomfort I had earlier felt in black cultural spaces came not from the black people there, but from myself. It was me who had felt I didn't have a place in the black community. That reggae club changed that feeling.

It was a beautiful thing to see people of all colours embracing Jamaican culture in a positive way without having to sacrifice any other identities they had. I realised that just like the black people I criticised for self-pigeonholing, I too had put myself in a damn box.

I had de facto accepted a narrowly defined identity based on the white cultural space I was used to and felt comfortable in. I had built up this one-dimensional person and was very scared of veering away from that. I realised it was now up to me to paint my own picture.

I remember looking at myself in the mirror in Australia and recognising the person staring back even though I got a really dark tan there. This time, I saw exactly what I thought I would see. Becoming more comfortable with who I was on the outside allowed me to start expressing who I was on the inside more openly. It changed my way of dressing. I wear more varied clothes now. My individuality started pushing itself into other realms of expression. Now, I don't really give a shit if people think I'm this or that because I know I can be both this and that. My identity is all-encompassing. There is an overwhelming comfort in not needing to be anything. Embracing all of my cultures and heritages has allowed me to let go of all of them and just be who I am.

Before, when people asked me about my roots, my answer was a party trick. I'd list all the identities my parents were connected to in rapid succession: I'm Jamaican, Saint Lucian, English, Indian, Irish, Spanish and Latvian-Jewish. But that was just a party trick, I didn't feel most of those identities or even know what they meant to me. It was when I started travelling things started becoming clearer. Travelling is great because it helps hit home just how much we are a product of our environment and its cultural perceptions. When you are in the same place for a long time, you don't see this. But when you remove yourself from your normal environment, you give yourself the opportunity to breathe and to examine everything you believe about yourself and others.

I know I've enjoyed white-passing privilege. I've been told that a lot by darker-skinned people. In fact, most of the prejudice I've had has come from people wanting to emphasise that to me. But racial prejudices are not the only prejudices. Being a woman, especially an outspoken woman, has its drawbacks, too. I've worked in a place where I was paid several grand less than a mixed-race guy in the same position even though I had five years' experience and he'd never done the job before!

Prejudice isn't just about culture, race or gender, it's an amalgamation of all these and many things. Because I am considered white-passing, my own experiences with prejudice are often shrugged off by darker-skinned people, like, 'Meh.' I don't think that's fair at all. I am not saying I've faced huge struggles in my life, but I would think it should not be a competition about whose struggle really counts, but an acknowledgement that we all face struggles.

We should all be fighting for rights and equality; no one should be made to feel less than in that fight. Also, while I know it is not so easy to detach yourself and pretend your bad experiences with race never happened, I think you still have to find a way to look for the good in others, and not judge an entire race based on your own personal experiences. If I treated every black man like the twenty or thirty black men who yelled sexually explicit comments to me in public and made me feel uncomfortable, I would be rightly considered ridiculous by black people. But I knew those prejudices were my problem and I had to rid myself of them. The same should apply to people of any skin colour who've had negative experiences with people of other races. No colour has just good or bad people.

As individuals, I also believe it is our responsibility to step outside of our comfort zones and engage in conversations that help build trust and understanding between various groups. Even if those conversations may be awkward and uncomfortable for us at first. When I was in Australia, I was once sat next to a drag queen by accident. I didn't know what to do. I had a choice. I could act like I was totally comfortable and go away with the feeling of still not knowing anything about how people like her were or felt. Or I could feel like a fool for five minutes by asking the question we are asked so often, 'Who are you really?' I chose the latter option and enjoyed the beautiful experience of this person telling me her life story and struggles. I learnt so much I would never have learnt if I hadn't asked a question that took me out of my comfort zone. We have the power to start a conversation and learn about other people and their perspectives as well as enlighten them about our point of view. That's how understanding is built.

Unlike Bea and Isabella, Dion grew up identifying as white, imagining her future 'as this woman in V-neck cashmere sweaters and khaki pants with great hair and a degree from Oxbridge'. It is only in recent years that she has started to think of herself as a woman of colour capable of navigating several worlds.

The incident in her Aylesham school when she was assumed to be 'a Paki' was clearly a key moment in her life story. It was the first time she was denied whiteness, always a traumatic event in the life of mixed-race people who grow up identifying as white. Nothing is quite the same after that. While Dion still identified white after that incident, it was, as she acknowledged, chiefly because white was the only identity she knew. But it was probably always just a matter of time before she started reimagining herself. Whiteness once denied can never truly be regained.

None of the white-passing people I spoke to who grew up identifying as white, only to experience the denial of whiteness, identify as white today. While this does not apply to Dion, I sensed that some of them, especially those who had been raised in very white environments, *would* identify as white if it were up to them. But they didn't feel it was. It's as if you can only be white by unanimous decision. Even one dissenting white vote has the power to deny you entry into the shrine of whiteness.

Tom, a thirty-four-year-old from Newcastle whose father is white English and mother mixed Scottish-Jamaican, said: 'My mother was estranged from her Jamaican family, so I grew up around white English and Scottish people. I've never been to Jamaica; there is nothing culturally Jamaican about me. I listen to rock, not reggae. I don't really relate to black culture in general. My friends are all white. We are interested in the same kind of things. I generally look white. But once the white kids in my schools found out my mum was half-Jamaican, I instantly became this exotic person of colour in their eyes. So I've just kind of gone with that label since childhood because I know that's how people will see me anyway once they learn my family background.'

This too cannot be a very comfortable position to be in; to internally identify as white but be seen by white people as a person of colour because of a family connection that has little bearing in your everyday life. It is another manifestation of the continuing adherence to the one-drop rule, in this case by white people.

If whiteness is reimagined to be more inclusive in twenty-first-century Britain the way it was reimagined in twentieth-century America to include the previously excluded Italians and Irish, then I suspect a higher proportion of white-passing Britons would openly identify as white than do today, especially those brought up in what we might describe as 'white culture'. But for now it doesn't make sense to say you identify as white if you know someone around is going to say, 'But isn't your mother half-Jamaican?' That opens you up to mocking accusations of being 'desperate' to be seen as white. Who needs that?

Of course, there is currently a trend in woke culture to portray whiteness as passé. What is cool and ennobling is being a person of colour. I find this a fascinating development that reminds me of the parable by Jesus in the Book of Matthew about a world in which 'the last shall be first, and the first shall be last'. In the woke order, groups at the bottom of the world's material hierarchy are elevated to the top of its moral hierarchy while those at the material top are relegated to the moral bottom. Crucially, group moral status is now deemed more important than group material status. The last have become first, and the first last.

However, I find it hard to believe this can ever become a widespread attitude of *Homo capitalismus*; it is rather one I expect to remain restricted to academic, cultural and social media circles in the affluent West while the rest of the world continues to reserve its admiration for those at the material top. Contempt for material success is a luxury most of the world cannot afford. Ultimately, I think if whiteness is reimagined in Britain this century to be less exclusivist, quite a few white-passing Britons will end up self-identifying as white.

Of the many interesting points Dion raised, another one I found particularly intriguing was when she talked about how historically, the racial divide 'started from whites evaluating others – including blacks – in their literature, art and other forms of expression'. This is so true.

For centuries, it was only white people who had the power to define other people and make those definitions stick: black people were like this, Indians were like that, Arabs were such and such, Latinos were so and so. Meanwhile, white people were only examined and defined by other white people – writers, intellectuals and academics.

Thanks to social media, however, hundreds of millions of black and brown people around the world now have a stage from where they can turn the lights in the opposite direction. In today's social media world, the gaze is now on white people more than anyone else. This is making more than a few white people quite uncomfortable. It is not much fun being constantly and intently peered at through a critical lens, is it?

While I find some of the unflattering portrayals of 'whiteness' by people of colour on social media caricaturist, resentful and sometimes outrightly hateful, psychologically they should be understood as the exacting of sweet revenge for all those centuries of voicelessness and unflattering portrayals of blackness and brownness. Sometimes, whitebashers are motivated by genuine moral outrage at the racism that still exists in this world. Sometimes, they are motivated by feelings of envy and resentment as especially younger generations of black and brown people fume at growing up in a world where white people have so much more collective wealth and power. Are envy and resentment productive? Usually not, these are common feelings among the world's poorer groups, especially those with clear historical memories of exploitation at the hands of today's powerful groups. Hopefully, soon enough, people will get over the unproductive thrill of whitebashing and we'll be able to move on to more productive exchanges. God knows we need them now more than ever following the turbulent year of 2020.

As someone who is visibly not-white, I have never had to contend with being on the edge of whiteness the way Dion or Bea have. While I don't think my childhood would have been very different from what it was in Nigeria if I had been white-passing, it would definitely have been so in Poland where I would doubtless have been treated much better if people thought I was white. Overall, though, I'm glad to have not experienced being on the edge of whiteness. At least I've never had to deal with that level of mixed-race complication.

# Chapter 11

# To be like Daddy

My youngest interviewee, Gina (her name has been changed), is six. The daughter of a prominent figure in Britain, let's just say her mum is British with African roots while her father is white English. Gina lives in London. To kick off our interview, which her mum mostly helped me conduct, I placed six cards in front of her. On each of the cards was an identity label: 'British', 'white', 'black', 'mixed race', 'English' and one with her mum's African nationality. I asked Gina to pick the card which best describes her. Without any hesitation, she immediately reached for the card that read 'mixed race'. Her mum asked if she was absolutely sure, of all the cards in front of her, that particular one best described her. 'Yes, Mummy, *this* one,' Gina replied emphatically.

When you are mixed race, it means one part of your family is white and one part of your family is black. And then when you get to have a younger sibling, they are either lighter or darker. Like my younger brother Tony, he's lighter than me because he's a boy so he looks like Daddy. I'm a girl so I look like Mummy. Mixed-race children are different from other children. Sometimes when you have different parents, they have different eye colours, too, so you get a mix. If one parent's eyes are blue and the other parent's eyes are green, you get a sort of mix of blue and green. It's nice to have a mix like that because it means some people will say you have blue eyes and some people will say you have green eyes, and you can choose what colour eyes you have.

All the children in my class are white, I am the only dark person. Mummy says two of the girls in my class are Asian, but I don't know what 'Asian' means. I feel different from the other children in my class because I am the only dark one. The teachers treat everyone the same, but sometimes if someone has been naughty for the whole year or half of the year, they don't get to sit with all their friends. The other children don't talk about my hair or skin colour. I have never been to Mummy's country. I would like to go because my cousins are there, and Grandpa and Grandma are there. Grandpa and Grandma from Mummy visit us sometimes. Mummy's grandma is different from Daddy's grandma.

Mummy's grandma doesn't give me any sweets, only presents and clothes. She says sweets are not good for my teeth, but Daddy's grandma gives me sweets. Mummy asked if I would like to learn her language, I said no. She asked me why. I said because I don't want to. I know what 'British' means. They're in the United Kingdom. But Daddy says he's English, so I am half-English and half-[her mother's nationality].

I told Mummy I want straight hair. Mummy asked me why. I said because then I wouldn't have to sit in the bath for an hour while she does my hair. Mummy asked if it's because I want to have white hair, but I told her I just want straight hair. But I do wish I was white. I think about it every single day. Because then I would be the same as Daddy. But Mummy said if I was white, people wouldn't know she was my mummy and that would make her sad. Mummy asked if I want to be white because I think it's better to be white or if it's because I just want to look like Daddy. I said it's because I want to look like Daddy. I don't think one colour is better than another.

Afterwards, Gina's mum told me there wasn't much of her birth country's culture in her daughter's life. She's at work most of the time, so her husband is the 'dominant parent' at home who cooks for Gina and generally runs the house. He spends much more time with their daughter than she does, which helps explain why Gina is clearly a daddy's girl and perhaps at least partially explains why she wishes she was white like Daddy.

Gina's mum said she's done everything she can to try and make sure her daughter doesn't grow up with any racial complex. 'But where I grew up, everyone around me looked like me. So honestly speaking, it hasn't been easy for me to know what to say to her anytime she raises the issue of looking different from the other kids at school. She told you nobody points out she's different, but she's occasionally indicated to me someone said something in that direction,' she said.

The problem with knowing how to react to all this, Gina's mum continued, is that 'it's difficult to pin down a six-year-old and find out what's really going on inside her head. My husband thinks I read too much into some of the comments she makes. But I don't want to take anything for granted. I don't want to assume race will never be an issue for her. And I really don't know what to make of her saying she wishes she was white. Should I treat that as some kind of warning sign or is it just a girl who clearly adores her father simply wishing she looked like him? I really don't know.' Neither do I, obviously. But I was a bit struck by Gina wanting to be white like Daddy. One might have thought a mixed-race six-year-old in London, where half the population is either black or brown, would barely even notice her skin colour. But that was clearly not the case here.

I also spoke to a friend of mine who lives in Birmingham and has a mixed-race kid. He told me a story we both found very unsettling. My friend is Polish-Ghanaian while his wife is Ghanaian. But despite the fact their daughter – let's call her Sandra – is technically just a 'quarter' white, she's actually quite light-skinned and looks like a classic half-white, half-black mix. Sandra is ten.

My friend has a sister who is married to a black Briton. They also have a daughter – let's call her Keisha. But despite the two girls being of the same racial mix, Keisha is much darker-skinned than Sandra. Keisha is seven.

One day they were all in my friend's place when his daughter, Sandra, came home from school in a bad mood. She didn't want to eat or speak to anybody and had an angry look on her face. For hours my friend tried to cajole her into saying what had happened at school to upset her so much. She finally relented and said there's a boy in her school who she fancied. The boy is white. That day Sandra had told him how she felt about him.

'Sorry Sandra, I like black girls, but I don't fancy them like that,' the boy replied.

'Why?' Sandra asked.

'Look Sandra, I like you, but not *like that*,' the boy repeated.

Sandra couldn't understand why the boy thought she was black.

'But I am light, why did he describe me as black?' she asked her dad.

But before her father could answer, Keisha, her dark-skinned cousin, jumped in.

'But you're black, Sandra. You may be light, but you are black,' she said.

'No, YOU are black. I am brown, I am NOT BLACK,' Sandra screamed at her cousin with such fury Keisha burst into tears. It took all four parents a while to calm both girls down and get them speaking to each other again.

If these kinds of scenes are happening between kids born in the last decade, then there is clearly still quite a lot going on with attitudes to blackness in Britain, even among the very youngest generation.

# Part 2

## Mixed in BritAsia

Chapter 12

# Things more important than being brown

After mixed black and white, the next most oft-recurring mixed-race combination in Britain is mixed white and Asian. Of course, 'Asian' encompasses a vastly diverse selection of peoples and cultures, ranging from India to China and a few in between. The South Asian and white mix, however, is far more common than the East Asian and white mix in Britain, which is not that surprising since 71 per cent of British Asians are of Indian, Pakistani or Bangladeshi heritage, according to the last census.

Similar to the relationship between black and white, there is a complicated history and psychological dynamic here, too, born of the fact that Britain was once the colonial master of much of South Asia. As the great British-Sri Lankan writer and intellectual Ambalavaner Sivanandan famously said, 'We are here because you were there' – a memorable encapsulation of the history that has shaped the relationship between white Britain and both black and brown Britain.

Before I started speaking to people of mixed white and Asian heritage about their experiences, I expected I would hear some things from them that would resonate with me. To be human is to be like no one else while seeing flashes of yourself in everyone else.

But I had no idea whether the mixed white and Asian experience would be fundamentally similar or perhaps fundamentally very different from the mixed black and white experience. Would there be many common elements in our stories or is that combination a different territory altogether?

I started my questions with Ian, the son of an Indian father and German mother. Both his parents emigrated to Britain in the early 1960s. Ian was born here in 1965 and grew up in Southend, a seaside town in south-east Essex.

My mother was a farmgirl from Bavaria who came to Britain to work as an au pair. My father hailed from the Gujarat region in India and came here to become an engineer. They both ended up in Southend, Essex, which is where they met. They fell in love and decided they wanted to get married. But both their families were completely against the idea. Neither side thought it made sense to marry outside your race and culture. When my parents did eventually decide to tie the knot despite their families' objections, they were both promptly disowned. As a result, me and my younger brother grew up without any Indian or German family members around us.

We grew up poor. My father never got to fulfil his ambitions of becoming an engineer but ended up as a factory worker instead. Not having any family around to help with babysitting, my mum had to stay home and take care of me and my brother when we were younger. The family survived on my dad's wages until we were old enough for my mum to be able to leave home and do some secretarial work.

My mum was a very clever woman. She taught herself to read and write fluent English despite growing up on a Bavarian farm where no one around spoke anything but German. She definitely had the intellectual capacity to go to university and become anything she wanted to, really, but those were different times and life never made it possible for either her or my dad to fulfil their potential.

Since neither of them could speak the other's language, my parents communicated with each other and with us solely in English. Apart from our family often eating Indian curries and a lot of German salamis (both culinary rarities at the time), there was nothing really Indian or German about our home. My dad occasionally listened to Indian music. When VHS came out in the late 1970s, once in a while an Indian friend of his would come over with a Bollywood movie and they'd watch it together. But that was more or less the limit of Indianness I experienced growing up.

My parents brought me up to be English. They wanted me to think of myself as an English boy, not an Indian-German boy. Their chief desire was for me and my brother to keep our heads down and assimilate. To make something of our lives, do better than them. They didn't want us to learn their languages. There weren't many ethnic minorities in 1970s Southend where I was growing up. It was a very right-wing and very white working-class town. The war was still fresh in people's memories, so being half-Indian and half-German was almost a combination designed to annoy the locals. The last thing my parents wanted was me and my brother speaking German or Gujarati in public.

My mum often recalls an incident that gives a sense of the attitudes back then. She was walking me in my baby pram when a white English lady stopped to take a look at me. Fully expecting to see a white baby since my mother was white, she peered into the pram, smiling and ready to coo. When she saw I was brown she spat in my face. Spitting in a baby's face is a pretty incredible thing to do; my mum was so dumbfounded she had no idea how to react.

I went to Catholic primary and secondary schools attended by mostly white working-class kids. I remember a few black kids but no Indian kids in my primary school. I can't recall any incident related to race from that period, though. However, in my secondary school, which had a handful of black and Asian kids, it was pretty normal for us to get racist abuse. Most times I was called 'blackie', 'Paki' or something similar. But when the kids found out I was half-German, I'd get called a 'fucking Kraut' as well.

Luckily for me, I was never physically attacked, which was a pretty common experience for black and brown kids back then. The National Front was popular when I was growing up and there were quite a few boys in my school who were proud members. Their graffiti was everywhere. You felt they had you in their sights if you were brown, that they were coming for you. You could really smell the racism in the air, and I remember often feeling scared and vulnerable as a young boy. Some teachers were openly racist. Our history teacher thought the British Empire was God's gift to humanity and spent much of the class extolling its virtues. He often picked on me, the only brown kid in class, who he clearly disliked.

As a result of the atmosphere around me, by the time I was in my teens I felt very oppositional to the British establishment and to mainstream British society in general. I became interested in punk music and left-wing political movements. I read a lot of books about British history, philosophy and politics. Because of the way my parents were bringing me up, I didn't really have a racial identity from home. I didn't think of myself as Indian-German or as mixed race, which wasn't even a term people used back then. Punk music and leftism became the pillars of my identity rather than race. If someone had asked me back then who I was, I would have said I was a punk and a socialist rather than define myself in racial categories.

Because my parents wanted me to keep my head down and fit in, they were very unhappy with my interest in radical left-wing politics. Especially considering we were living in Margaret Thatcher's Britain by the time I was in my teens. They didn't want me opposing mainstream Britain but becoming part of it. My father was particularly desperate for me to embark on the path towards a 'respectable' profession. For him that meant becoming a doctor, dentist or following some other stereotypically Indian career path. This was really the main 'Indian' thing he wanted me to do in life.

He was furious when I said I wanted to study politics. He couldn't see the point in that. Neither could any of my friends, who were mostly white working-class kids. They didn't really see the point in going to university at all. To give an idea of my socioeconomic circle back then, I was the only one in my group of friends to go to sixth form. And then I became the only one to go to university. In those days, only 5 per cent of people got university degrees.

I ended up studying at a polytechnic in Plymouth where I stuck out both for being working class and an ethnic minority. This was the mid-1980s. There were towns I'd go to around Plymouth where I got the sense I was the first brown person some people there had ever laid their eyes on. Again, I was lucky never to be physically attacked, but I was also very careful about my movements.

In those days, the pubs in Plymouth used to close at 11 p.m. and the nightclubs at 2 a.m. In the immediate hour after closing time, you knew there'd be a lot of the locals about town, making their way home. I always avoided being in town at those times. If not, I'd have almost certainly been attacked one time or the other. I am one of the few male ethnic minorities I know who grew up during that era and never got beaten up.

As I grew older, my relationship with my dad grew increasingly difficult. Like I said, he had always been keen for me to be English and well-educated. The problem was that the better-educated I got, the less of a dutiful Indian son I became. He found that very difficult to deal with. Indian fathers expect obedience from their sons. What my father really wanted was for me to be educated, English and a dutiful Indian son at the same time. But it doesn't really work that way, does it? When I became as independent-minded as any typical young Englishman, he realised he'd created a monster he didn't really like.

He was always embarrassed by my choice to study politics. It is a big deal for Indian fathers to be able show off their children to their friends at Indian weddings. 'My son is training to become a doctor.' 'He's just finishing dentistry school.' These were the kinds of declarations that impressed other Indian men. When they'd ask me what I studied and I said politics, they always reacted scornfully, 'So what are you going to do with *that* when you finish? Become a politician?' Like that was obviously not something *we* did.

Back then, Indians and Asians generally were primarily concerned with assimilating and getting ahead economically in Britain. Indians were interested in commerce, not politics. They wanted to get rich, not become MPs. It was black Britain that was more ready to be the focus of attention back then. It was black people who were more ready to be confrontational with the police and challenge the status quo. Virtually all the race riots in those days were started in black communities.

There've always been major differences between the Indian and black community in their approach to life in Britain. These differences are still there today. Walk into any bookshop today and most of the books you will find about race and the minority experience in Britain will be by black Britons talking about the black experience. Indians are still focused on family and commerce. I guess the positive side of this is that the Indian community has done particularly well economically in this country.

I had a proper encounter with institutional racism after I completed a one-year journalism course following my politics studies. Me and half-a-dozen or so white friends completed the course at the same time. I had the best results out of all of us. We started applying for trainee reporter jobs in London. I'd get letters from newspapers telling me they weren't taking on any trainees that year. My friends would get invited to interviews by the same newspapers for jobs that were not supposed to exist.

The only interview I got was with the *Southall Gazette* and that was because they thought it would be a good idea to, for the first time, get an Indian reporter to cover Southall politics because the district hosted the largest concentration of Sikhs outside India. That was my lucky break. If not for that, I probably would never have gotten a job in journalism.

I'd never been interested in the idea of being Indian until I started covering Southall politics. Like I said, it was the first time the *Southall Gazette* had an Indian reporter and the people in the community reacted very positively to this and to me generally. This made me more interested in, and aware of, being half-Indian. The district had very strong leftist movements back then, even the Communist Party was a major force in Southall in the 1980s and 1990s. For the first time in my life, I met Asians who combined their racial identity with their politics in a manner that rendered both virtually inseparable.

Never before had I met people who were so aggressively Indian. They were very different from people like my dad and the other Indians I knew. They awoke in me a stronger sense of my own Indianness or part-Indianness than I'd ever gotten from home. I felt this awakening happening and it was a fascinating and exciting personal experience. But to be honest, once I stopped working the Southall patch, that whole connection to Indianness and Asianness fizzled out with time. Southall was an important experience in my life but, after that, I went back to thinking of myself in terms of my politics and musical interests rather than my racial identity.

Today I have mixed feelings about the way my parents raised me. On the one hand, I am very glad I'm not someone who is defined by race the way some ethnic minorities in this country are. I am defined by things I chose to be interested in, not by the accident of my skin colour. I know others may define me by race – this I cannot control. But what I can control is how I choose to think about myself. And there have always been things more important to me than being brown. I have always instinctively identified with people based on similar worldview rather than similar skin shade.

On the other hand, there are moments when I think I've missed out on something. I don't have an ethnic hinterland the way some of my Asian friends do. They speak lots of languages; I speak only English. They know more about their Asian families than I do. I've never even been to India. It's not like I feel a great desire to visit there to be honest, but when I hear my friends talking about their experiences in India, I feel like they have something I don't. Sometimes, I wish I had that something.

I definitely wish I could speak languages other than English. At the minimum, I should be able to speak German and Gujarati. It's a real shame I can't. But all this doesn't mean I would have preferred to grow up in a traditional Indian household with a strong emphasis on traditional Indian values. Indian households were pretty stifling and unpleasant places to grow up in back in those days, limiting places where your aspirations were decided for you. Places where your parents' plans for your future were always financially motivated.

They wanted you to become a doctor or dentist not because they thought these were noble professions, but because doctors and dentists earned well and enjoyed a high social status in Britain. Luckily for me, my father never had the power to force me to live my life the way he wanted. But many Indian kids of my generation grew up in more traditional homes where they never really had a choice in deciding their future lives and career paths.

When it comes to identity, I think my parents largely achieved their aims. If you ask me how I identify today, I'd say I think of myself as English or British, even though I have very ambivalent feelings about being British. I've always considered Britain a pretty racist country with a racist imperialist history. This changed somewhat in the 1990s when I felt Britain was becoming more inclusive and far less racist. Back then, I felt things were changing for good. That we'd won the battle. But then the Brexit referendum happened, and I realised British society hadn't changed that much at all. All that had happened was that people had stopped saying what they really thought in public. The referendum gave them the opportunity voice their true feelings once again.

After that brief interlude in the 1990s, race is once again a big deal in Britain, just like it was when I was growing up. It's a big deal now in a different way than it was in the 1970s – there's no National Front thugs marching the streets these days. But it is once again a big deal, nevertheless. Also, some things have really not moved forward that much since my younger years. In my newspaper days, you'd go to an industry event and there'd be one Asian in the room or one or two black people. Things have changed somewhat since then, there's a few more now, but not that many more from what I hear from young journalists.

Having said all that, I truly cannot imagine living anywhere other than Britain. And London where I currently stay is obviously a huge multicultural bubble where I don't even think about my skin colour. So yes, I do think of myself as British, though not in the same way as white people. In lots of ways, I'm very culturally English. I have many white tastes, if you like. But I do still feel like an outsider in this country, someone slightly separated from the society. However, it is a sense of difference and otherness that does not make me feel uncomfortable at all. I'm quite happy with it. As a matter of fact, it fits neatly into how I like to think of myself, as someone slightly different from everyone else anyway.

Ian's experience shows how you can be born into an identity but never actually live it. While there's been some contact with Indianness in his life, Germanness has played virtually no role in shaping his experiences apart from the German salamis he used to eat as a kid. Extended family play a key role in making mixed-raceness a truly diverse cultural experience. If they are not in the picture, as in Ian's case, the experience loses much of that diversity.

Ian's parents wanted him to think of himself as 'an English boy, not an Indian-German boy'. Their parents wanting them to assimilate and *feel* British is something most people of mixed Indian heritage to whom I spoke emphasised particularly strongly, consistently more so than those of any other mix. In teenage Ian's case, however, his view of Britain as a racist society, combined with the fact he 'didn't really have a racial identity from home', led him to seek a sense of self not in Britishness or brownness, but in oppositional music and politics.

Race is identity by birth, ideology is identity by choice. Ideologies, especially universalist ideologies, can have a very powerful appeal for mixed-race people that race lacks. Race can reject you based on how you look, ideology will not. As long as you believe, you're in. Ideology is a club that can never have enough members.

Ian is glad he defines himself by things he 'chose', not by the accident of his skin colour. I found this an interesting position for someone who grew up in a time when race seemed a defining feature of minority life in Britain. Ian argues that while we cannot control how others define us, we can control how we think about ourselves. I love the empowering message behind this stance, but I suspect some black and brown Britons would argue that is easier said than done. I know from personal experience how difficult it can be to 'control' how you think about yourself if people around you are constantly defining you by your race.

As I mentioned before, my first years in Warsaw were pretty horrible in terms of racial abuse. I was constantly reminded of my skin colour and never allowed to forget I wasn't white. It wasn't long before I started thinking of myself primarily in racial terms. This had not been the case in Nigeria where I thought of myself either as an individual or in class terms. We don't think about our racial identities until they start having an influence on our everyday lives. Nothing creates a racialist mindset as effectively as racism.

My mum noticed this the first time she visited me in Warsaw a couple years after I'd moved there. By then I was quoting Malcolm X every second sentence. 'Why is it you hardly ever speak of yourself outside a racial context any more?' she asked me. 'You start virtually every sentence with "we Nigerians" this, "we black people" that. You never used to talk this way before. Now you seem to constantly feel the need to emphasise your Nigerianness and your blackness. I know what you're going through here, but why are you allowing Polish racists to decide how you think of yourself? Where have *you* disappeared to?'

I knew my mum was right. I'd stopped thinking of myself as 'Remi' and started thinking of myself as a black boy from Nigeria, which was how Polish society saw me. But even though intellectually I was aware I was losing my individual sense of self to a racialist worldview, Poland was such a hostile environment for people of colour then that I stayed in that mindset emotionally for many years. It was not until the mid-2000s when it became easier for people of colour to breathe in Poland that I returned to thinking about myself primarily as an individual.

It is difficult not to define yourself by race when that is how everyone around you defines you. The question, of course, is whether white Britain today constantly reminds black and brown Britons of their skin colour. That has certainly not been my experience in my six years living in Sheffield. Nor did I feel that way when travelling around the country interviewing mixed-race Britons. I've never felt as unselfconscious about my skin colour as I do in Britain.

The white Britons I interact with on a daily basis do not remind me of my skin colour. The only reason I started thinking a lot about race again is because it is an inescapable topic in British traditional and social media. It's everywhere, to the extent that you can't *not* think about it, even if you tried. But the fact I've started thinking of myself in a racial context does not mean I feel defined by race in Britain. Ian, however, obviously grew up in a very different Britain from the one to which I came in 2015, so the fact he never allowed racism to force him into defining himself by race is something I find quite incredible.

I also find it very interesting how Ian's perspective changed for a while when he came into contact with what he found to be an appealingly assertive Indianness in Southall. There is something particularly exciting about assertive expressions of identities that have historically been suppressed and demeaned. This was why black and brown people all over the world fell in love with Muhammad Ali in his heyday. I must have read Ali's autobiography at least half a dozen times growing up. Ali was a great boxer and wonderful showman, but he was so much more than that. He was the guy who said to white America, 'I don't have to be what you want me to be. I'm free to be what I want.'

Those words expressed the aspirations of millions of black and brown formerly enslaved and colonised peoples around the world who yearned to be themselves. Not people forced to imitate the white man's ways to survive and get ahead, but themselves. It is one thing for someone to take off your chains and say, 'There, now you're free'; quite another for you to actually *feel* free. You can never truly feel free until you feel free to be yourself. So I can imagine Ian's fascination with the Southall Indians who were saying to white Britain what Ali said to white America: *We don't have to be what you want us to be. We will be what we want to be.* I adored Ali because he inspired me when I was struggling to find the courage to be myself growing up in Nigeria. When you're mixed race, being yourself will require some courage wherever you are.

After Ian stopped covering Southall, however, his connection to Indianness returned to its previous low-intensity level. People around us stimulate various aspects of our various identities. Hanging around Nigerians always awakens the Nigerian in me. Since I moved to Britain, I've had limited contact with Poles. Although I read Polish news every day, I am aware the Polishness I have in me lies mostly dormant these days. But it's there. A stimulating chance encounter with a Pole could awaken it in an instant. Our identities are like the music lurking beneath the keys of a piano: they require touch to come alive.

There are moments Ian feels he's missed out on having a deeper Indian experience, a 'something' his Asian friends seem to have that he occasionally wishes he had, too. Personally, I am very grateful I had the experience of growing up in Africa. It has shaped me more than any other life experience I've had; most importantly, by making me grateful for many things those who grew up in rich societies such as Britain often take for granted.

Some complain of 'white privilege' in Britain. Yes, there is such a thing. But there is also such a thing as British privilege, and that no one seems to talk about. To have British privilege is to have access to the kind of healthcare, education, security and economic opportunities of which 90 per cent of the world can only dream. When I first moved to Britain, I couldn't understand why people seemed to make such a fuss about the NHS. I had never before lived in a country where any public institution aroused such emotions and was a staple of everyday general debate. I really couldn't get it. Not until my wife needed an operation. It was not just the world-class medical service available to us and that I didn't have to worry about paying for, it was the care I saw in the eyes of the nurses and doctors who attended to my wife. I saw a compassion that I found incredibly moving and which gave me some much-needed reassurance. I saw the best of what humanity has to offer. It was then I understood what all the fuss was about. And then what can one add to the stories of the heroics performed by NHS staff to save lives when Covid-19 hit? It is an absolute privilege to live in a country with an institution like the NHS, and so many other institutions working to improve people's lives. My wife works in social care, so I know what kind of sacrifices and resources go into improving people's lives there as well.

These are privileges enjoyed by people of all skin shades living in Britain. There is nothing obvious or natural about any of this, but I guess you need to have grown up in a country where there is no functioning social security system and most things don't work to truly appreciate one where they do.

I'm also happy I had my Nigerian upbringing because it has made me a more multidimensional person than I would have been if I had spent all my life in Europe. It gave me a spirituality I would likely never have had if I had been brought up in secular Europe. Finally, and this is more useful than pleasant, I think growing up in Nigeria also left me with a more realistic view of the world than I find in the average Westerner.

There is an almost childlike naivety in many Westerners that is the preserve of those who have been shielded from the most desperate face of humanity. Innocence can be endearing, but it can also be very ignorant. Westerners often see the world through rose-tinted glasses when, for half the people on this planet who live on less than £2 a day, the logic of survival is the only logic that matters.

You need to have grown up where scarcity is the norm to truly understand how different the paradigms of thinking can be between people from the well-fed north and the still-often-hungry south. I had no problem understanding the Indian fathers of which Ian spoke, whose plans for their children's futures are always 'financially motivated'. He could as well have been describing the average Nigerian father or probably any other average father from the global south. Western parents can tell their children to pursue careers that will make them 'happy'. But the pursuit of happiness is a luxury most people from developing societies don't believe they can afford. Westerners are focused on escaping unhappiness; the rest of the world is focused on escaping poverty. As I mentioned earlier with regards to Nigeria, money is the main thing on most people's minds most of the time.

Finally, Ian said he does not have a problem with the otherness he feels in Britain as it chimes with his general self-perception of being different from everyone else anyway. This is a stance on otherness not commonly spoken of in the discussion on race. The assumption always seems to be that feelings of racial otherness automatically lead to feelings of stigmatisation and marginalisation. The idea some people might actually embrace the idea of being seen as different from mainstream Britain is rarely imagined.

# Chapter 13

# No longer in a corner

Fiaz is the son of an Italian father and Pakistani mother whose family came to Britain in 1975 when he was four. He currently lives in Sheffield but grew up in Bradford.

Although my mum would call herself 'Pakistani' today, she grew up in Kashmir back when all of Kashmir was still in India. My parents met in the 1940s. My father was a sailor who used to travel the world with the Italian navy. However, at one point, he got tired of being on the move all the time and decided to settle down somewhere. He chose India. He got a job working on a farm and soon found himself falling in love with one of the five daughters of the farm's owner – my mother. She felt the same way about him, and after a while they decided they wanted to get married.

My mother's father was completely against the idea. He threatened to disown her if she went ahead with it. Luckily for my parents, her grandfather was still alive at the time and he was the patriarch of the family. Like my father, he too had been a sailor and had travelled round the world, mixing with people from different nations and races. He was much more open-minded than his son – my mum's dad – and persuaded him to allow the marriage.

My grandfather reluctantly agreed but insisted on one non-negotiable condition – that my father convert to Islam.

Catholicism is an integral part of Italian identity; it was especially so back in the mid-twentieth century. This was a decisive moment in my father's life. He loved my mother, so he agreed and changed his surname from Salvietto to Saddiq. His Italian family disowned him immediately, said they didn't want to have anything to do with him. When my father would tell us this story later on, he would always say he never regretted the decision despite the cost, because it was done for love. My mum's eyes always lit up whenever he told that story.

After they married, my parents continued living on the farm. My dad started attending mosque and became a devout Muslim. But following India's independence in 1947, the fighting started over Kashmir and after witnessing years of conflict, my parents finally decided it wasn't the best place to raise a family. That was when they made the decision we would move to Britain.

My dad came first – in 1974. The rest of us joined him a year later. I was four when we arrived. I came with a sister who was twelve years older than me, a brother two years older and another sister a year younger. Before coming to Britain, we all spoke Kashmiri at home. My dad had learnt the language to be able to communicate with my mum. When we arrived in England, everything was new for us, the language, the culture, the surroundings. We had to adapt pretty fast.

We came straight to Bradford and for the first couple of years we lived with my mum's older brother and his family. Our family shared a room in their house, so it was pretty tight considering there were six of us. We felt quite alienated. Even though my father was a devout Muslim with a long beard and all, my mum's Bradford family let him know they viewed him as an outsider. The same went for us, his children.

Some of my dad's family members lived in Birmingham at the time and he tried reconnecting with them. But they said the only way they would accept him back into the fold was if he renounced Islam, changed his surname back to his Italian family name and returned to the Catholic faith. He wasn't ready to do any of that, but it was a real struggle for him to deal with their rejection. Family is as big a deal in Italian culture as it is in Pakistani culture, and for them to cut him off like that was a heavy blow he never truly recovered from.

My dad was an only child and had no siblings, so when his family cut him off, he was completely cut off. There was no sympathetic brother or sister he could get in touch with from time to time to maintain some kind of link to the family and to Italianness. Having grown up with the support of my siblings, I can't imagine what that must have been like for him. As the years passed, my dad went all in with Islam. Aside from us, it became the central point of his life. I think it was where he found his refuge from the turmoil with his family.

As for me and my siblings, our Pakistani cousins in Bradford would tell us we weren't 'really Pakistani' quite often. 'You're not one of us,' they'd say to our faces. They really suppressed us and did what they could to make us feel 'worse than'. We hardly ever went to family gatherings because we always felt like we didn't belong. I still feel that way at Pakistani family gatherings.

My dad worked long hours in a factory, doing night shifts six days a week. But on Sundays, he'd cook for us, always halal, usually curries. Though he had officially renounced Catholicism, looking back now, I see there were some elements of Catholic culture that remained with him. He was always very big on discipline and respect. He made sure we always dressed neatly. We had to go to the mosque on Fridays, no ifs, no buts.

But there were no conscious elements of Italian culture in our home. I think the pain of his family turning their back on him was too much for my dad to bear and still retain an emotional connection to Italianness. He replaced his Italian identity with his Muslim identity. Asian and Islamic culture shaped the dominant values in our home, the first thanks to my mum, the second thanks to both my parents. While I am ethnically half-Italian, there is nothing culturally Italian about me. I wouldn't even know what that would mean, to be honest.

We all felt very lonely growing up. The only thing that kept us going was the love in our family, which was a very tight unit. Even though my dad was usually out of the house working, there was a bond between us all that was unbreakable. I still remember scenes from when we shared a room in my mum's brother's house. I'd fall asleep on the bed, watching my mum and sister knit. Those moments always gave me comfort. Memories of them still make me feel warm inside.

My dad really played a big role in emphasising that as long as we loved and supported each other, we would all be fine. The feeling of not belonging is a difficult one for a child. We saw the conflict in our wider families, but we couldn't do anything about it. Nobody wanted to own us. We were nobody's people. We had no ground to stand on, so to speak. But what we did have was our unified family unit.

The love we had for each other was what kept us sane. No matter what I experienced on a given day, when I came home and told my siblings about it, they'd always say, 'Don't worry. We are here for you.' That always made me feel better. We always ate together, no matter what. Even if we'd had the biggest of arguments, we'd all sit together at the table and eat, even if it was in complete silence. No matter what was going on, we had to remain a unified family. My parents really imbued that in us.

We eventually bought our own house not far from where my mum's brother lived, but in a predominantly white neighbourhood. It was tough for us to make friends there. We were seen as an oddity of a family. I went to predominantly white schools. I loved playing football, and this helped me make some friendships with the white kids at school. The problem was that when the Pakistani kids in my neighbourhood saw me with my football buddies, they said I couldn't be friends with them. That it was either the white kids or them. I couldn't be in both worlds, they said.

I was confused. I asked my dad what to do. He said if I really loved football, I should ignore the neighbourhood kids and continue hanging out with my white football buddies. 'No one who wants you to leave something you love is your friend,' he told me. I think my dad saw Islam and sport as two things he really wanted us to pursue because he felt they would make us stronger inside, better equipped to cope with all the problems on the outside.

Me and my siblings did try to assimilate through sport. My brother chose cricket while my younger sister joined a basketball team. Only my older sister chose a different path. She was always a very devout Muslim who spent all her free time at the mosque. She's always been the most culturally Asian of us all, perhaps because she was already sixteen when we moved here.

Sometimes in school I had issues with the white kids I met through sports. In our younger years, football brought us close. But once we became teenagers and started competing for girls, I became a 'Paki'. Or if I did too well at football, some of them would get angry and want to pull me down to show me my place. My dad raised us saying skin colour didn't matter, but the world around us didn't seem to share this view.

The Asian kids were always reluctant to invite me back to their homes, like they didn't know how their parents would react to me. When they did invite me, their parents would indeed observe me suspiciously, as if wondering whether I wouldn't be a bad influence on their children, lead them astray. Perhaps to Catholicism, which maybe they thought I somehow had in my blood because my father was Italian. Before eating in their homes, the parents would always ask me if I'd washed my hands. They'd never have asked that if I were full-Pakistani because they would just clearly assume I had, it's such a basic requirement of the culture. Moments like that reminded me I was seen as an outsider.

I was constantly kept at arm's length by the Pakistani community, like someone on permanent probation. As long as I abided by the rules of Pakistani culture to the letter, I was allowed to hang around. But I always knew that if they ever saw me break any of the rules, that would be it, I would be out, cut off immediately. If a full-Pakistani broke the same rule, they would never get cut off. They would get scolded or harshly criticised, but not cut off. With Pakistanis, it's all about blood. Once you're not full-Pakistani, they never see you as one of them.

They feel people like me can't be trusted. They believe any day you could just walk away and go become whatever your non-Pakistani parent is. There's this traditional Pakistani lending system: a group of people sign up, everyone pays an amount of money into a pot and when someone needs a loan, they borrow the money from that pot. When I was around eighteen, I wanted to join the scheme, but I was told they couldn't accept me. Because I was mixed race, they didn't trust me.

Looking back now, I know some of the Pakistani kids and their parents were simply confused by us. This was Bradford four decades ago. People like us were really rarities at the time. Nobody really understood where we fitted. They tried to deal with that confusion in their own way and perhaps didn't always mean to make us feel bad. But their clear messages that we didn't belong – badly intentioned or not – only magnified our own insecurities and got our defences up. Defences build barriers. Barriers separate people.

The alienation we all felt in my family sometimes caused tensions at home between my parents. For many years, my dad held on to the hope of someday reconciling with his family. Sometimes, he'd suggest to my mum that perhaps he should make some gesture towards them, something that might soften their hearts, at least towards us kids. Maybe his parents might want to see their grandchildren even if they didn't want to see him. This kind of talk usually got my mum upset. She'd tell my dad it was best he left it alone. 'The children are confused enough as it is. They come back from school with all sorts of questions about where they belong and who they are. Do we want to confuse them even more?' she'd say.

By the time I was twenty, I was desperate to get out of Bradford. I was confused about who I was, and I found the Pakistani culture I was surrounded with a bit too stifling. At twenty-one, I wedded a Pakistani girl in an arranged marriage, and we moved to London. The marriage was my mum's idea. She thought if I married a Pakistani girl, her family would become more accepting of me. She also thought it would help me become more authentically Pakistani, more confident in my identity. It didn't.

Even though there was a big mixed-race community in London, I still felt lost there. I became very interested in religion. I studied Buddhism, Judaism and Hinduism. I visited black churches to see what that was like. I was searching for some meaning to life, some identity that would resonate with my soul. After about two years, me and my wife knew our marriage was not going to work.

She was very family-oriented. Every weekend, we'd be back in Bradford for this or that cousin's wedding. I had wanted to leave Bradford behind me and be as far away from it as possible, but here I was back every weekend in the same community I was trying to escape. Her mother was constantly interfering in our marriage, telling us what we should and shouldn't be doing. I'd have personal conversations with my wife and before I knew it, my mother-in-law would have heard every detail. 'I am married to you, not to your family. This was supposed to be between us. Why must you tell your mother everything and let her interfere in our marriage?' I'd ask her.

But my wife saw things differently. For her it was normal for her parents to be actively involved in our married life because that is the way Pakistani culture works. But I wasn't up for this, and so we eventually parted ways amicably. We're still good friends today. After we separated – I was twenty-three at the time – I decided I wanted to go to Tibet and become a monk. Buddhism was the religion that had resonated with me the most.

But as fate would have it, on the day I was booking my flight at the travel agency, I met an English woman there. We started talking. She'd travelled the world, been to India, Australia, America. Turned out we shared the same birthday and so much else. We just clicked immediately. Four months later we were married. We lived in Leeds for a while and then moved to Sheffield, where we've been for over fifteen years now. We have very similar views on family. By that I mean we are both focused on each other and our children, not on our extended families. This is a major difference in comparison to my first marriage. I guess I am very Western in this respect.

This will sound strange, but it was in the aftermath of the September 11 attacks that I discovered the identity I had been searching for my whole life. I was thirty at the time and living in Leeds. The days following the attacks were very tense. Some people would cross to the other side of the road at the sight of a Muslim or walk away whispering. Some Muslims responded by retreating into their communities. 'Ah, so you think we're different? OK, so we'll be different then.' That kind of attitude.

The attacks and what happened after them forced me to search deep in my soul and ask myself: 'OK, so where do I fit into all of this? Who do I actually identify with here? Who am I actually?' And then it came to me, just like that. I am a British Muslim. I am a Muslim yes, but I am British, and I empathise with the fears of British society. I understand why they're angry. But we are not a they, we are part of the community, too. We live on the same streets, go the same shops and employ each other. We're all in this together. And just like that, as the realisation hit me that this was how I actually felt, a calmness descended on me with regards to identity.

The feeling that there was a large community – British people – who I really empathised with, felt good. Identity hasn't been an issue for me since then. I still perhaps find the mixed-race bit a little tricky. I recently set up a Twitter account and my initial instinct was to write 'Dad. Husband. Mixed Race' in my profile bio. But after some thought, I decided not to add the 'mixed-race' bit. It's difficult to say why – I guess I was wary I'd receive loads of negative comments and questions like, 'What do you mean mixed race?' and all that. I just wanted to avoid any of that. I guess if I were to add anything to the category I now identify as, it would be 'Mixed-race British Muslim'.

But 'Muslim' is more of a cultural identity for me than a religious one. I still read the Quran from time to time because I enjoy reading it but, while I am very spiritual, I wouldn't describe myself as very religious. I also read Buddhist books sometimes. I think the way Muslims are portrayed in Britain has improved since the years following 9/11. Up till a few years back, after any terrorist attack, the spotlight would be turned on the entire Muslim community and British media would virtually equate 'Muslim' with terrorist. But I noticed that the coverage following the 2017 Manchester Arena bombing was much more focused on the victims of the attack, including the Muslim victims, rather than on how the Muslim community had 'allowed' this happen. It was much more balanced.

There is still discrimination in Britain, though, it's just more subtle now compared to when I was growing up. Ethnic minorities still have to work twice as hard and be twice as smart to get ahead. I am an IT consultant. Sometimes, I still feel a kind of 'well, you were able to achieve such and such because we let you' attitude towards me. You do need a thicker skin as a minority here.

Though I am very comfortable with my British-Muslim identity these days, I still feel an element of outsiderness in Britain, which is perhaps why some of my best friends today are British Jews. We share a commonality in that while they are very British in many ways, there are still some important aspects of their value system that come from a very different place and differ from British cultural values. For me, Britishness means Sunday roast and accepting people's values without being offended if they clash with yours. In the end, people will believe what they want to believe.

I would like to visit Italy some day with my two daughters, just to see what kind of country it is. It's funny, my daughters – one nine, the other eleven – tell me sometimes the Asian kids in Sheffield ask them whether they are Muslim, Buddhist or what? When they say they are nothing, the kids say, 'No, you can't be nothing. What are you?' Then when they mention their dad is half-Pakistani, the kids say, 'Ah, so you're Muslim then.'

So my eleven-year-old daughter has now started asking me, 'Daddy, what are we?' I'm starting to hear the same questions me and my siblings used to ask our parents as kids. So many things have changed in Britain since I came here in the 1970s, but one thing hasn't changed: people still need an identity. I tell my daughter she can be whoever she wants to be. The world has changed since I was a child: today there are so many kids like her from mixed heritages and cultures. 'You've got double to give. This is your time,' I tell my daughters.

Those of us who grew up mixed race in Britain thirty or forty years ago faced many struggles not knowing who we were, but we've evolved. We are now realising we have so much to give. We no longer sit in a corner, not feeling a part of anything. If I were to give any advice to young mixed-race people, it would be that they read books about being mixed race, listen to podcasts, YouTube videos, anything to help them understand what it means in daily life. But ultimately, it's important for them to find their own path.

My father, even ostracised from his entire family, still managed to find his peace in the end. We are all capable of that. Mixed-raceness is a blank canvas. It's up to us to write whatever we want on it.

'Nobody wanted to own us. We were nobody's people,' recalled Fiaz, describing the situation of himself and his siblings growing up in Bradford. 'But have you thought about the children?' was a standard question interracial couples were often asked in the past by those sceptical of such relationships. Behind that question lay the rather unsubtle accusation that while falling in love with someone of a different race was one thing, condemning the potential offspring of such a relationship to the confusion of mixed-raceness and a world often harsh to their kind was downright irresponsible and selfish. I've often wondered how it must have felt for couples such as Fiaz's parents who were probably asked that question before they got married to later see their children indeed being alienated by their communities and confused about their identities. It must have felt pretty terrible.

Being 'nobody's people' was the harsh punishment meted out to Fiaz and his siblings for their parents' love. There is a confidence knowing you are part of a larger tribe gives you in dealing with the world. *I'm not alone, there are others with me. Mess with me, you mess with them.* Having no 'them' behind you weakens your negotiating position with society. Identity is not just about the sense of self on which we often focus. It is also about the reassuring feeling of belonging to a tribe that has your back. Even if that feeling is illusory, illusions are no less empowering than realities. To be deprived of an empowering illusion can be every bit as bad as being deprived of an empowering reality.

Luckily for Fiaz and his siblings, they weren't completely defenceless. The clearly strong bond of love his family shared provided them all with a powerful emotional buffer. We need oxygen to survive, but we need love to thrive. Fiaz's parents couldn't give him the psychological comfort that comes with an easy identity, but they did give him the assurance a child gets from growing up in a loving home. That is priceless, and something for which many children in mono-racial homes would gladly give up their easy identities.

But outside his home, Fiaz still had to deal with being on 'permanent probation' with the Pakistani community, ever on standby to confirm their suspicions someone like him could never really be like them. Maybe for a while, but surely not for good. 'They believe any day you could just walk away and go become whatever your non-Pakistani parent is,' Fiaz recalled. This assumption he was probably not a permanent feature in the Pakistani world but could 'go become' Italian any day reflects a transience associated with mixed-raceness that I knew from my own childhood.

I was always seen as a temporary element of the Nigerian landscape. Here today, gone tomorrow. Because I had a white mother. Even though many Nigerians were emigrating abroad for economic reasons during the period I was growing up, it was never considered an inevitability a full-Nigerian would leave. The assumption was that personal circumstance would decide: some would go, some would stay. But it never crossed anyone's mind that someone like me might *not* leave. Mixed-race kids were always seen as having one leg in, one leg out. It was assumed we would all eventually go off and become British, American or whatever other identity people felt was available to us thanks to our white parent.

This takes us back to the 'same boat' question. People feel less of a connection to you when they don't believe you are in the same boat as them or think you can switch boats easily in a way they cannot. If Fiaz had been full-Pakistani, the Pakistani community in Bradford would have known he had no option but to always be Pakistani – at most he could become British-Pakistani. That would have made them feel surer of him. But the whole Italian dad thing was too much for them. The fact many people believe that when you are mixed race you can switch identities at will makes them less certain of where our loyalties lie. Groups don't like that. Hence we are often on 'permanent probation'.

But switching is far from always that straightforward in real life. As Fiaz acknowledged, his Italianness existed largely on paper. 'While I am ethnically half-Italian, there is nothing culturally Italian about me. I wouldn't even know what that would mean, to be honest.' Yet the Pakistani community believed he could 'become' Italian whenever he wanted. It doesn't really work that way. Barack Obama's father was Kenyan. But the idea he can 'become Kenyan' one day and actually persuade himself and others that he is Kenyan is pretty far-fetched. Most mixed-race people have a limited set of feasible identities to which they can switch in a manner convincing to themselves, let alone others.

Fiaz went through a lot of pain and rejection at the hands of the Pakistani community, which is why I found it incredibly mature when he said: 'Looking back now, I know some of the Pakistani kids and their parents were simply confused by us . . . People like us were really rarities at the time. Nobody really understood where we fitted. They tried to deal with that confusion in their own way and perhaps didn't always mean to make us feel bad.'

While I think our empathy should always be focused primarily on the individual, understanding the group psychology that drives attitudes towards mixed-race people is vital to understanding the experience. I mentioned in the introduction that when we think of race, we usually focus on skin colour, but at their heart, racial differences are often really about cultural differences. Race is merely what signals that difference to the naked eye. I talked about how my father's family was displeased he married my mother due to cultural anxieties rather than pathological xenophobia or racism. The fact of the matter is a mixed-race child presents a cultural uncertainty.

As Fiaz recalled, before he ate at his Pakistani friend's homes, he would be asked whether he had washed his hands: 'They'd never have asked that if I were full-Pakistani because they would just clearly assume I had, it's such a basic requirement of the culture.' But the Pakistanis didn't feel they could make that assumption because who knows how a boy being raised by an Italian man eats at home? These cultural uncertainties the mixed-race child inspires in others is, as Fiaz wisely acknowledges, 'confusing' for them, too. It is important we acknowledge this because you cannot hope to influence human behaviour if you do not try to understand it first.

Fiaz's search for a life story that made sense to him took him from an arranged marriage with a Pakistani wife to Buddhism, Judaism, Hinduism and even the black church experience. Fascinatingly for me, it was the aftermath of 9/11 that led him to discover his Britishness or, more precisely, his self-identification as a British-Muslim. Sometimes we need to be shocked into discovering who we are by a major event that brings the big picture sharply into focus in a way everyday life does not.

# Chapter 14

# What's all this mixed-race nonsense?

Sunder is the son of an Indian father and Irish mother. He was born in Doncaster in 1974 but spent much of his childhood in the north-western county of Cheshire.

My father came to Britain in 1970 as a twenty-four-year old doctor. He hopped on a plane here from India with no specific destination city in mind. On the flight, he struck up a conversation with someone who asked where he was headed to in England. 'I don't know, you tell me,' my dad replied. Luckily for him, this person was more clued in than he was, and through him my dad ended up at a hospital in Surrey where he met my mum. She came to England from Cork in 1968 to work as a nurse.

When my dad's Hindu family heard he was planning to get married to a Catholic Irish girl, they were not happy at all. My dad's father tried to stop the wedding. He told my dad he had already arranged for him to marry an Indian girl from a family he knew. My father was faced with a life-changing decision at this point. Even today, it is very difficult for an Indian man to refuse his father such a request and embarrass him in front of the family he has given his word to. In 1970, it was virtually unheard of. But my dad stood his ground. As a result, there were more work colleagues at my parents' wedding than family members. Initially, my mum's Irish family wasn't thrilled with the marriage either.

My dad eventually converted to Catholicism, which won him some points with them but further aggravated his own family. Catholicism was a core element of my mother's identity and she was very involved with the church throughout her life. My dad was more pragmatic about religion. He officially converted to Catholicism without ever really giving up his Hinduism. He kept icons of the elephant god in his room and would visit the Hindu temple on one day while attending church with us the next.

However, thanks to my mum and her family, I had a very Irish-Catholic upbringing. I went to Catholic schools. I was an altar boy at church. I still remember Pope John Paul II's visit to Liverpool in 1982. I was one of the million people who lined the streets of the city to greet him on his arrival. I was seven at the time. The Irish element of my heritage was really pronounced in my early childhood because of this connection to Catholicism. But there was also a lot of traditional Irish culture at home. Me and my siblings learnt Irish dancing, we listened to Irish music. When people look at me, they immediately see the Indian-Asian angle, but the Irish-Catholic angle is less obvious to them.

My parents were very different in terms of personality and affinity with their cultures. My mother was quite the contradiction. She was a fervent Irish nationalist who wanted the English out and a united Ireland. She was a soft supporter of Sinn Féin. At the same time, she was a huge fan of Margaret Thatcher, who generally took a hard line on Anglo-Irish relations. She voted Tory and was a keen reader of the *Daily Mail*. She was ultra-conservative, completely anti-abortion and very worked up about crime and drugs. When I got older and asked her how she could reconcile her Irish nationalism with being pro-Thatcher and pro-Tory, she could never give me a straightforward answer. My dad, meanwhile, voted Labour. Not for any strong ideological reasons, but because as soon as he started working in a hospital, he was told by his doctor colleagues, 'Here in the NHS we vote Labour.' So he went with that. This reflects my dad's very pragmatic approach to life.

He never tried to nudge me towards developing an affinity for India. He didn't even try to get me to support India in cricket, a game he was fanatical about. I still remember when India won the cricket World Cup in 1983 and how my dad was jumping up and down the living room dementedly. I remember being pleased for him that his India had won the World Cup, not that our India had won the World Cup.

I don't speak any Indian languages – my dad never tried to teach us. I never asked him why but, thinking back, I realise his priority was always that we did well at school here. My dad is a typical Indian man in the sense he places a huge emphasis on education. What mattered to him was us doing well in school rather than learning about our Indian roots.

However, we did visit India five times between when I was born and the age of sixteen. We'd usually stay about six weeks at a time, so these were long holidays where I'd meet members of my family I had no clue how I was related to. So I do have a good sense of the sounds and smells of India. But I always felt out of place there culturally. I am definitely more at home in England and Ireland than in India. I have more in common with my Irish family than my Indian family. Irish culture feels more accessible to me than Indian culture. India is hard to wrap your head round.

I did become quite interested in India's history, its politics and Britain's colonial involvement there. But this was intellectual not emotional interest. I felt I could navigate my way into understanding India politically and historically, but it's not a place I can access from the inside. Sometimes our family would go watch the big Bollywood movies, but I could never really get them.

To me, India was always more like, 'OK, so this is where my dad is from.' I was very much a British kid with Indian heritage trying to figure out what I thought about India. Indian food is probably the only real connection I've ever had with Indian culture. My sister went through a phase of being really Indian when she was a teenager. She would listen to Indian music all the time, light joss sticks in her room and wear Indian clothes. I generally found it all a bit amusingly performative and suspected it wouldn't last long. It didn't.

I had friends who got caught up in performing a minority identity. One of my best friends from childhood was also part-Asian but had always been very culturally British. We both ended up at Oxford University. Because he started hanging out with mostly Asian friends, he was constantly trying to show them how Asian he was. I knew this wasn't really him, that it was an act. What happens in a place like Oxford, which can be very intimidating, is that people search for their comfort zones, and in his case it was Asian groups. I guess he felt he had to perform Asianness to be acceptable to them.

While I did get called a 'Paki' in primary and secondary schools, my real introduction to racism was in football stadiums. It was not my dad who introduced me to football but my mum. For some reason she was very keen I knew all about Kevin Keegan and all the other top players. Perhaps she thought it would help me blend in. By the time I was six, I was mad about football. I became an Everton fan and started going to games from when I was ten.

Back then, Everton had no black players. Club policy. By the time I was around eleven or twelve, teams like Aston Villa and Arsenal had several black players and Liverpool had signed John Barnes. Whenever these teams would come to Goodison Park, Everton fans would turn out to be ferociously racist. When we played Liverpool, the fans would be chanting, 'Everton are white, Everton are white,' at the Liverpool fans because they had John Barnes. The assumption was that Liverpool fans would be jealous Everton had an all-white team because Liverpool was basically a black team now. Whenever a black player from one of the other teams was on the ball, Everton fans would chant, 'Shoot that nigger.' I realised I'd picked a club which seemed quite proud to be racist.

But by this time I was addicted to football so I can't say I stopped supporting Everton because of this. I still went to games and cheered the team. I still wanted us to win the league. However, what I also did was get involved in anti-racism initiatives in football. It was through football I began to get involved in social issues. By the early 1990s, it was becoming normal for teams to have black players. But it was not until after the 1994 World Cup that Everton signed its first black player, Daniel Amokachi from Nigeria. And overnight, just like that, the racist chants stopped at Goodison Park.

When the other kids called me a 'Paki' or other derogatory names, I'd usually try to say something clever back like, 'What you on about, you wally, you dickhead, is your dad French or what?' At the time, I felt the French thing was a great zinger. Looking back now, it doesn't seem that great a zinger. My mum had an incredibly aggressive stance towards racism. She'd tell me if anyone called me a racist name, I should punch them. Unfortunately, this was never going to be an effective strategy for me as I was quite a small kid.

Another strategy she had was to drum into my head that I was the son of a doctor, that I was the one who had social standing, not the kids calling me names. There was a bit of class snobbery there. But I really bought into that and it gave me enormous confidence. I felt I was the one who better understood the history of Britain and it was these kids calling me names who needed to get it into their head that I was as British as they were. It was they who had the problem, not me.

I think there's been some regression in how race is thought about in Britain these past few years and in how free mixed-race Brits can feel to be themselves. Obviously, in the 1970s my parents had to deal with a society that considered interracial relationships abnormal, as did the offspring of such relationships, kids like myself.

Up till the 1980s, interracial relationships were still frowned upon by British society. But by the 1990s, people like me could breathe more easily in most places in Britain. We could just be ourselves. However, there is now something of the past back in the politics of the moment, with Brexit, Trump and all the rest. The atmosphere can sometimes feel suffocating again. People are thinking in us-versus-them terms again, with mixed-race people caught somewhere in the middle.

Some years back, a very prominent black broadcaster and race activist tried to persuade me to the 'if you're not white, you're black' worldview. We were both waiting to go on *Newsnight* in the so-called Green Room at the BBC. We started talking about race and he says, 'Mixed race? What's all this mixed-race nonsense? If you're not white, you're black.'

I told him I'd never felt I was black, and shouldn't it be up to me to decide who I thought I was? 'What are you then?' he asked. I replied I was British. My parents were Indian and Irish, so I was half-Asian and mixed race as well. 'British? Why don't you call yourself Indian? Are you ashamed of your father, boy?' he retorted.

I found this an odd thing to suggest. I am not ashamed of my mother, but that doesn't mean I would call myself Irish either. There is definitely an 'it's all of us minorities against them white people' school of thought that remains attractive to some minority intellectuals today. But I've never really been able to think that way. To be honest, I don't know any full-Indians who consider themselves 'black' either.

I run a think tank that deals with racial issues and identity. There is an understandable radicalism among younger-generation ethnic minorities in their demand for absolute equality. They are impatient and want everything fixed now. So you have all these highly intellectualised ideas about white structures of power. I don't believe there are organised structures of white power in Britain today, especially in the economic sphere. Of course, there were financial benefits from slavery and colonialism, but the idea bankers today give a damn about the colour of your skin is ludicrous. They are quite happy to make money with anybody.

Of course, it is difficult for children born in less affluent homes to make the kind of progress that has never been made in their families, but that is a class issue. Frankly speaking, I think Britain is doing much better on race than on class. But there is now a split between academic, media and political environments and the lived experience of the rest of the country.

These ideas about 'white structures' will probably continue to thrive in academic and political settings, which will become clashing points on race. These ideas will not only be driven by young students. I've noticed a pattern of radicalism among some middle-aged minorities in these settings who've gotten to a certain age and are not quite where they'd want to be in their careers. They then become radicalised and say the twenty-year-olds are right, there is still structural racism in Britain. These groups will make up their myths and narratives about twenty-first-century Britain, which they will attempt to spread. Some are already resorting to regressive racist language, calling minorities who disagree with them 'coconuts' and all that.

I believe there are legitimate reasons to reproblematise race in this country, and I do think there is a lot of prejudice still going on towards Muslims, for instance. This has led to a lot of people becoming re-Muslimised and feeling alienated. This is very real and needs to be addressed. But the problem is that the race discourse is dominated by people who spend all their time on it – we don't hear enough from people who just get on with their everyday lives and are not defined by race.

Perhaps I have a more nuanced approach because race has not really affected my life. In fact, I more often get the 'where are you really from' question from British Asians than white Brits. They are usually disappointed when they find out I can't speak any Asian language. My wife is white British, and I can see that my children instinctively identify as white. Though my eleven-year-old son has worked out he is mixed, for both my kids India is a million miles away from their world. It was hard for me to identify with India, much less for them.

I remember my ten-year-old daughter telling me how in school they'd been told about Nelson Mandela and apartheid. She said her black friends today would not have been able to sit in the same class with her back then. She was instinctively telling me this story from the perspective of a white girl. Both my kids believe they can choose how to identify. I asked them if they felt I could choose how to identify as well and they grabbed my arm, looked at it and said, 'No, Dad, you can't choose, you are definitely dark and mixed race.'

My kids go to a school in Dartford, which is where we live. While Dartford is a pretty white area, the school my kids go to is very diverse. In my son's class of about thirty kids, there are only five or six white British kids. I noticed that, after the games, there is an instinctive clustering of kids along racial lines. The black kids stand around each other, Asian kids cluster together and so forth. I noticed my son clusters with the minority white group. I find this very interesting, but I've never raised the issue with him. Clearly, he is doing this instinctively.

I think the one-drop rule is slowly disappearing in Britain and people like my kids will increasingly come to be seen as white. Eighty-five per cent of this country is white, 75 per cent of the people who are mixed race are partly white. Thanks to those numbers alone, I think we will be seeing more part-white mixed-race people getting married to white people and their children essentially identifying and being seen as white. I could have married an Asian woman, but that would have meant me having to navigate a rather unfamiliar cultural background with her family rather than the more familiar cultural values of my Irish-English wife. I think it would be hard for my kids to decide to be Malcolm X. And this will be the case for most children born into families like ours.

People say mixed-race minorities have it easier in Britain than full minorities. There is something in that. There is definitely a marked preference for people with lighter skin in the Asian community. And there is definitely a level of threat associated with full-black males that is not associated with part-black mixed-race males. It is also true that more opportunities go to people who are seen as fitting the prevalent cultural norms of a society and that applies to mixed-race Britons. Mixed-race people are often celebrated as bridge builders and empathisers.

But a lot depends on which mixes we are talking about. For instance, mixed-race people with one Muslim parent who are keen on their faith and visibly Muslim will face different pressures from, say, a mixed black and white kid raised in a Christian or secular home. I've given my kids Indian names as first names, Zarina and Indira. This is me on the one hand acknowledging my Indian backstory and, on the other, making a bet that when my kids get to working age, CVs from Indira Katwala and Zarina Katwala will be judged on the merits of their content, and not on how English-sounding they are not.

Despite visiting India several times in his childhood and taking an interest in its history and politics, Britishness and Irishness have always come easier to Sunder than Indianness. As I mentioned in the context of mixed-race Britons of African descent who felt out of place in Africa, it is difficult to understand the logic of a culture if you have never really been immersed in it. Like Ian's Indian father, Sunder's dad's priority was for him to get a good education and assimilate in Britain rather than cultivate his Indian heritage. This, too, likely contributed to his cultural distance from Indianness.

I started this book with a quote from Sunder's story of his encounter with the prominent black broadcaster and race activist who claimed, 'if you're not white, you're black' and then went on to also reprimand Sunder for calling himself 'British' instead of 'Indian'. With all the respect due such people for standing up to racism in Britain back when it was really not an easy thing to do, this is a very twentieth-century approach to race and identity.

Unless we go by the old patriarchal rule that you are what your father is, Sunder has as much claim to Irishness as to Indianness. No one, however, would think of castigating him for not calling himself Irish. Yet some ethnic minorities will think it wrong he doesn't pronounce himself Indian. They will suggest, as in the story Sunder recalled, that people like him are 'ashamed' of their Indian/brown/ Asian roots. What is the logic behind such accusations?

There is a long history of inferiority complexes in the formerly subjugated peoples of Africa and Asia, who often came to believe their cultures were inherently worse than that of their conquerors. Some of this was the result of white indoctrination, some of it was based on an instinctive respect for power. This inferiority complex did not end with the demise of colonialism.

As I suggested in an earlier chapter, *Homo capitalismus* values money and success. Because the former colonising nations are still way ahead of the formerly colonised ones in economic and developmental terms, there does exist a tendency for some black and brown people born in nations such as Britain to want to disassociate themselves from their ancestral homelands. To feel . . . yes . . . even a certain shame in being associated with the less-developed 'Third World'.

This is not just a matter of a colonial mentality, but of general human psychology. People of any skin colour prefer to be associated with achievement and success than with failure. So yes, there probably are some British-Indians, British-Nigerians and British-Pakistanis who prefer to emphasise their Britishness over their other heritages for this particular reason.

But that does not give anyone the right to assume that whenever a mixed-race person such as Sunder says he feels British rather than Indian, he is being motivated by this kind of 'shame'. In effect, such accusations amount to emotional blackmail; mixed-race people must claim their non-white heritages or face mockery and accusations of being ashamed of them. Of being 'self-hating'. Meanwhile, it is entirely plausible for someone of Sunder's heritage and life experience not to feel Indian while simultaneously not feeling ashamed of his Indian father and Indian roots. The idea that lack of identification automatically equates to shame seems rather too much of a sweeping generalisation. No one should feel they have the right to try and pressure or ridicule anyone in a similar situation to that of Sunder who says they feel British first and foremost.

# Chapter 15

# Performing Indianness

Amy's mother is British-Indian while her father is British-Jewish. She is twenty-six years old and grew up in London.

My mum's family arrived in London in the early 1960s just before she was born. They were one of the first Asian families to settle in the Whitechapel district in the East End. The first fifteen years of her life were a back-and-forth between India and London, so Punjabi was her first language. She grew up very Indian. The only brown child in her school, she struggled with English and was bullied a lot. On the streets of Whitechapel, white kids would throw rocks at her, hurl racial insults and sometimes chase her all the way home from school. She never spoke about these experiences when I was growing up. I've had to prise them out of her in recent years.

As for my dad, he doesn't really know where exactly in Europe his Jewish roots lie. He's not very interested in that kind of stuff. I figure Poland or Germany. But all that matters to him is that he was born and raised a London Jew. While his family was not very religious, he was definitely raised culturally Jewish. He had his bar mitzvah and observes all the Jewish traditional celebrations.

My mum never went to university, but she was always very creative and good with her hands, so she became a fashion designer.

That was a very white career path in 1980s London when she started. The people she worked with were all white. It was then she first started trying to blend into a world which was very different from the Indian world she had been raised in. This immediately caused friction with her family, who frowned on anything not considered acceptable in the Indian village they hailed from. For instance, when my mum pierced her ears at the age of nineteen, her family was furious, especially her older brothers. They were such a traditional family that for years my mum handed over all her wages to my grand-mum rather than keep anything for herself.

My dad worked in the fashion industry, too. His company dealt in trimmings my mum often used, which was how they met. She became quite besotted with him. Coming from her background, she had a very romanticised vision of whiteness. A white man interested in her meant she was acceptable to white society.

My parents had me in 1993. We lived in Hampstead Garden Suburb till I was four, before moving to Cockfosters in north London where my younger sister was born. My mum paid a heavy price for marrying my father. Her family disowned her. Her brothers cut her off completely. Back then, interracial marriages were big no-nos in the Indian community.

My dad's family's reaction was not that explicitly negative. His mother died when he was young, so it was just his father and grandparents around. They never openly voiced dissatisfaction my mum wasn't Jewish, but her relations with them were always a bit frosty. She didn't feel welcomed into their family. The reactions of both my parents' families to their marriage makes me really sad because I know all my mother has ever wanted was to have a happy family where everyone felt accepted. But she never got that.

Her quest for white validation coupled with her family's rejection led her to distance herself from Indianness in the twenty-five years she was married to my father. He didn't help matters in this sphere.

As far back as I can remember, he never made any effort to show an interest in Indian culture or to make my mum feel comfortable being Indian. This reinforced her instincts not to associate herself with Indianness, to keep that side of herself hidden, almost like a dirty secret.

My mum is quite light-skinned, just a bit darker than me. She is not very visibly Indian and plays on that a lot. Sometimes even Indians don't recognise her as Indian. She'll be in shops and people will start making comments about her in Punjabi, never imagining she understands what they're saying.

My earliest childhood memories are from Cockfosters, which was a very white suburban area. I went to a private Catholic school. In my early years, it never occurred to me I wasn't white. Something always felt a bit off, but I couldn't put a finger on it. I was surrounded by white kids. I never had any issues with them because of my appearance, but I could see I didn't exactly look like them. I wasn't the skinny fair-haired girl I saw everywhere I turned. I was darker and heavier. However, I didn't think of myself as racially different. I didn't feel like the odd one out in my primary-school years.

My mum never spoke about India at home. She rarely made Indian food when my father was around because he didn't like the smells. In the earlier years, she would sometimes cook Indian food, slaving for hours to make four or five different dishes. My dad would take his seat at the table, spoon a bit of everything onto his plate, pour some yoghurt, and mix it all into one big brown sludge. I'd see the disappointment on my mum's face. She'd spent hours making several distinctly flavoured dishes and my dad just mixed them all into a mush without as much as a word on whether he found it tasty or not. After a while, she stopped bothering altogether.

To be honest, on the rare occasions she did make Indian food, neither me nor my sister particularly enjoyed it. There was nothing in our house to suggest we were Indian, no typical curry smell, no

Indian decorations. My mum never wore traditional Indian clothes but dressed like a typical Western woman. And by the time I was growing up, she spoke English without an Indian accent, which is interesting considering her first language was Punjabi. We ate mostly white food at home and had white family friends. We lived in a large house which my Jewish granddad had bought for us after my younger sister was born. Everyone on our road was wealthy and white.

It was not until secondary school that some notion of difference started creeping in. I have some typical Indian features like very thick eyebrows and hairy arms. When I was around twelve, I remember my best friend staring at me intently one day and announcing in a solemn voice, 'Amy, I think you need to get your eyebrows threaded.' She wasn't being malicious or anything, just giving me what she considered good best-friend advice. But I started feeling self-conscious after that.

I know this sounds shallow but the main thing that stuck with me in secondary school were the comments about my eyebrows. I felt like I had the bushiest eyebrows ever. I still didn't connect this to race, though. I felt I was just hairy, not Indian and hairy. Though I look a bit foreign, I'm quite light-skinned so I never experienced racism the way my mum did. Such experiences would have definitely brought about a sharper feeling of difference much earlier.

One other thing that made me realise I wasn't quite like the other kids, though, was the discipline my mum imposed on us. My white friends' parents were all very liberal and slack in terms of what time they could come home and where they could go. Not my mum. We had strict curfews. Sometimes she'd come pick me up in the middle of nowhere just to make sure I got home on time.

None of the white parents I knew did this sort of thing. Hence, my teenage years were shrouded in lies I'd tell my mum about where I was going. My dad, just like the other white parents, was very liberal in this sphere. 'You go do your own thing' was his general attitude. So I'd usually tell him the truth about where I was going and lie to my mum. She was the stereotypical Asian mother in terms of discipline.

But it was only as I approached twenty it really started registering in my brain that I wasn't white. Just before I went off to university, my mum taught me how to cook some basic Indian dishes so I wouldn't have to live on junk food. The reactions of my university peers to my cooking was a key moment in terms of my mental separation from the white majority. I went to Reading University where there were lots of white students from the countryside. I was the only person in my hostel who wasn't white.

Whenever I'd cook my Indian food, the other students would be like, 'Oh my God, what on earth are you eating? That smells so awful!' I found this very hurtful because, hey, that's the food of my mum's country. It reminds me of my mum. Dissing it feels like dissing my mum. I think being mixed race makes you inherently more tolerant than the average person. I would never tell someone the food they were cooking stank even if I felt that way, because it could be something their grandma made them or taught them how to make. University was when I really started thinking about who I was and what my roots were.

The way my parents raised me had a lot to do with these thoughts coming so late. I once asked my mum why she hadn't pushed Indianness on me and my sister when we were growing up. She said she'd had such horrible experiences with racism and being seen as different when she was a child that she hadn't wanted us to go through the same pain. 'I feel like this was a lose–lose for me,' she said. 'Today, you ask me why I didn't teach you Punjabi, why I didn't cook Indian food more and why I didn't bring Indian culture into our home. But if I had done that when you were growing up, it would have made you feel very different from the kids around you. And it would have likely also made them see you as different.'

She's right on this count. Because of how she raised us, I did not feel particularly different from the other kids growing up. We all ate the same food and did the same things. Can I blame her for deciding to raise us this way? I agree it was a lose–lose situation for her. Truth is, if she had pushed Indian culture on us, I am pretty sure I would probably have rebelled and said, 'No, I don't want to be Indian. I just want to be like everybody else around me.'

While I will probably raise my kids differently, considering my mum's background and reasoning at the time, what she did made absolute sense. The negative consequence of this approach, though, is that you get kids who reach young adulthood and start feeling confused about who they are. In my early twenties, the 'who am I?' question started popping up more and more often in my head.

Right until my grandfather died when I was sixteen, we had regular Friday-night dinners with my dad's family, which is a Jewish tradition. We'd go to my granddad's house or the family would come to ours. These dinners were probably my only real taste of Jewish culture in childhood. It wasn't much, but it was more than the Indian side. However, I have mixed feelings about my relations with my Jewish family. I can't say I've ever felt uncomfortable around them, but I don't remember any warm fuzzy feelings either.

My parents getting divorced changed my cultural life completely. Me, my sister and my mum started stepping into Indianness a lot more. But it was a difficult journey and still is. Even after my dad left, I could see my mum still didn't feel that comfortable being Indian. I wanted her to know I felt it was OK to be Indian so she should, too. So I started going to a Sikh temple and wearing Indian ornaments. I started asking her to make Indian food virtually all the time. I became a lot more invested in Indianness and, with time, I could see this made my mother more willing to re-embrace it herself.

But stepping into the world of Indianness brought many uncomfortable situations for me and my sister. We felt very foreign in Indian settings, including around the members of my mum's family she reunited with. At family gatherings, they'd all be speaking Punjabi so we couldn't understand a word they were saying. They saw me and my sister as different from them. To them, we were white children. They assumed we wouldn't even eat the same food they ate. It's the age-old problem of being mixed race; you feel different around white people and different around brown people. There is no group in whose company you do not feel an underlying sense of difference.

My mum hadn't been to India for thirty years, so we decided to visit in 2016. We went to the village her family is from and stayed with her brother. This was my first trip to India. In the run-up to it, I saw this as a return to my homeland. I was going to feel so connected to India. It was going to be this incredible experience where I would come to the realisation that this is who I am. But that feeling never came.

Rather than it being this nice incredible experience, there were so many rules and regulations in my uncle's household it felt really stifling. 'You can't do this, you can't do that,' was what we kept hearing. There was an endless list of things we weren't allowed to do because my uncle was so conservative. It wasn't even the rules per se that really bothered me, it was the assumption we had to constantly be reminded of them. Because we were spoilt Western brats who probably had no manners. My mother's family simply assumed we wouldn't be respectful and probably didn't even know how to be if we wanted.

'I'm never doing this again!' I told myself by the end of the trip. That visit to India made me realise that while I may feel different around my white British peers, that doesn't mean I fit in with my mum's Indian family. I don't. I've never felt as white as I did when we were in India.

However, generally speaking, in terms of cultural values, my mum has definitely had a stronger influence on me than my dad. It was she who instilled in me the very Indian belief that family must always be number one. That it is my absolute responsibility to look after my sister since she is younger than me. That when we go out, I have to pay for her. That we had to be generous and share what we had with the family. My dad never emphasised any of these things.

To be fair, I think a major reason he wasn't a big cultural influence on me was because he is generally a detached person who, like I mentioned, is not even interested in his own family roots, much less in spreading any sort of cultural values.

A few years ago, my dad told me I am not mixed race, that I am white. I'd just had a conversation with my boyfriend who is also mixed race, but half-black, half-white. It was he who sparked the idea in my head that being mixed race was its own thing, different from any other identity. So I brought this up with my dad, thinking I'd have a mature conversation about race and identity with him. But his response to me talking about being mixed race and not white was, 'What do you mean you're not white?'

'Er . . . Mum's from India and I am half of her,' I replied.

'But you were born and raised in London. Why on earth would you feel anything other than British?' he asked, with a puzzled look on his face.

I hadn't been prepared for that reaction. I didn't know what to say. It was later it struck me that he didn't even separate whiteness from Britishness but used the two terms interchangeably in our exchange. He couldn't fathom why I would feel different from anyone around me.

Today, Jewishness doesn't mean anything to me. I know this has a lot to do with the fact I associate it with my dad and am not on great terms with him right now. I don't think I will be this distanced from Jewishness forever. I can imagine a time later in life when I become interested in learning about that aspect of my heritage. But for now, I don't have the emotional space for both cultures. I think my mum's culture deserves the interest I am giving it right now.

Food is the main route I use to connect to Indianness these days. It's a way of establishing rapport with my mum's family. I eat with my hands when I'm with them, Indian-style. I do this to send a clear signal I am not different from them and don't want them to treat me as a white person. I know they have registered the way I eat approvingly. I've also made it my mission to cook Indian food really well.

Food is a means of validating identity. I don't know why we assume it has these magical powers that can give us an identity, but we do. I don't know why eating Indian food with my hands makes me any more Indian than someone who eats with a fork and knife, but that's the way it works.

I guess there is something particularly communal in the ritual of eating the same food together in the same way. Family meals are not a big deal in British culture. In Indian culture, cooking and eating together, that's what a family does. I don't look Indian so I need to grasp anything I can that is a symbol of Indianness. I can't make myself look more Indian. Food is the easiest way for me to perform an Indian persona.

It doesn't bother me that I know it's a performance. We all perform different social identities in different situations. There are so many hats and masks we wear every day, depending on who we're with and where we are. Many of these masks have nothing to do with race, some are linked to it. At the end of the day, what I do with my Indian family is a social performance no different from other social performances.

Though I generally want society to see me as mixed race, when I'm around Asian people, I want to be recognised as an Indian woman. I definitely do not want to be viewed as a white person the way my dad views me. I'm not that.

I'm generally not a fan of the Western obsession with racial classifications. In some places, people are so mixed no one is interested in whether you are 25 per cent this or 50 per cent that. In two British generations, you won't even be able to say what you are any more because everyone will be so mixed. By then, the very concept of 'mixed race' will likely become obsolete. It only exists today because most Brits are still monoracial.

Amy's disappointment with her visit to India and realisation she was more British and even more 'white' than she had imagined echoes some of the stories from earlier chapters about 'going back'. As did her realisation that India, like the rest of the non-Western world, is significantly more conservative than Britain. Some other Britons with Indian roots, however, had different stories to tell.

Naomi, who is the twenty-seven-year-old daughter of a South African Indian father and Scottish mother, told me she enjoyed her first visit to India very much. Unlike Amy, however, she didn't have to stay under the roof of a conservative Indian uncle reeling out dos and don'ts for her.

Instead, she went with a family friend with whom she toured the country for three months. She was seventeen at the time. 'The pace of life is crazy there, but I loved it. I really felt at home for the first time in my life. I started wearing Indian clothes. By the end of my stay there, random people would often assume I was Indian. Indians usually pay lower ticket prices for trains than foreigners and I was getting charged "Indian prices" instead of foreigner prices. When I was leaving India, the airport official asked where my Indian passport was. That all felt nice and made me feel at home.' The fact she was often assumed to be Indian clearly played a big role in Naomi feeling positive about her Indian experience. Few things make a mixed-race person's heart warm like the feeling of being seen as one of us.

Going back to Amy's story, her mother faced the classic dilemma many parents of mixed-race children face. Do I want my child to feel like everybody else or different from everybody else? Both options have their pluses and drawbacks. Amy's mum chose the former option, which Amy understands today. Yet 'the negative consequence of this approach, though, is that you get kids who reach young adulthood and start feeling confused about who they are. In my early twenties, the "who am I?" question started popping up more and more often in my head.'

I guess one thing parents of mixed-race kids should be prepared for is that the 'who am I?' question will come sooner or later no matter how much they try to help their kids to blend in with everyone else. I think Amy summed it up perfectly when she said that, being mixed race, 'there is no group in whose company you do not feel an underlying sense of difference'. That is exactly how I have always felt.

It's not like you feel this difference strongly every time you are with a group of people. Oftentimes this feeling remains way below your subconscious or surfaces for the most fleeting of moments, too short for you to even think about afterwards. But it is there. Triggered by a comment, a memory, a random thought. Something that reminded you that your life experiences and feelings have been quite different from everyone else in the room. By no means does it always have to be an uncomfortable feeling or one that leaves you alienated. But it's there.

I loved what Amy said about performing an Indian persona and how we all don various masks to suit the social situation we are in. Sunder touched on the issue of how some mixed-race Asians feel the need to perform an Asian identity, but Amy really went into some detail about this. I think she was spot on when she said, 'We all perform different social identities in different situations. There are so many hats and masks we wear every day, depending on who we're with and where we are.'

When she said that, I thought, *Yeah, I do a half-decent perform-ance of Nigerianness myself.* Like in Amy's case, food is a major element of my repertoire. Not just what I eat, but how I eat. Growing up in Nigeria, we always ate with cutlery at home. I knew most Nigerians ate many Nigerian dishes with their hands, but we always used a fork and knife. I never saw my dad eat with his hands.

My dad was born to a very poor family in a village during the colonial era. He would never have received an education if not for the fact a pair of white missionaries turned up at his home one day and told his father they were opening a school in the village, which would be free. My dad ended up going to primary and secondary schools run by white Catholic missionaries. They taught him how to use cutlery and he never again ate with his hands. Neither did I while in Nigeria. Nobody ever expected me to – after all, I was an *oyinbo*.

But when I moved to Poland, I noticed most of the Nigerians there ate with their hands and I was starting to look like the odd one out. Keen to be a full part of an in-group in a hostile environment, I started eating Nigerian food with my hands instead of cutlery. Nigerians were always surprised the first time they saw me do that. 'Wow, so you eat with your hands! You're a real Nigerian,' they'd say. I liked hearing that.

The first time I went back to Nigeria, I went out with my dad for a meal. We ordered a Nigerian dish. I asked the waiter to bring me a bowl of water, which is a sign you plan to eat with your hands and need to wash them first.

'You want to eat with your hands?' my dad asked me, visibly surprised.

'Yes, Dad.'

'Why would you want to eat with your hands?'

'Why not, Dad? Many people in many different cultures eat with their hands. In the Middle East, they eat with their hands, too.'

222

'Those are primitive cultures,' my dad observed.

'Why would you say they're primitive, Dad? What's wrong with eating with your hands?'

'It's not hygienic, that's what. But if you want to eat with your hands, that's fine, go ahead,' he smiled.

It would be easy to scoff at my dad for being one of those Africans who were 'brainwashed' by the colonialists and now believed their ways of doing things were the best ways while his people's ways were the 'primitive' ways. But that would be far too simplistic a tale. The colonised African was as complex and contradictory a being as any other. My dad embraced some Western ways of doing things as better than the pre-colonial African ways while rejecting others. Those who completely accepted the one and rejected the other belong more in the realm of caricaturist imaginations than flesh-and-blood people.

The difference between me and my dad, though, was that he did not need to perform Nigerianness by eating with his hands. All he had to do was open his mouth and speak Yoruba for everyone to know he was a Yoruba man from south-western Nigeria. I couldn't speak any Nigerian language, but I could eat with my hands.

During one of my first trips back to Nigeria, a friend called me aside after a meal of pounded yam at a gathering one day.

'Dude, you're doing it all wrong,' he said.

'Doing what wrong?'

'The way you're eating. You're only supposed to dip your hand into the bowl of water beside you before eating and after eating, both times to clean your hands. But you kept dipping your hands into the water while eating.'

'That's because the pounded yam was so hot I had to cool my hand down from time to time,' I exclaimed.

'Ah, but you see, there's a way you roll the pounded yam in your palm to cool it down before eating. That way you don't need to dip your hand in the water all the time. When you went to the toilet, everyone was laughing at the way you were doing that,' my friend told me.

Well, I guess nobody said this performance business would be easy.

# Chapter 16

# I expected to see white hands

Danyal is the twenty-three-year-old son of an English father and Pakistani mother. He was born and raised in Ipswich where he currently lives and works as a graphic designer.

My parents faced some resistance when they wanted to get married in the 1990s. While my father's family had nothing against their son marrying a Pakistani woman, my mother's parents were initially against the idea of her getting married to an English man. Not because they have anything against white people in general, but because they feared she would become Westernised and lose the values they had tried to instil in her all their lives. By 'Westernised' I mean they feared she would start smoking and drinking, going to pubs with my dad and his English friends, generally getting involved in English pub culture and all that comes with that.

To calm their nerves, my dad converted to Islam. This helped smooth things over, and my mum's parents relented, so she was able to marry my dad. But now that her parents have gotten to know my dad, they love him and there are absolutely no problems between them at all. They get along fantastically. My dad's conversion to Islam was purely for formality, though. After the wedding, he pretty much forgot all about being a Muslim. He was never much of a

225

Christian before that either: he is generally not a very religious or spiritual man.

But my mum and her parents are very spiritual people. My Pakistani grandfather in particular. He never tried to impose Islam on me. Today, I am pretty much an agnostic and he knows that, but I am very happy he imbued in me a keen interest in the spiritual aspects of our existence. When I was growing up, he'd ask me questions like, 'Danyal, why are we here? What is the purpose of life? What makes people feel truly content and fulfilled? What gives their life a sense of meaning? What makes them happy?'

He taught me to think deeply about a lot of things I would never have thought about on my own, definitely not at so young an age. I really enjoyed our conversations about that kind of stuff. People often say I'm very mature for my age. If they are right then I think my grandfather's influence in my upbringing definitely had a lot to do with that.

When my parents got married, they lived in London at first. I asked them how it was being a Pakistani-English couple in the 1990s. However, even back then, London was a very multicultural place with loads of interracial couples, so no one took much notice of them there. Only when they visited places like Cornwall and other virtually all-white cities would people literally stop in the streets and stare at them.

My mum usually laughs when she recalls such scenes. I've always remembered her as a very confident woman. Those kinds of things never affected her negatively. She is generally very secure in who she is. She sees people as inherently good and always tries to flip things in a positive way. I know some people laugh at this kind of talk today, but my mum doesn't see colour, the only thing she sees is culture. She tells me people are mostly shaped by the expectations of their culture. She says if she had walked on the streets of a Pakistani city holding hands with my white dad in the 1990s, Pakistanis would have stopped to stare, too. Because people are always curious at seeing the unexpected in their cultural world.

I never recall my parents arguing about the right way to bring me up or which values were best for me. Generally speaking, I would say I was brought up in very Western fashion, like anyone else on our street in Ipswich. However, because both my parents were busy professionals, I did spend a lot of time with my Pakistani grandparents who definitely had an influence in shaping my value system.

In addition to the interest in spirituality my grandfather passed on to me, he constantly reminded me to always treat people respectfully, to always keep calm and take time to think even during the most heated of conversations or moments. Tranquillity was key for him. My grandparents taught me some Urdu as well, but unfortunately I've forgotten most of it. There was no Pakistani community to speak of in Ipswich where I was growing up, so I didn't really have anyone to practise the language with.

I regret not remembering how to speak Urdu today. I would like to know the language as I think it would make me feel more connected to my Pakistani heritage. As it stands, because there was no Pakistani community around me growing up, my links to Pakistan are very personal, through my mum and my grandparents, but nothing beyond that really. I do feel some sort of connection to Pakistan, but it is quite abstract and theoretical, not something I can really put my finger on. I've never been there because my mum is worried it's too dangerous. Quite frankly, so am I. When I weigh up the benefits of connecting more with my Pakistani roots by visiting there and the dangers involved in potentially getting caught up in some violence, I'm not sure it's a risk I'd be willing to take. I would like to visit someday, though.

Out of about a hundred kids in my secondary-school year, only five of us were not white. While I generally don't remember any explicitly racist experiences like people saying, 'Dan is this and this because he is half-Pakistani,' I was often reminded I was different because of my skin colour. This would mostly happen through offhand comments and jokes from the other kids, which centred around the fact I was darker-skinned than them. I can't recall any specific ones, but I do know they triggered an identity crisis in me when I was in my teenage years.

I wondered who I really was. I hated the fact I was being treated differently when I felt the same as everyone else. I was born here. I was brought up here. I thought like everyone else here. I was fully ingrained in British culture. Looking down at myself, I instinctively expected to see white hands and would have forgotten I wasn't white if I hadn't been reminded of it by the other kids.

I did sometimes wish I was white. It would have been easier to fit in. I would look just like everyone else, no one would notice me and that would be great. All I wanted back then was to conform, to be like everyone else. I spoke to my mum about my frustrations once or twice when I felt really upset.

Apart from the fact my mum is a person of colour, I chose to speak to her and not my dad about my identity issues because she is generally much better with words than he is. I always went to her with all my problems. When I told her how I was feeling, she said I was 'unique' but then so was everyone else. 'You are different, but that's not because you have a different skin colour. It's because every single person is different, everyone has unique experiences. So don't ever feel like you are some sort of outcast. You're just visibly different here in Ipswich because everyone else is white,' she told me. At the time, my mum's words didn't help me feel any better, though. I'd say something along the lines of, 'everybody hates me, Mum' and storm off like an upset prima donna.

However, by the time I was eighteen, my attitude to looking different from everyone around me had changed quite drastically. I started meeting loads of girls and getting noticed for being different in a positive way. When girls think you look cool, that certainly affects the way you see yourself, and in a nice way! Female attention completely changed the way I viewed myself. I started feeling happy I stood out from all the other guys, thinking it would actually be pretty boring to look like everyone else because then I wouldn't get noticed by pretty girls. Comments about my skin colour nowadays are very positive. People will say things like, 'Wow, you've got a gorgeous skin tone,' which is a nice thing to hear. Looking like everyone else doesn't seem that appealing any more.

In terms of identity, 'British' sums me up best. I was born here. I share British values. By 'British values', I mean a sense of pride in Britain, a habit of politeness, and of being a bit reserved. I feel quite personally detached from the Muslim aspect of my Pakistani heritage. Islam was what my grandparents believed in. I think my mum would tell them she believes in it, too, but I'm not sure she really does. She doesn't practise Islam or read the Quran very often. I suspect she thinks about the Quran in an abstract way, as stories told to instil morals in us.

However, while I've never personally been disparaged for being associated with Islam, when I hear the media saying negative things about Muslims, I do take it personally. At such moments, I think of my grandparents who are Muslims. I wonder how they feel listening to such negative stories. I imagine them going to town and someone saying something horrible to them because they are Muslims. This makes me feel sad not just because they are my grandparents but because I know they are good people.

People aren't bad because they are Muslim – that's a ridiculous thing to think. I know the majority of British people don't think this way, but those who do tend to be the loudest, so their negative opinions get heard. Some people associate Muslims with terrorists while others say they are trying to impose their values on the rest

229

of Britain. But the number trying to do one or the other is a tiny percentage of a large group of people.

Personally, I don't think it is white supremacist or anti-Muslim ideology on the part of journalists that motivates these negative stories about Muslims in the British press. I think it is a cynical business calculation. The media know their audience demographics and pander to whatever demographic reads their paper. Whether it's the *Guardian* or the *Sun*, the mechanism is the same: those writing the headlines know the trigger words their reader base will react to. So they make sure to use those words to grab their attention.

Most readers of papers like the *Sun* will be white and very right-wing so 'Muslim' and 'terrorist' are words that are likely to get their attention. I'm sure even those right-wing tabloids have black and brown people working for them, writing sensationalist articles and playing on stereotypes. This is sad if you think about it, but I think what motivates a lot of people, including journalists, is money.

Journalists want people to read their articles, so they do everything they think they need to do to get them to do that. There definitely should be better vetting processes determining what kind of headlines can be chosen but I think we won't stop greed and ambition among journalists anytime soon. It will also be difficult to stop politicians saying things to get themselves attention or to play to their audience just like the media. Like when Boris Johnson made those comments about women in burqas looking like letterboxes. Why did he have to say that, make fun of them in that way? Even then he was someone in a position of power so people like that should be particularly careful with their words. I think that was racist because it's always racist when someone in a position of power singles out a minority group for ridicule like that.

My friends, who mostly tend to be white, sometimes ask me how I feel in Britain, considering my racial background. I usually tell them I am happy with who I am and kill the conversation. I respond in this way because I feel like they are wanting to hear a specific thing from me, essentially that I think there is a lot of racism in Britain, and I am being oppressed. But I can't say this because this has not been my experience. So I feel it's just better to end the conversation. I am not comfortable speaking for huge numbers of people dealing with different problems. I can only speak for myself. I wouldn't like others to speak in my name either.

However, with regards to race relations in Ipswich in the past couple of years, I have definitely noticed a difference in the atmosphere. In the pubs, it is now much more common to hear complaints about foreigners and immigrants. Mostly about those from eastern Europe. Most of these complaints are related to crime: people feel the eastern Europeans have made some of the neighbourhoods in Ipswich more dangerous.

It's funny, just a few days after the Brexit vote, someone I know, not a friend, but someone I see in town from time to time, came up to me in a club and said in a sad voice, 'Hey Dan, I'm really sorry you'll have to leave now.'

'What do you mean, leave?' I asked.

'You know, because of Brexit,' he replied.

I laughed and told him, 'Dude, Pakistan doesn't have anything to do with Brexit, so this doesn't affect me at all. Apart from that I'm a British citizen so don't worry, I'll be fine.'

He seemed quite relieved I wouldn't have to leave. He was a fair-minded bloke, but that exchange left me feeling quite sad. I was sad that someone who had probably voted in the referendum had no idea what he was actually voting about and thought Pakistan was somehow connected to the European Union and Brexit.

When it comes to people making comments that could be deemed racially offensive, I think your reaction has a lot to do with how secure you feel as a person in general. If you are insecure, you will immediately get defensive or lash out at those making such comments or jokes. But if you are truly secure in who you are, such incidents will never really bother you. Just like they never bothered my mum.

Personally, I've never felt my skin colour be an obstacle to me getting what I want in Britain. Nor do I feel there is anything that has been taken away from me because of how I look or where my mother is from. My parents worked really hard, put me through university and I am now on my second (good) job after finishing my studies. Me and my girlfriend are about to buy a home soon. I've never been a victim of any kind of institutional racism in Britain. I am not saying racism does not exist in Britain, I am just saying I haven't experienced it. And of course I don't know what it's like to be very dark-skinned in Britain.

We don't really discuss race at home; politics yes, but race only occasionally. My mum sometimes talks about race, usually emphasising how Britain is definitely more tolerant today than it used to be. Twenty years ago, when my grandfather would be speaking on the phone in Urdu in a public place, people around would sometimes say, 'Speak English, we don't understand what you're saying.' Now no one cares about things like that. Of course, there is still a small group who do, but I think they are definitely in the minority.

Most people I meet today are not obsessed with race and identity. In the real world outside the media bubble, most people just get on with their lives and get along with the people around them whatever their race or background. If I eventually get married to my current girlfriend, who is white, our kids will probably be indistinguishable from white kids.

Sometimes I wonder if they would identify as white, full stop. I don't think I'd be upset by that. Everyone has to choose their own path and figure out where they fit in. My children would just have to come to grips with the fact their father is mixed race and that's that.

You need to accept who you are and live life to the fullest. While you cannot choose your skin colour, you can choose your culture. It is entirely up to each of us which values and morals we decide to live by once we are adults.

The days of racial purity, be it black, white or Asian, are over and are a pretty old-school idea. My generation won't accept the idea of fixed racial and identity boundaries or people imposing on them who they are allowed to feel like, they just won't. I believe Britain is a fair society though I know perfectly well that I have never lived in poor neighbourhoods in cities like London where minorities might feel differently. In Ipswich, most of the people living in council estates and deprived neighbourhoods are white so I personally don't associate poverty and suffering in this country with being black or brown. But I get that others elsewhere might feel differently.

Danyal's mixed-race experiences were shaped by his relationship with his white peers in Ipswich rather than with the Pakistani community, as was the case with Fiaz who we read about a couple chapters earlier. His biggest struggle with being English-Pakistani stemmed from the kind of subtle otherings many ethnic minorities complain about in modern-day Britain, 'offhand comments and jokes' from other kids revolving around his darker skin colour. This led to him suffering an identity crisis in his teenage years.

Danyal hated the fact he was seen as different even though he felt 'the same' as everyone else and 'thought like everyone else' around him. This is something not just mixed-race people but people of colour in general who were raised in Britain often complain about. Having grown up completely immersed in British culture, they feel they are no different from their white peers, yet the latter can often see them as different just because they have a darker skin shade.

Meanwhile, in cases such as that of Danyal, take away his darker skin colour and contact with Pakistani grandparents and he really is just another British kid raised in Ipswich. So much so that looking down at himself when he was younger, he 'instinctively expected to see white hands' and would have forgotten he wasn't white if he hadn't constantly been reminded of it by other kids.

While he says now that one's reactions to racial othering depends on how secure you are as a person, expecting a teenager to be secure enough not to be fazed by this is setting the bar a bit too high. Danyal seems to have ultimately emerged from his experiences a confident and happy young man (thanks no doubt in large part to the female attention he talked about) but the general rule is that people who have been hurt want to hurt others. Any society that wants its young ones growing up to be adults who don't feel a need to hurt others needs to do what it can to absolutely minimise the hurt they experience in their vulnerable years. Otherwise, you will get a society full of people craving revenge.

The spiritual aspect of his personality that Danyal attributes to his Pakistani grandfather is something that chimed with me and the spirituality I also feel I got from my contact with a non-Western culture growing up. I liked Danyal's mother's comment about people being 'mostly shaped by the expectations of their culture'. In her case, as with many of the other stories I heard, opposition to her interracial marriage was grounded in cultural anxieties about her becoming 'Westernised' rather than her Pakistani parents simply hating white people. As I've mentioned before, I've come to see the logic behind these anxieties. I suspect many readers will, too. If we are ready to accept that Nigerian, Indian or Pakistani families can be opposed to interracial marriages out of cultural rather than racial motivations, however, then we should be ready to acknowledge that so too can white families.

The real history of widespread white racism means that we have come to a place where a white family exhibiting scepticism at their son or daughter marrying a black or brown person raised in another culture will immediately be deemed racist by many people. But if a Nigerian family does not want their child to marry a white person and we don't call them racist for that, then on what grounds do we automatically label a white family that feels the same way 'racist'?

This whole race discussion really has to be a two-way street for it to make any sense and for people on all sides to feel it is fair. Otherwise, it is just a discussion in which we use history to justify having one set of standards for white people and another for everyone else. That is a recipe for resentment, not constructive dialogue.

To those families of any race who might feel anxious at the idea of one of their own marrying outside their race, I would quote Danyal's wise words: 'While you cannot choose your skin colour, you can choose your culture. It is entirely up to each of us which values and morals we decide to live by once we are adults.' The power of race has always lain in its claim that it is capable of distinguishing qualitatively different types of human beings. But it isn't. My skin colour and even my family background tell you absolutely nothing about the quality of person I am. I could look the way I look and be the noblest man in Britain or I could be an absolute piece of shit. But you'll never know which if you don't come closer.

# Chapter 17

# Can I pray to God in Chinese?

Linxi is the twenty-three-year-old daughter of an English father and Chinese mother. She grew up in London.

My father used to volunteer at a refugee centre in London where he struck up a friendship with a cousin of my mother who persuaded him to start writing letters to her in China. Obviously, her cousin was trying to matchmake them, but I don't think my dad realised it at the time! After a few years of correspondence, he and my mum indeed decided to get married and she came to the UK. My dad was forty-nine at the time while she was much younger.

I grew up on a council estate in Kingston upon Thames in London, the kind of place where most of the guys either end up in jail or in the army. My dad never had a steady job and my mum stopped her waitressing after I was born, so my family has survived on benefits for as long as I can remember. Our grocery shopping consisted of going around all the supermarkets on Sunday with a granny trolley and buying whatever products were on offer that day. Because of this, our meals were a real mishmash; we could be having potatoes and spring rolls one day and rice with tofu and sausages the next.

It wasn't just race that messed up my identity, but also class, everything from my accent to how I walk and how I talk. I am still confused about who I am and haven't quite decided yet. Growing up, I sought refuge in Harry Potter books and the Bible. I got my Christian faith from my father who is a devout Christian. It is the one stable thing in my life, my one sure identity; I am a child of God. For many Brits, their Christianity is just something they tick on a box; for me it's real. I try to read the Bible every day even if just for five minutes on the bus. God is the first thing I think of when I wake up and the last thing before I sleep. This makes me quite countercultural in today's Britain, definitely so among my generation.

To the left of our council estate was Surbiton, a posh suburban neighbourhood where people lived in big beautiful houses. My school was five minutes away from where we lived. Because of the area the school was in, there were people from council estates like me as well as loads of middle-class kids, kids whose parents were in politics, and some rich kids. The school was so diverse with so many mixed-race people that race wasn't a problem. What really divided us was class. Though of course it was the case that most of the middle- and upper-class kids were white while most of the minority kids were lower-class like me.

I probably shouldn't be saying this, but the kids from similar class backgrounds to mine weren't really serious at school. They'd be messing around all the time, never paying attention to the teachers, doing stuff I'd never dream of doing because my mum was so strict. She was the stereotypical Chinese mum who didn't allow me go out and play with other kids after school for most of my childhood. All she wanted me to do was study. I had to take all the extra classes offered at school and join every single study club.

The working-class kids were more in charge at school than the middle-class kids. It was so funny, there'd be these tall middle-class white boys scared silly of the lower-class kids who often bullied and intimidated them. The lower-class kids had the power in school. There were these two girls all the middle-class white boys were terrified of, so I became something of a go-between for them. They'd say, 'Hey Linxi, could you please ask Paysia and Asia if we can pass the corridor because they're standing there talking now, blocking the hallway?' I'd be like, 'Just walk through, you idiots.' But middle-class kids are such scaredy-cats, it's so easy to intimidate them.

My mum was definitely the dominant parent in my home. She was fierce and very demanding. My dad was way more tolerant and relaxed, but he never had the character to fight my mum. Even when he tried, she would win every single time. After a while, he stopped trying. My mum totally ran the show. All my dad could get away with was going to church whenever he wanted to even though my mum has little patience for Christianity. But even when it came to faith, she would still force both of us to accompany her to Chinese religious festivals despite the fact they conflicted with our Christian beliefs.

There were many practices my mother imposed in our home because that was how it was done in China when she was growing up. There was no way I could put my knickers and socks in the washing machine without handwashing them first. Why? Because! Also, you always had to wear shoes or slippers going into the kitchen, even if you were just stepping in for two seconds.

She couldn't accept the idea tap water could be clean enough to drink, so the rule was that you had to boil the water in a kettle first and then filter it. Only after this could you drink it. I was shocked when I first saw a friend drink water from the tap at home. My wardrobe was divided into outdoor clothes and indoor clothes. What you wear outside couldn't be worn at home and vice versa. I could never understand all of this, but there was no negotiation with her.

My mum wasn't like British mums who have conversations with their children. She simply shouted orders at me and that was that. These things stick with you. Recently at university, a friend came to my room and got into my bed and it bothered me because I was thinking how can you get into my bed with outside clothes? My mum had drilled it into my head this was wrong.

I remember us having terrible arguments about me not wanting to wear a bra. I don't have big boobs, so when I was around sixteen, I told my mum I didn't really see the point in wearing a bra. She was furious. 'You're a whore, you're a slut, a street girl. No decent girl would ever walk around without a bra,' she'd yell. My mum was very theatrical and deployed all sorts of dramatic language when trying to win an argument. Perhaps I got my fascination with acting from her. I studied English and Drama at the University of Exeter.

As reflected in our bra debate, my mum has significant problems coming to terms with my liberal British view of womanhood. She has very fixed ideas of what a woman should and shouldn't do. I was a tomboy growing up – my mum hated this. She couldn't accept the fact I wanted to play football or that I'd climb trees all over the place. She told me that was not how girls behaved, that I wanted to break her heart and then eat it, that I wanted to kill her. Like I said, she was very dramatic.

I can speak both Mandarin and Cantonese, which I learnt from my mum yelling at me, but unfortunately I can't read or write in either language. It's a pity because when I was younger, my mum asked me if I wanted to go to a Chinese school where I could have learnt that. But at the time, I only associated China with negative things so I didn't want to go. Unfortunately for me, on this issue, my mum didn't push.

My negative perceptions of China were mostly down to my experiences there during our visits. We went to China a couple of times when I was a child, and I always felt lonely there, a real outsider. The other kids would treat me like this little celebrity because I looked white and I would feel like I was being paraded around because of this. It made me feel uncomfortable. My mum wouldn't let me go out and play with the other kids there as well, this time because it was apparently too dangerous.

Also, it's difficult for a child who doesn't understand there are loads of different cultures with different ways of doing things. If you are a child and you think the British way is the only way, and then you're thrown somewhere else, you're like, 'Everyone here is doing things the wrong way.' I thought Chinese people weren't efficient. I thought they had no manners because they wouldn't queue properly and would spit on the pavements like it was nothing. I thought it was disgusting they threw rubbish on the ground like they weren't bothered with how dirty their surroundings were. And I couldn't understand why they ate with their mouths wide open all the time. It all seemed so wrong to me. *These people are crazy*, I thought to myself.

Also, the city we were in was quite dirty and infested with rats and cockroaches. In general, Chinese people lived in very poor conditions compared to Britain. The whole place just seemed like rubbish to me. It wasn't until I was fifteen I was able to have my first enjoyable experience in China and appreciate that people simply did things differently there.

During those earlier visits, I clearly remember reading my Harry Potter books and the Bible all the time. I clung to my Harry Potter books because they were entrenched in British culture and thus very relatable to me in this alien world which was not at all relatable to me. As for the Bible, God was my only friend then. But this also got a bit confusing for me in China. You see, I had always just assumed God was English, so when I was in China I wondered whether it was enough to pray to God in Chinese. I remember feeling so weird because I saw God as English but then I also knew

God was in this country, too, so in what language should I speak to him here?

So those early experiences in China were why, when my mum asked if I wanted to go to a Chinese school, I said, 'No way, China is stupid.' I think what I really wanted and lacked was a Chinese community around where I lived. I'd have liked someone to tell me what it meant to be half-Chinese and half-English. Is there a way to go about it? I still don't know the answer to this.

In China, I am perceived as white, which is very desirable there. White skin is fetishised and symbolises greatness in China. So I get special treatment there not because I'm Linxi, but because I am seen as white. It's confusing thinking of yourself as the other because to yourself you are not the other, you are just you. On the other hand, there's a part of you that you know is different and that you want to learn about, so you also feel that trying to be just like everyone else is cheating yourself out of that authentic experience.

I keep asking myself, *What does it mean to be Chinese and how does that differ from being half-Chinese? Is it simply what other people perceive me to be? Is there a particular way of behaving that encapsulates being half-Chinese or even full-Chinese?* I really don't know. But I do know a part of me is looking for that connection and understanding. For instance, I keep two Chinese knots in my room. I don't know what they mean but they have my middle name and also symbolise a rat because I was born in the year of the rat. I don't really know what it means, but I keep it anyway and feel a connection to it.

Today, there are definitely things I've come to appreciate about China. The men squatting on pavements playing cards, the noodle bars, people everywhere, even the spitting doesn't bug me that much any more. The place is quite amazing, actually, and I miss it sometimes now. I know how to cook some Chinese dishes, which I really enjoy. I wouldn't say my mum taught me how to make them;

she shouted orders at me to bring her this, and give her that, and add this or that to the pot while she was cooking, so I picked it up that way.

My mum made a lot of Chinese dishes at home but, like I mentioned earlier, there was also a mishmash of meals depending on which food products happened to have been on sale the last time we were at the shops. Whether we'd have Chinese dumplings for breakfast or English cereal depended on that. My favourite meal is shepherd's pie, which my mum makes better than anyone else in the world.

My dad is a generally anxious and timid person with low self-esteem. I know he had wanted to go back to school when he was in his late forties to get a degree in landscape architecture. But then he met my mum, had a kid, and that was that. He did odd jobs here and there. He'd be a cab driver for a while, then something else. I always saw him as the odd-job man. Every other week, he would say it would probably be better for us if he left because he was failing us both as a father and as a husband. My mum would just yell at him to shut up. My dad is quite a sad case, actually. I see him as a guy who once had dreams and now he's seventy. But one thing I do like about him is his gentleness and affection. He was very affectionate towards me, the kind of father who would hold your hand as a kid. He would constantly tell me he loved me. I liked that because my mum wasn't that way at all. I don't think she was ever taught how to show affection to a child. So, my dad's kindness is something I try to emulate in my own life.

While I never felt out of place on account of my racial heritage in diverse London, my experience at the University of Exeter was somewhat different. Exeter attracts a rather elite type of Britishness, a class of white people who have their own traditions and cultural codes. It's weird to describe, but they are just a bit posh and demeaning to people like me.

Much of it had to do with class, but I think there was a racial element there, too. It would be little things like, for instance, someone would come up to me and say, 'Could you please get your Chinese tea leaves out of the kitchen drain?' I wouldn't have thought anything of it if they were any tidier than I was, but I was the one who actually cleaned up after myself the most in the kitchen, courtesy of my mother's home drilling. These kids always left the kitchen in an absolute mess but seemed to think that was all right. Or they'd complain about the smells from my Chinese cooking, that sort of stuff.

Sometimes, it's difficult to distinguish whether people are looking down their noses at you because of class or because of race. These rich white kids in my university, sometimes they might have a rich Indian friend who'd roll with them, suggesting what mattered more was class. But then I don't know how they would react if that Indian friend started speaking Hindu or cooking 'smelly' Indian food. I suspect they might take the piss out of them.

Anyway, in my case, the combination of my ethnic and social background meant I was viewed as clearly different from these kids. What really surprised me was when a girl who had been my best friend in my London primary school met me at Exeter. She was middle-class back in primary school, but that hadn't been a problem for our friendship then. However, when she saw me in Exeter, first of all, she seemed pretty pissed off we'd ended up at the same university, and second, she didn't want to have anything to do with me. Whenever we ran into each other, she'd just say 'hello' and walk away quickly.

There was also a guy I went to secondary school with, white, middle-class as well. We used to be good buddies back in London, but he too acted like he didn't know me in Exeter. Ultimately, what happened in the first few weeks of university was that most of the ethnic minorities gravitated towards each other. What was funny was that because I was seen as the whitest of the ethnic minority students, I was usually the one delegated by the rest to go speak on their behalf to the white students whenever there was a problem.

However, while I usually had a great rapport with fellow British-Chinese kids, I found it very hard to connect with my full-Chinese peers at university. They just have such a different mindset from me. They think study is the most important thing in life. They believe everything the Chinese government says. This is something I really can't wrap my head round.

Even my mum, who has been in this country for over twenty years, still believes everything the Chinese government says. When I tell here there are millions of people protesting in Hong Kong, she says it's all nonsense and propaganda. She believes her government was right to do what they did in Tiananmen Square where so many people were massacred. It's like talking to a wall. Chinese people can be incredibly insular. I know this sounds very stereotypical, but whenever I am talking to a Chinese person, I feel like I am talking to a robot. Even the young ones, there's no bantering with them, we just can't relate. And then of course they do this 'Oh, wow, you are white, that's so cool' thing, which I just can't stand.

An issue I definitely had as a drama student was that when it came to casting, the white teachers usually chose their own. The only main role I got was when they needed a character who could talk in a chav London accent, which no one other student could do apart from me. In general, people of mixed-East Asian heritage like myself are hardly represented at all in British film and media. Blacks and mixed-race blacks have representation and that's fine. But people like myself are hardly anywhere to be seen on the screen.

I recently watched an animated movie *Big Hero 6* in which the main character was half-white, half-Japanese, and I was so excited. I was like, 'Yay that's me!' Of course, I am half-Chinese, not half-Japanese, but it was still the closest thing to me I'd seen on the big screen! Chinese people have been settling down in Britain since the early twentieth century, but still there are hardly any East Asian characters on British telly. There are lots of Southeast Asian characters, but no East Asian characters. Where are the stories about us?

I identify as mixed British-Chinese which is how I would like to be seen and treated by the rest of society. I usually face the 'where are you really from?' question when I'm abroad rather than in the UK. I was in Malta recently, and all sorts of people from Italians to Macedonians would be asking where I was from. When I said I was from Britain, they would then say something like, 'Ah, but you are . . . yes?' holding their hands in a gesture slanting their eyes. What they meant, of course, was that I was probably originally East Asian, as in Chinese or Japanese. I used to find this gesture quite annoying, but honestly speaking it's stopped bothering me now.

I did have some experiences of prejudice in my childhood. A kid in the playground once told me to 'go back home'. That was a big one. I was half-hurt and half-like, 'Dude, that doesn't make no sense.' But most of the prejudice I witnessed back then happened when I'd be with my mother. We'd go to shops and people would pretend not to understand her English or mimic her Chinese accent. Or they'd simply be very rude to her.

Sometimes, I would try to intervene and sort the situation out. I would usually try to posh up my English accent just to convince the people involved that I was British. And sometimes – this I am quite embarrassed about now – but sometimes I would feel ashamed of my Chinese mother, and rather than take her side, I would take the side of the white people attacking or mimicking her. I'd be like, 'Yes, Mum, why don't you do so and so or behave such and such?' That's one thing I would definitely do all over if I could go back in time. Generally, though, I think it's quite nice to be mixed race.

Sometimes, you look in the mirror and are like, 'Wow, that's so cool.' It's nice to know you are unique. And we are on the rise. Yay!

Linxi's case highlights that the individual character-type of parents also plays a role in shaping the identity of a mixed-race person. Her mum being the dominant parent who ran the house and raised Linxi as she saw fit meant there was no way she was going to end up without a strong element of her mother's 'Chinese' ways imbued in her. On the other hand, having grown up in socially liberal Britain meant she and her mum clashed regularly on issues revolving around gender roles and 'proper behaviour' for a girl. Linxi clearly had her own ideas about this.

So while a dominant parent will certainly be influential in moulding the cultural worldview of a mixed-race child, they cannot make that child unsee the things they see in the society in which they live; just like nothing my mum told me about how the world should work could make me unsee a way very different from hers, the Nigerian way. She couldn't stop me soaking up the Nigerianness with which I was surrounded. Location is key to identity. The way things are done in the place we come of age will always be a reference point in our interpretation of the world. Nigeria will never leave me just as Britain will never leave Linxi.

I completely got what she said about wishing she'd had someone to tell her how to be half-Chinese and half-English. 'Is there a way to go about it?' I could say the same for being half-Nigerian and half-Polish. I guess the answer to that is that the way is whatever way we make it. Today. Tomorrow. But as she said, it is confusing thinking about yourself as this constant other in the eyes of people when to yourself you just feel like you. It's like people see in you something you can't see. A weird feeling.

But then, as Linxi says, there's this part of you that you know is different and that you want to explore. You know just trying to be like everyone else would be cheating yourself out of that experience. Perhaps we just want to have our cake and eat it, too. We want to be treated like everybody, but at the same time be different. Is this fair to ask of the world? Perhaps not. Perhaps the price to pay for these unique life experiences we have is constantly being perceived as other or otherish wherever we are. Perhaps it is a fair price to pay for a ticket to multiple worlds.

# Chapter 18

# Technically, I'm mixed race,
# but I identify as white

Alexandra's mother is Scottish. Her father is Ian, the Indian-German man we spoke to at the beginning of this section of the book. She is twenty years old and grew up in Hackney, London.

Because the relationship between my father and his Indian family was non-existent, I never met a single one of them. Anytime me and my brother would ask about them, my dad would tell us they were generally not nice people and leave it at that. I grew up in Stoke Newington, Hackney. There's been a huge change in the area since I was born there twenty years ago. I lived through its gentrification, a process my family has very much been a part of. My dad is a journalist while my mum is an architect. However, Stoke Newington is also very multicultural with large Asian, Turkish, Jewish, Somali and Caribbean communities so I grew up in a very diverse environment. It's also an uber-liberal part of London. Suffice to say, Diane Abbott has been our MP since 1987.

My childhood memories are pretty idyllic; my mum leaving us in a neighbourhood shop where me and my brother would read comic books for hours, my dad making delicious curries, generally happy stuff. You can tell my dad is mixed race. In the summer he gets quite dark and people often assume he is from Turkey or some other Middle-Eastern country. But while I tick the 'mixed white and Asian' box in official forms because technically I'm mixed race, in practise I view myself as white. I identify as a white girl.

I am blonde with bluish eyes, as is my brother. We often joke we wonder what Hitler would have thought of us. Either he would have considered our appearance a triumph of strong German genes, considering we look more Aryan than anything else despite being just quarter-German, or he would have hated the fact we existed.

I never thought of my dad as Indian. I've always thought of him as British, English even. This definitely affected the way I viewed myself as well. My dad has never been to India. We didn't watch Bollywood movies. I've never been to an Indian wedding. My dad didn't have Indian friends. He is not in the least bit culturally Indian.

Our only contact with Indianness at home was through food. My dad loves cooking and knows how to make many Indian dishes. So, we've always eaten a lot of spicy Indian food. When I came home for my first break from uni last year, my dad made chicken wings to celebrate. I literally doused them all in hot sauce before eating. 'I'm so proud you're my daughter,' my dad said, looking at me with a happy smile. I felt good when he said that. But that is where the Indian connection ends, with food. I don't feel Indian in any iota of my being.

If my dad was culturally Indian, I would probably identify differently, too. However, it's not just because of culture I describe myself as white, it's also very much to do with how I look. If I was dark-skinned, I'm sure I'd feel more Indian because that darker skin colour would have affected my life experiences. I would probably have been subject to some form of racism at some point in my life. Experiencing racism ties you to the feeling of being a minority. But I've never had that kind of experience, so I've never had that feeling.

The fact my dad had bad relations with his Indian family also definitely increased the divide between me and Indianness.

I never even internalised the fact my parents were an interracial couple until I was sixteen. I was home watching a documentary on such couples one day and it hit me. 'Dad, you and Mum are an interracial couple!' I exclaimed. 'Yes Alex, your mum is a ginger-haired white Scottish woman and I am brown,' my dad responded bemusedly. To me, being an interracial couple involved struggle, something people had to fight for, something controversial. I'd never personally witnessed any of that growing up where I grew up; that kind of experience seemed so distant from my family the thought just never clicked in my head.

Throughout our childhood, my dad deliberately shielded me from his experiences with racism growing up in 1970s Essex. When I'd ask him how it had been for him, he'd always say, 'Fine, no problems.' Only recently has he started opening up and talking about some of the horrible racism he experienced as a child. I think he wanted to protect us from the nastiness of this world, keep me and my brother happy children, that's why he never talked about it.

Only when my dad talks about his experiences with racism do I realise I've had a very different life from him. My life experiences have been shaped by being a white girl. I grew up around white people, my mum and her Scottish family. I definitely feel a connection to Scotland, which we used to visit, and to Scottishness. Despite going to very liberal multi-ethnic schools, my friends were all white. I can't really explain why or how this happened, it just did. The only Indian kids I sometimes hung out with were the ones who hung out with the white kids. In school, kids tended to group along racial lines. Black kids hung out with black kids, Turkish kids hung out with Turkish kids, etc.

The more I think of it, the clearer it becomes to me how different my life experiences have been from my dad's. There was a time he used to work a lot and every year me, my brother and my mum would go camping to this little English village while he stayed back. There's literally no black or brown person in that village. For years we went, and no one ever batted an eyelid. The first year my dad went with us, I noticed all of a sudden people would stare at us.

In the years we'd only go with my mum, there was this shop we went to, like every day. We became friendly with the shopkeeper. One day, he asked me and my brother if we could help him keep an eye out for a white van making deliveries. 'There'll be a coloured boy driving it,' he described casually. I had to ask my brother, 'What the fuck is coloured?' No one would use that word in our liberal bubble back in London.

But even in London, there are awkward situations related to how our family looks. When I'm out with my dad, people often think I'm his girlfriend because it doesn't cross their mind I could be his daughter. Sometimes people look at us weird. My dad notices it more and I see it makes him feel very uncomfortable. We bond through our mutual love for politics, punk music and lager, so we often go to the pub for a drink together.

When we walk in, I always say, 'Daaad, can you get me a pint?' very loudly so everyone is clear what's going on here. Once my dad and my brother, who is a strawberry blond, were on the tube during Gay Pride. My brother innocently sat on my dad's knee. People on the tube started giving my dad gross looks, like he was this perverted man preying on this really young boy. That really upset him. He was with his own son, but people were looking at him like he was a paedophile.

When I'd tell kids at school my dad was half-Indian, they'd flat out tell me my mum had cheated on him, that there was no way a half-Indian man could be my biological father. 'He can't be your dad, it's just impossible,' they'd say. Once during a science lesson, we were doing a class on genetics, what influences how children look.

I remember sticking my hand up and asking, 'Um, my mum is ginger, my dad is Indian with brown eyes, so why am I blonde with bluey eyes?' My teacher gave me a 'well, obviously, your real daddy is the milkman' look and sidestepped the question. One Spanish teacher asked me outright why I wasn't brown considering my surname is Patel. Even my dad's mum thinks my brother is not really my dad's son. She's willing to accept I might be my dad's child because she sees some resemblance there, but she thinks my brother isn't.

My surname always causes confusion and elicits all sorts of comments. People simply can't wrap their heads round me being a Patel. This happens everywhere; in banks, the post office, the pharmacy or in nightclubs and parties where I have to show my ID. People just look and say, 'Come on, there's no way this is your ID.' Interestingly, it's often people of colour who question it more. I think some white people don't register the name 'Patel' as classically Indian, so they don't react. But people of colour, especially Asian people, often react disbelievingly. The fact people are always shocked my surname is Patel also reaffirms my whiteness in my mind.

All the doubts raised about me being my father's daughter have never unsettled me. If you look very closely, you will see I have some of his features. I have never doubted he is my biological father, so I always find such comments quite amusing. I have ten jokes in my head ready to go anytime the Patel question comes up. My favourite is the one of me and my brother being Hitler's wet dream. I know that one shocks people. Even though I've never discussed this explicitly with my dad, he knows I identify white. I think he too views me and my brother as white.

As I said earlier, it took a while before I even had a concept of race. I remember one scene from my childhood when I was really young. We used to play a game where you'd pick two things and say which was your favourite – which grandma you liked best, that sort of thing. I remember taking my parents' hands together and saying, 'Mm, which skin colour do I like best?' But my parents both responded sharply, 'No, you can't do that, that's wrong.' I remember thinking to myself that I had been about to say I like both of them best anyway because, somewhere deep down, I had a vague feeling it would have been wrong to choose, but I didn't know why.

I've definitely benefitted from being white and middle-class. There were incidents in school when this became clear to me. Once I forgot my homework at home and told my teacher about it. 'No problem, just bring it in tomorrow,' he said. A black boy in my class said exactly the same thing a minute later and he was given a right bollocking by the teacher.

Nowadays, me and my dad talk about race a lot. Though he says things are a lot better in Britain now, he still gets very frustrated with how Indian people are stereotyped and mocked in mainstream culture. It's funny but the way it works today is people choose which ethnic minority groups can be stereotyped and mocked, and which can't.

Just a few weeks ago there was a situation in an office I worked in this summer. Someone sent round a video of the mixed-race comedian Trevor Noah in which he did a skit on why Russians were often cast as evil characters in movies, but no one would ever cast Indians as evil characters. The key to the joke was that while Russian men are intimidating and manly, Indian men are subservient, effeminate and nerdy so who would ever take seriously an Indian bad guy in a movie? It played on the whole colonial image of the serving Indian. The women in the office, all very liberal well-educated ladies who marched with Extinction Rebellion, thought the jokes were hilarious and were laughing their heads off.

I felt so uncomfortable I finally had to tell them I thought the video was racist. They were shocked I thought so. I was shocked thirty-something-year-old professional well-educated women living in London didn't see anything wrong with jokes emasculating Indian men. I told my dad about it and he said it's because you are allowed to be racist to Indians. Liberals mock Indians in a way they would never mock black people. He told me the emasculation of Indian men in popular culture was something that has been around ever since he was growing up. Black men were seen as cool, Indian men as nerdy. This continues till today.

My dad was very much into punk culture growing up. But while young punks would listen to reggae and ska, they'd never dream of listening to Punjabi music or any kind of Indian music. People didn't think Indian culture was cool, something to emulate: it was rather something to mock. It's interesting how the stereotype of Indian men is the exact opposite of the stereotype of black men. Black men are seen as oversexed aggressive types while Indian men are seen as subservient nerdy types. Not manly at all.

This is probably why those ladies in my office thought that Trevor Noah video, which played on these popular stereotypes about Indian men, was hilarious. I don't identify Indian at all, but if I was an Indian man I think I'd be pretty annoyed at such jokes. I'm sure these same 'progressive' women would also giggle at the stereotypes of Asian men having small dicks. There's lots about that on social media as well.

During the 2017 elections, Labour campaigners came knocking on our door. When they saw my mum, they immediately blurted, 'You're not Mrs Patel.'

'Yeah, I fucking am,' my mum barked at them. It made her really angry because she knew the instinctive assumption the campaigners had made was that a white woman who looked like her – my mum is quite pretty – would not have married an Indian man. The emasculating stereotypes of Indian men make this kind of thinking possible. Why else would those campaigners think she definitely couldn't be Mrs Patel?

It's not just older generations who seem to have drawn lines between what is acceptable prejudice and what isn't. From my observations at my university in Sheffield, it's clear to me there is a belief you are allowed to pick on certain groups. The criteria is simple. It boils down to which groups people think can be mocked without negative consequences and which can't. People my age who would never say anything racist about black people, feel free to mock East Asian students quite publicly. I find that quite depressing because there should be none of any of that directed at anyone. But if you complain too much, they'll ask you why you are so triggered, why you make everything such a big deal.

What would I say to those who might accuse me of trying to deny my Indianness by identifying white? Or suggest I am ashamed of my Indian roots? I will never try to pretend I'm Indian because I think that would be rude. There are people out there fighting battles I have never had to fight because I am viewed as white. Me claiming Indianness would be me laying claim to someone else's experience. I am definitely not ashamed of my Indian roots. I love having the name Patel and love seeing how it confuses people me having that name.

I am a feminist and generally very into social movements. But while I feel like an insider in the feminist movement, I view myself as an outsider in race-equality movements like Black Lives Matter. I'm an ally but not someone directly affected. I'm like a man involved in feminism. When I think about gender-equality issues in Britain, I think about myself. But when I think about racial-equality issues, I never think about myself. I get angry at the bad experiences my dad and other people of colour have had, but it's never personally relatable to me.

I think the identity you feel boils down mostly to how you look, not your genetic fractions. Our self-perception is completely shaped by the people around us and how they perceive us. People meeting me for the first time have asked me if I am Danish or Swedish; no one has ever asked me if I am Indian. With everyone perceiving me as white, thinking myself as anything but white is impossible in my head. It's just who I am. And no, this doesn't generate any conflict in my mind. I am perfectly comfortable in my skin as a white girl.

When I'm in Scotland, I feel quite at home, definitely more than I can imagine feeling in India. I don't feel any particular pull to visit India. I feel a general interest in visiting what is a huge and definitely amazing country, but not the way some mixed-race people want to visit where their minority parent is from because they are looking for a place to connect to. To be honest, I think this is often people looking for something to tell them who they are. I have never felt not at home in London. The geographical space that has been the most important cultural influence in my life is London. London has shaped me, not Britishness.

I don't feel any pride in being British. I think this is the way many people of my generation who grew up in London feel. We feel very separate from Britishness and the rest of Britain. I am ashamed of the many horrible things Britain did in the past and of British hyper-nationalism. Many Brits clearly don't seem able to accept the fact we are insignificant in the grand scheme of affairs today.

Have I ever been accused of being racist considering I look white? I did catering classes for GCSE because I wanted to learn how to bake. There was just one other white kid in this class. The rest of the class was all people of colour who'd been pushed there because the school didn't expect them to do well academically based on their results to date and whatnot. Once we were in class talking and a black guy said to me out of nowhere, 'Why did you say the n-word, you white bitch?'

I said I hadn't said that word, which I would never do. I think what he was trying to do was to make me feel uncomfortable. And it did to a certain extent, because being a racist is an awful thing to be. But I didn't feel degraded in any way by that incident because white people don't undergo a system of oppression in Britain. Hence, when someone says something like that to me, it doesn't have that kind of weight, it doesn't really bother me. I was more annoyed at being called a 'bitch' than being called a 'white bitch'.

I found Alexandra's story fascinating because of the fact she can boldly say she identifies white, something of a rarity for any mixed-race person with an ethnic minority parent. As she herself suggests, though, aside from her father's lack of 'cultural Indianness' playing a role in this, it would seem what really enables her to feel secure in her whiteness is the fact she doesn't just look white-passing, she looks white, period. She has thus never faced a situation in which she has been denied whiteness like some of the other white-passing people I spoke about earlier. The doors to the shrine have always been left wide open for her. Her experience has actually been of having to convince people that she really is a biological Patel.

# Part 3

Mixed other

# Chapter 19

# Searching for that other part

If you are not of mixed black and white or mixed white and Asian heritage, then you are classified as 'mixed other' by the UK census. Close to a quarter of Britain's mixed-race population is assigned this category, the one we know and talk about the least. I started out discussing how it is being 'mixed other' by speaking to Pauline, who was born to a British mother and American father of Mexican heritage during the Second World War. Pauline has lived all her life in Southampton, which is where I went to see her.

My mother was born in Southampton to parents of English, Scottish and Welsh heritage. When the war broke out she joined the Women's Land Army, which sent her to work on farms in Winchester, in Hampshire. Meanwhile, the US Army posted my father, an American soldier, to Winchester to work as a medic. My parents did not, however, meet in Winchester, but in the nearby town of Eastleigh.

Given a pass to leave camp one evening, my father and a couple of his army mates headed to Southampton looking for some song and dance to lift their spirits. They had no idea how badly the city had been destroyed by German bombings. When they arrived there and saw the state it was in, they realised there wasn't much fun and games to be had in Southampton and decided to head back to base.

But on the train ride back to Winchester my dad hopped off in Eastleigh because he could hear music playing from somewhere near the tracks. He headed in the direction of the sound and walked into a dance. There he met my mum. They hit it off immediately. When they discovered they were both based in Winchester, they started dating and, by April 1944, my mum was pregnant.

But with D-Day fast approaching, American soldiers were cut off from communication with the outside world lest any word of the Allied plans leaked out. My mum lost contact with my dad, who was eventually transferred to Gosport near Portsmouth from where he left for Normandy in the wee hours of D-Day. He made it out alive but was brought back to England with a shrapnel injury. My mum was finally allowed to visit him and took me with her to see him. I had been born in January 1945.

However, as soon as my dad got better he was shipped off to France and we completely lost contact with him after that. When the war ended he returned to his wife in America. He told my mum he was married as soon as they met so she knew what she was getting into. I guess in wartime everything is so uncertain people just take things one day at a time, not focusing on long-term consequences like we do in peacetime.

After the war my mother eventually married an Englishman and had two daughters with him. Then at the age of twenty-eight she suddenly collapsed one day and was rushed to hospital. I never saw her again. Back then children weren't allowed to visit hospitals and a few days later my mum was dead. It turned out she'd had a brain tumour. I was eight at the time.

Fortunately for me, I had very loving grandparents, and a particularly wonderful grandmother. She immediately insisted she and my granddad would take me in and raise me rather than leaving me with my stepfather. This really helped because I had spent the first three-and-a-half years of my life in their Southampton home where me and my mum lived before she married. So going back to my grandparents' house felt like going back home, to a place where I felt safe and loved.

Aside from my mother's early and tragic death, my memories of childhood are very happy ones. My grandmother was the matriarch of the family so there were always lots of uncles, aunties and cousins coming to visit us. The house was always so lively that even though I missed my mum terribly I never felt lonely.

Despite the massive destruction Southampton had suffered from the bombings, the 1950s were a wonderful time to grow up here. After the war people just got on with things. 'We are going to get through this. We survived the Blitz, so we made it through the worst' was the general attitude of Southamptoners. There was a wonderful sense of freedom and community in the air. People went out of their way to help each other. Back then, nobody locked their doors, we just walked in and out of each other's houses. I'd go out and play with my friends and only come back home when I was hungry.

I cannot recall a single incident in which I was called a name or any other unpleasant experience connected to my brown skin colour. The only bad thing I remember getting called was a 'bastard' when I was around eleven. But I don't think that was connected to race. Unfortunately, back then any kid whose mum or dad were not in the picture could get called that. It wasn't like today where there are so many kids being brought up by single parents. In those days virtually everybody grew up with both parents.

I don't recall any racial incidents at school either. Or in any of the places I started working after secondary school. I never went to university but started out as a cashier at the Southampton bus station where I worked for many years. When I was an adult I once asked my grandma how she and granddad had felt raising a brown child in those days. 'We never thought of you that way, you were just our Pauline that was all,' she replied. The one racial incident I do recall experiencing, and it was quite an unpleasant one, was connected to my ex-husband's family, specifically his grandmother.

I was married to my husband for fourteen years. During that time, I had a good relationship with his family. But after we got divorced I found out his grandmother had warned him against having children with me. 'With her roots you never do know how those children might turn out looking, now do you?' she had told him. We never had children because I couldn't for medical reasons, but I was shocked when I heard his grandmother had said that to him. Her behaviour towards me during the years we were married never once suggested to me she could think that way. So you really do never know what's going on in people's minds.

However, I grew up thinking of myself as a girl from Southampton and nobody ever told me this wasn't what I was. I could obviously see I was brown, but my grandparents in particular never allowed me to feel this was an issue within the family. They never let me think I was different in any way because of my heritage. In my case, my main problem with identity revolved not around the way I looked but around my father. As I grew older without a mother I started thinking about him more often.

While I was happy growing up in my grandparents' house, I felt a deep void I never shared with anyone. By the time I was around ten I thought about my father virtually all the time. I wondered how he looked, where he lived, what kind of person he was. But I never asked my grandparents about him. I was afraid of the answer I might hear; either that he was dead or that he didn't want me. So I preferred not to ask. It was safer that way.

I remember once walking to the local telephone box, pulling open the big heavy iron door and taking the Southampton phonebook down from the shelf. I can still remember how heavy it felt in my ten-year-old hands. I had my father's surname and I knew his first name, so I started looking for him in the Southampton phonebook. I believed the whole world was in there. Of course, I didn't find him.

As I grew up, I embarked on an on-and-off solo search for my father. Anytime I passed a war memorial in a city I would go read the names to see if I'd find his. Anytime I passed a phone box in a city I would go through the phonebook searching for his name. I never told anybody I was looking for him, but I was.

When I was thirteen, my granny gave me a small jewel box that had belonged to my mother. It contained two photos of my dad and a few letters and greeting cards he had sent to my mum. One card was signed 'Kisses for Pauline from her daddy.' I felt so happy when I read that. I had a daddy. That box became my most prized possession, I kept it under my pillow.

However, when I got married, I generally got on with life and for some years I thought much less about my father. It was only after my divorce that the need to find that other part of myself became overwhelming. I finally started sharing with my friends just how incomplete I felt not knowing my dad. Two of them helped me start actively searching for him. This was the pre-internet 1980s so our search basically involved writing letters to all the US Army institutions we could think of asking for any information they might have on my father. Years went by with no results. It was only thanks to the incredible encouragement I got from my friends that I didn't give up looking.

The breakthrough came in 1988 when I finally tracked down my stepbrother who lived in Texas. When I called and told him my story, he gasped, 'Oh boy, you must be my sister.' He gave me a number to call my father on. I was trembling when I dialled the number, petrified he might reject me and not be interested in knowing me. But he was delighted I had found him. It was one of the most wonderful conversations of my life.

The next day I was buzzing so hard at work in the bus station I couldn't focus. Around midday the office secretary called me up. I suspected it was because they had noticed I wasn't focusing on my work that day. So I started explaining I'd make up the time. 'Shut up,' she said. 'While you've been floating around on your clouds all morning, we've been having a collection. We already have five hundred pounds in the pot for your airfare.' This was 1988 in an office made up mostly of basic admin staff, bus drivers and mechanics. That was really a lot of money back then. I was shocked. People can be so incredible.

In no time I was on my way to America to meet my Hispanic family. My stepbrother and -sister were waiting for me in El Paso airport together with other family members and friends. There were also some little children holding up a sign saying, 'Welcome Pauline, we love you!' I scanned the group and spotted my father. I immediately knew it was him and rushed into his arms. It was the most beautiful moment of my life.

I found my long-lost father to be an extremely caring man. My new family comprised of countless uncles, aunties and cousins who were all shades of brown. They were so warm and welcoming, I quickly felt very comfortable around them. It was only when I found my dad and his family that my identity felt complete for the first time in my life. At last, I now knew the other half of me and who else I belonged to. Where I had come from.

While I felt totally accepted by my Hispanic family, there were some moments that brought home to me the fact I was brought up in a different culture from them. One thing that immediately struck me was how many children they had. They all have lots of children and their lives often revolve around family and kids. Anytime I was introduced to a new family member, one of the first questions they would ask me was how many children I had. Not *if* I had children, but how many.

When I explained I didn't have any children there would be an awkward silence, and sometimes that would be the end of the conversation. In Hispanic culture it is simply expected you must have children. Here in Britain it is not seen as a must and no one will act awkward if you tell them you don't have kids. So this was definitely something that differentiated me from the rest of my Hispanic family.

Despite the fact my Hispanic side is now very much a part of me, and I felt like someone had cut off my arm when I stepped on the plane back after that first visit, I still feel very English inside. Not British, but English. I was born in England and raised English, so I feel English more than British. We often speak about this with others friends my age in Southampton, how we all feel English rather than British.

Some people have pointed out to me that I have no strong family ties here; I am divorced, I have no kids, my grandparents are dead. So why don't I move to America to be with my Hispanic family? they ask me. But I tell them this is home for me. Southampton, England, is where I belong. I love visiting El Paso for a while, I feel a part of the place and a part of my family there. But I still like to come home. I could never imagine living there. I've never wanted to leave Southampton, I am very tied to the city. It's where I was born and where I would like to die.

My feeling of Englishness is connected to culture rather than race. In earlier years, when I was required to tick an ethnicity box in administrative forms, I would usually tick 'white'. Back then there wasn't any option for a mixed-race Hispanic. However, when doing that I always used to think to myself, *Mm . . . I'm not completely white though*. Luckily, nowadays there are lots more options to tick on those forms, so I usually have more fun with them now.

I was lucky to enjoy a beautiful twenty-seven-year relationship with my father before he died in 2015. I regret not having been able to have children because I know the Hispanic side I discovered at forty-four is going to die with me. It would have been great to have had kids who could have grown up spending time with my family in Texas, learning their traditions and cultural values. But that's the way it goes. Ultimately, I can say that in my case, my search for identity has never been to do with a sense of cultural displacement or otherness, but simply with a desire to meet the man who fathered me. I just wanted to meet my daddy, whoever he was going to be, that was all. And once I did, I felt whole.

When Pauline told me she had never experienced any racial abuse growing up in 1950s Southampton, I found it hard to believe at first. I really pushed her on this. 'Really? Nothing? No incidents, no jokes, no comments about you being brown?' I asked, searching her face for signs of some long-suppressed memories. But I saw nothing there, and Pauline insisted there had been nothing of the sort. She had shown me pictures of herself when she was a young girl and she had been visibly brown, especially when she was younger. She'd also used her father's surname, which signalled her Mexican roots.

Remember Rita, who was sexually abused by her stepfather growing up in Eastleigh? She and Pauline were both 'war babies' who grew up barely five miles from each other during the same period. Yet their experiences could not have been more different. Although Rita was a shade darker than Pauline, she had suffered horrific racial abuse while Pauline had been spared any of that. I asked Pauline if she had any idea why. 'Perhaps because I grew up in what was a very tight-knit community that had been hit hard by the war and was determined to be there for each other,' she'd replied. I had no idea myself. The randomness of it all was a little scary.

Perhaps it was because she had not been associated with blackness and that carried a special kind of stigma in Britain as opposed to having Mexican roots. It is difficult to do more than speculate here. But what I think Rita's and Pauline's stories do show is just how different the mixed-race experience could be even back in the 1950s and even in such close proximity to each other.

Of course, despite the unimaginable tragedy of losing her mother at the age of eight, Pauline also had the good fortune to be raised in a loving home where she felt safe and protected, as opposed to Rita whose mum never showed her any affection. This was a fundamental difference that shaped their lives and sense of self in their formative years. It is frightening to think the luck of the draw can have such an effect on how we come to see ourselves. But it does.

Pauline was the only mixed-race person I spoke to who emphasised she identified as English rather than British. As she suggested in reference to friends of her age in Southampton, there is probably a strong generational angle to this. It would likely be rare to find a mixed-race person in Britain from a much younger generation who would be so emphatic they identify as English rather than British.

Another thing that really struck me about Pauline's story was how strongly our sense of identity can be connected to a single person (usually a parent) rather than a group, because we usually think about identity in terms of group connection. Someone wants to connect to their blackness or their Asianness or their Jewishness. In other words, they want to plug in to a group identity and feel part of a larger collective. But as Pauline said, in her case she just wanted to connect with her father. The Hispanicness she came into contact with when she did was more of an added bonus. I think we may underestimate how much our sense of identity can be shaped by our feelings towards a particular parent. Either present or absent.

# Chapter 20

# Balancing Identity

Andreas is the son of a Uruguayan father and German mother. He was born in the United Kingdom in 1970 and has lived in Britain for much of his life.

My parents met on a train from Germany to London in the late 1960s. My father was coming to stay with his uncle, a Uruguayan diplomat, who was posted here. My mother had always wanted to live in London. Neither of their families had a problem with the relationship. In those days, people from the so-called 'new world' nations of South America looked to Europe – the 'old world' – to get a better sense of themselves and who they might like to be. Putting it simply, being of European extraction, especially northern European extraction, was seen as better than being wholly Latin American. As for my mother's family, they saw my father as someone positively exotic. There was no opposition to the relationship from either party.

I thus grew up the son of two parents from very different cultures, being raised in a third culture. I remember my father teasing me about my identity when I was a child. 'Where are you from?' he'd ask. My response was that I was from nowhere. I suspect behind his teasing tone lay slight confusion. He probably wondered where my roots would ultimately lie.

I don't remember ever feeling uncomfortable with my situation in terms of racial background. It helped that both my parents had a strong sense of who they were. My father was proud of being Uruguayan and had a deep knowledge of his country's history. The same went for my mother who knew a lot about German culture and literature. Both my parents always emphasised that I wasn't from here, that I was this strange hybrid: Uruguayan-German. The name they chose for me was no coincidence. They could have opted for an English first name, but they didn't. They gave me a name that could be pronounced both in Germany and in the Spanish-speaking world.

My first language was German because that was the language my mother spoke to me as a child. My father sang me nursery rhymes and lullabies in Spanish. The third language in our home was broken English (with the odd German and Spanish phrase thrown in), the language my parents communicated in. And, of course, I learnt 'proper' English at school. I grew up a real hybrid, but one whose parents had a clear sense of identity, which in turn helped me develop a strong sense of self.

Apart from my parents' influence, another reason I identified strongly with my Uruguayan-German roots was my father worked for the Uruguayan foreign office. I grew up with the feeling we'd leave Britain one day. And so I never felt the need to become British and put down roots here.

Of course, I was perceived differently by my different families. In Uruguay, I was the German-English cousin, the one from Europe. In Germany, I was the Uruguayan-English cousin, the one with the Latin connection. It required adjusting to different family members' assumptions about me. People pigeonhole because it's the most expedient thing to do. They don't have the time to think about your identity in a complex and nuanced way, so they make snap judgements. 'You're the European cousin.'

After a while, I made a conscious decision to be more Uruguayan around my Uruguayan family and more German around my German family, to be more palatable to them. I think this has shaped my general attitude towards identity. I've had this attitude towards British society as well.

I believed I had to learn how to balance my identities. My mother likes to tell a story about how once when we arrived back from a visit to Germany, she continued speaking in German to me. 'Don't speak to me in that language, Mummy. We're in England now,' I said. There was, of course, an element of wanting to fit in here as well.

Moreover, those were different times in Britain. This incident at Heathrow airport happened when I was three or four. There was generally more conformity in those days. It was believed that if you were going to live here in Britain as a foreigner, you should make an effort to fit in, which included speaking English.

To succeed at school, I had to learn the advantages and disadvantages of both the cultures I came from. It wasn't lost on me that those who knew where Uruguay was considered it a 'Third World' country, generally far behind Britain politically and economically. It ranked rather low in their global hierarchy. In some ways, Latin America has always been the forgotten continent. North America doesn't understand it, and Europe has always been more fascinated with what it sees as the 'exoticness' of Africa, Asia and the Far East.

When I was growing up in the '70s, memories of Empire were still fresh in British minds. There were, of course, dismissive or racist comments about Latin America. But I had one trump card to play that was a winner in a boy's world – football. While we only come to the world's attention once every four years when the World Cup is being played, we do so in quite a memorable way. For that one month, South America is on everyone's lips. We are always contenders for the title, and perhaps even more importantly, we don't just win games, we entertain the world. The World Cup is not just football, it's an arena for collective achievement and national pride. The sense of worth the Pelés, the Maradonas, the Messis have brought Latin Americans is something that is undervalued. In response to jibes, I could always come back with, 'Well, how many World Cups have you guys won? You've only won one and you're still talking about it today.' And then when Maradona came along, there was no discussion. 'You couldn't produce a Maradona even if you tried for two hundred years.'

Growing up in a foreign country, it's important to know what your culture or cultures do well. Perhaps it's as defence mechanism. My father taught me how to embrace my Uruguayan identity through football. And, of course, aside from football, the continent had that sense of mystique and otherness.

As for digs at my German roots, as might be expected, there were sometimes comments about Nazis and general suspicion about Germans. But whatever you want to say about Germany, you can't gainsay its literature, its philosophy, its classical music. The Germans used to describe Britain as 'a country without music'. And if someone wanted to belittle me because Uruguay was inferior politically and economically, I could always bring up my German side. I guess I was lucky to have come from the right countries, so to speak.

My parents I don't think had an inferiority complex in relation to the British. My mother definitely not; my father, even if he did, never showed it. While there were many elements in Anglo culture that I liked and respected, I never felt in any way inferior growing up Uruguayan-German in Britain. I saw English culture for what it was.

I was fortunate to be educated privately and generally gravitated towards friendship groups made up of foreigners and English boys. There was a sense of solidarity I felt with the former. At my prep school, we used to play this game, British Bulldog. It was always us, the foreigners, against the English boys. There was a palpable feeling of difference there. I remember thinking at the time that even in an international city like London there weren't many biracial people around. I felt different from those around me. But I tended to see my difference in a positive light, as uniqueness.

Growing up, I soon sensed where my bread was buttered. I realised being Uruguayan was far more exotic than being German. Nobody thought being German was interesting, but people thought being Uruguayan was. I learnt how to use my difference in a positive way, how to leverage it. I think kids sense these things early. If you embrace an identity, then you have to take everything that comes with it, both the good and bad.

Of course, there were racist and prejudiced comments about Latin Americans and Germans. However, my trips to both my parents' countries taught me to be realistic about the world. There is no racial Utopia anywhere. The British, in spite of their Empire, can sometimes be very parochial and even reflexively xenophobic, but could I really say Uruguayans and Germans are free of this?

Sometimes, people born here to a non-British parent or parents view their parents' countries and cultures through rose-tinted glasses. But if we are really being honest about these things, Britain has long been a more tolerant and easy-going nation than many others, including where both my parents come from. It's not a question of not seeing British flaws, but of weighing their behaviour against that of other societies and seeing their good as well as their bad sides.

I realise today that my benign attitude towards Britishness and its shortcomings was largely shaped by the fact that, growing up, I always felt I had another home to go to. When you feel you have somewhere else to go and where you will be accepted, even if realistically that isn't the case, as long as you *feel* it is the case, you are more relaxed wherever you are. You have that sense of autonomy, that feeling of choice. But if you feel you don't really have anywhere else to go where you'll be accepted, then you probably develop a more acute sensitivity to racism or xenophobia.

I always had the sense I was choosing to stay in Britain but could leave anytime I wanted. I think this feeling of having somewhere else to go to, or not, is really key to how people experience this country.

I remember an incident from when I was around ten or eleven – this would have been in the early '80s. I was walking down the street with a Nigerian friend of mine when an English builder yelled out, 'Hello choccy!' Obviously racist behaviour. What I remember making an impression was not what that builder said but the way my friend reacted. He just brushed it off with a shrug and a 'what an idiot', and went on as if nothing happened.

Why had my friend brushed it off so casually? I think it was due to a strong sense of self or identity. He had come from a well-established Nigerian family and knew he was going back home after his schooling. He genuinely couldn't care less what an English guy on the street thought of him. If you know there's a homeland waiting for you, those kinds of comments might seem more idiotic and even amusing than anything else. Their effect is ephemeral. These are the aspects of foreignness that I don't think have yet been well explored in the current debate.

My father told me a story about how he was once stopped by customs. He was asked who he would be staying with in London. He replied that he was staying with his uncle. They asked what his uncle did. He said his uncle was a diplomat at the Uruguayan embassy. 'But how do I know he's not a cleaner there?' the customs officer demanded. This begets questions about how important class is in your experience of foreignness in Britain.

The class-conscious British have always tended to treat more respectfully those from other cultures who they see as having a higher social standing within their own societies. The English will treat a Nigerian prince very differently from a Nigerian economic migrant. We don't really talk about this aspect of attitudes towards foreigners, but I think a lot of xenophobic bias is camouflaged class bias. My traditional English education meant I had the advantage of never being viewed as an economic migrant.

At a dinner party years ago, I remember someone asking loudly, 'So who runs Uruguay now? Is it a dictatorship?' I replied Uruguay was a democracy. 'Yes, but who *really* runs it?' this person demanded, arrogantly dismissing notions of *Uruguayan democracy*. 'Ah, one of our relatives,' I replied with an equally arrogant shrug. That shut him up. In retrospect, I should have been more balanced.

When I started applying for jobs in the 1990s, a recruiter once suggested I might want to change my name. 'You could pass for an English person. Just change your name and don't write Uruguayan-German in the nationality segment of your application forms, just put British.' But this was never an option. It's one thing to make yourself palatable to the culture you are living in, it's another to try and pretend you are something that you don't feel.

I've never been able to call myself 'British'. Even though I was born here and, for the most part, grew up here, I just can't call myself British. It doesn't feel right. The word just won't come out of my mouth. I suppose I've always *wanted* people to ask me where I'm from. I need them to know I'm Uruguayan-German, that despite my English accent, I've never thought of myself as from here. Which doesn't mean I don't get misty-eyed when I sing 'Jerusalem'. Or that I don't experience a surge of emotion when confronted by the beauty of the British landscape.

I love this country, but that doesn't mean I feel wholly British. My people are not from here. I have family in Uruguay and in Germany, but I don't have any real roots here. I think for mixed-race people your relationship with your parents is also very important in whether you decide to embrace their cultures or reject them. As are one's observations of how one's parents interact with their own.

Personally, I think parents who emigrated here and try to make their children feel British above all else without really thinking about what that means are doing them a great disservice. It is for us to find our way. If someone grows up here and finds their way to Britishness or Englishness or Scottishness or Welshness then fine, good for them. These identities shouldn't be forced down their throats just because they live here. As long as one fulfil one's obligations to be a constructive member of British society – someone who recognises both its flaws and its strengths, rather than just carping about the former – then Britishness does not have to be a must. Or that's the way I see it. There is something inside me that just makes it impossible for me to buy into any culture wholesale, not Britishness, and not even Uruguayanness or Germanness. I've always cherry-picked what I like from each culture. I guess I've always wanted to have my cake and eat it, too.

That feeling of being stuck here when you feel like an outsider must really grate. Like Andreas observed, 'when you feel you have somewhere else to go where you will be accepted, you are more relaxed wherever you are. You have that sense of autonomy, that feeling of choice'. But when you don't have that feeling, as is likely the case with many ethnic minorities in Britain, including some mixed-race people who have lived here all their lives, 'you develop a more acute sensitivity to British shortcomings'.

Like Andreas, I have never felt trapped in Britain because there are other societies I know and could imagine living in. I intend to stay in Britain, but I don't feel like I have to stay in Britain. The thought I could leave tomorrow if I wanted is always at the back of my head, and it is a thought that gives me a strong feeling of freedom and agency. So, Britain has never felt like a prison to me. That is indeed a more comfortable vantage point from which to observe British society and likely explains to a significant extent why I share

Andreas's more benign attitude towards British shortcomings than some other ethnic minorities in this country. Not having deep roots in a place can be a very liberating feeling.

Andreas's stories about how he leveraged Uruguay's footballing success and Germany's economic status to his advantage in dealing with his British peers shows again just how much the associations people have with the country and part of the world you are seen as being from matters. While Uruguay and Latin America in general may be much less economically developed than Britain, they have something Brits envy them for: consistent World Cup success. Growing up in football-mad Nigeria, we all fantasised about Nigeria or any African team for that matter, winning the World Cup. In 1990, Cameroon got our hopes up, in 1994 Nigeria did, in 2002 Senegal looked strong, 2006 Ivory Coast, 2010 Ghana. We all knew that if an African team could win the World Cup, it would do more to end the stereotype of Africans as collectively disorganised and ineffective than a century's worth of books arguing that case could do. A tiny fraction of the world reads books, but everybody watches the World Cup. But it didn't happen. And hasn't happened yet. No African team has ever gone beyond the quarter-finals of a World Cup, a huge let-down for a continent crazier about football than Europe.

France winning the World Cup with players of predominantly African descent is not the same thing because, while nobody doubts African footballing talent, the questions that have always been raised have alluded to our organisational and tactical capacities. France being able to use players of African descent to win the World Cup simply helps perpetuate the view that Africa does not yet know how to effectively organise and utilise its own potential. Latin American teams have demonstrated time and again the ability to often organise more effectively than European teams at World Cups. Effectiveness commands respect.

So Andreas was fortunate to have the football card, as he called it, at his disposal in his interactions with peers growing up. Meanwhile, Germany is a bigger economy than Britain, so none of his British peers could assume a position of superiority towards him on that level either. As Andreas said, he was 'lucky to come from the right countries'. This helped him to develop a confidence about his roots that may be more difficult for someone not from the 'right' countries to develop. Being Uruguayan-German in Britain is probably easier than being Guatemalan-Albanian, with all respect to the latter nations. It's all about the associations you can draw on.

# Chapter 21

# Becoming black in Iran

Sereena was born to an Iranian father and Jamaican mother. She lives in Bristol, which is where we met, but she grew up mostly in London. She is thirty-five.

My parents met in a KFC in Catford, south-east London, thirty-six years ago. My Iranian father was working there at the time. My Jamaican mother walked in, saw him, and said to herself, 'Yeah, that's the one.' Three dates later I was conceived. My mother's grandfather had come to Britain from Jamaica in the 1950s as part of the Windrush generation, heading straight to Birmingham. My mother's father joined him in the late 1960s, but he went to live in Brockley, south London, which is where my mum grew up.

My father came to the UK to study microbiology in November 1978, just a few weeks before the Iranian Revolution. When he arrived, he needed to improve his English before starting his studies, so he moved in with a host family in Eastbourne, a small resort town on England's south-east coast. His host family cautioned him to be careful because the National Front was very active there at the time. They warned him NF members wore heavy Dr Martens boots and that if he ever got into a fight with them, one thing he could never do was fall down because, if he did, they'd kick his head in and he'd be done.

Like many Iranians, my dad looks Mediterranean and can pass for Spanish or Italian. So to avoid hostility he pretended he was Spanish when people in Eastbourne asked where he was from. It was an incredibly hostile experience to be a person of colour outside London in 1970s Britain. My dad had never thought himself as a person of colour before he came to Britain because Iranians generally classify themselves as white people not brown people.

My dad was born to a wealthy Iranian family. His grandfather owned several large poultry farms. But after the Ayatollahs took over in 1979, it was no longer possible to send money out of Iran, so he had to fend for himself. That's how he started working at KFC, which was a bit ironic considering he was the scion of a family with a large poultry business back home.

Psychologically, this was very difficult for him. Iranian society is all about status and hierarchy. Prestige and money are more important there than they are here. For someone of his background to work in KFC was a humiliation for him. He was an angry twenty-nine-year-old man when he met my mum, and he remained an angry man throughout my childhood. When my mum, who was ten years younger than him, told him she was pregnant, he said he didn't want a child. But she decided to keep me anyway.

After I was born, my dad didn't even bother to come see us. But when I was around six months old, one of my mum's fierce sisters went to his workplace, pinned him to the wall, and basically told him to live up to his responsibilities as a man. After that, he came to visit us and apparently melted at the sight of me. My parents decided to try and make a life as a family.

For the first few years, we all lived in my grandma's home in Brockley. Afterwards, we moved to Clapham where we shared a house with his friend. But my dad was always an incredibly violent man and, when I was five, he tried to kill me. He was literally trying to strangle me to death, but fortunately for me his friend was around and pulled him off me.

After that, me and my mum went into a shelter for a while, I can't remember how long. This was the first time my parents broke up. I can imagine how frustrating life was turning out to be for my father. He was not realising his full potential. He had come here to become a doctor but was doing menial jobs instead. I think he felt a resentment towards me and my mum and saw us as obstacles to achieving his dreams.

He'd gone from riches to rags and was clearly having a problem dealing with that. I've been through a lot of therapy to try and understand his behaviour. Violence is a form of communication for those who can't communicate otherwise. There were also vast differences in personality and culture between my parents, which contributed to the tensions between them. However, after we left the shelter, they decided to give it another shot, and we all moved to South Croydon. My dad continued being super-aggressive and within the next three years, my parents broke up at least three times.

My father is a walking contradiction. He calls himself a feminist and always told me I could be whatever I wanted to be in life, that I could do anything. He repeated it so often I've carried those words with me all my thirty-five years and they've helped me become successful in the corporate world I now function in. On the other hand, whenever he and my mum would break up and she'd start dating other men, he'd call her a whore in front of me.

Imagine a young girl hearing her mother repeatedly called a whore by her father. This affected my psyche and is one of the reasons I did not lose my virginity until I was in my mid-twenties. For a long time I was apathetic towards men and didn't want sexual relations with them. So when it came to sexuality and ideas about what a woman was allowed to do in this sphere, my dad was incredibly conservative. My mum was definitely too 'Western' for him in this regard.

But my father was also an incredibly strong personality, one of those people who walk into a room and everyone flocks around him. So when he did live with us, he completely dominated our home. As a young girl, I never felt the sense of displacement or confusion about identity that many mixed-race people speak of. This was because I was brought up with a really strong Persian identity.

We didn't speak Farsi at home, but we ate virtually only Persian dishes. My dad taught my mum how to make them. We ate Persian-style, on a beautiful mat set on the floor. We celebrated the Iranian New Year in March. We listened to Persian music. My dad told us about Persian history and culture. The only reason he never taught me Farsi was because he wanted me to speak 'Queen's English' and, back in the 1980s, parents still believed a child can only master one language fluently.

I have a younger brother and my dad would always tell us that as a family we were different from others in Britain. But in his telling, this difference made us special. It was something to be proud of. I can remember being very confident in my Persian identity as a child. I felt fine being different from the other kids.

My dad was violent, but the truth is I've always been closer to him than to my mum. I think this is why I have always leaned more towards the Persian side of me than the Jamaican side. I've never really connected with Jamaicanness. This is also probably because my mum herself was never very Jamaican. On the contrary, she was very English. To me, Englishness means being white, conservative, restrained and stoic. A closed book. My mum was all these things except white.

Other than skin colour, there was nothing to distinguish her from a white Englishwoman in mannerisms, behaviour or way of speaking. My mother's parents played a role in the fact she was like this. They hadn't wanted her Britishness to be diluted by her Jamaicanness, so they purposefully didn't raise her oriented towards that aspect of her identity. Hence, while both my parents told me and my brother we were British and should feel that way, it was my dad who emphasised there was another layer to us that was not from here. My mum did not.

She was so white-oriented she even converted to Mormonism at one point, a religion where a core belief is that the darker-skinned you are, the worse your sins were in your previous life. Blacks were not even allowed to join the church until the 1980s. Yet my mum would drag us to this Mormon church in London, which was a special kind of white. You think you know what conservative is, but nothing compares to Mormon conservatism.

The women sat separated from the men in church. I hated it so much I thought I would screw with them by hammering at this piano we had in the church as loudly and disruptively as I could. But they were so conservative no one would even tell me I was making too much noise! Every single part of me rejected that experience. Thank God my mum is no longer a member of the church, but she never wants to discuss the issue when I try to ask her why she joined in the first place. Interestingly enough, while my mum was oriented towards Englishness, she always had a thing for Middle Eastern men, not white men, but Middle Eastern men specifically. The stuff that goes on in people's heads is so complicated, no?

So growing up, I never had a black identity. The fact I was othered by my Jamaican cousins also contributed to this. When I was a little girl, my Jamaican aunts always wanted to play with my hair. I was like the first dolly to arrive. They'd virtually queue up to plait my hair, unplait and replait it again. I enjoyed when they did that. But it affected the dynamics between me and my cousins who felt I was being favoured. That caused them to resent me. Loudly enough so I could hear, they would say things like, 'She's not really Jamaican anyway, she's not one of us.' This created a barrier between us, so we were never really close.

Because we moved around a lot I went to eight different primary and secondary schools. I was never picked on by the white kids but by the black kids. I remember one school incident when we lived in Roehampton where my mum, who was an English and history teacher, was doing a university degree. I was about eight or nine at the time. There was this black girl called Chivonne. For some reason, Chivonne hated the fact I was hanging out with the white kids.

I had this white friend called Maxine. One day, I was standing holding hands with Maxine when Chivonne walked up to us and physically ripped our hands apart. 'You two can't hang out with each other,' she screamed. I was so shocked I didn't think to ask why. Neither did Maxine. Till today, I have no idea why Chivonne did that. But I do know it made me very confused and upset. Maxine had been my best friend at school, but after that we were afraid to hang out with each other because we were both scared of Chivonne. I became a loner in that school. I would sit and draw on my own. I remember feeling very isolated. That incident definitely scarred me.

By the time I was eleven, my mum had finished her degree in Roehampton, and we were back in Croydon. I went to a school in Selsdon with mostly white working-class kids. I can't recall any issue with my skin colour in this school. The only racial incident I remember from this period happened outside of school when I was walking to my friend's house one day and someone called me a 'Paki'. I remember having no idea what that meant at the time. It was the first time I'd had a racial slur directed at me.

During my later secondary-school years, my mum got a job in Berkshire in the Home Counties, so we moved there. Our new surroundings were the polar opposite of our neighbourhood in Croydon. We lived in a tiny village called Finchampstead, surrounded by massive eight-bedroom houses. It was really beautiful, and I loved it there.

However, by the age of fourteen, I really wasn't getting along with my mum who was so focused on her career she had no time for me or my brother. So I returned to London to live with my dad. This was a tough experience. I had no freedom. My dad was repulsed by my short skirts and make-up, so he took away all my clothes and gave me a new wardrobe of clothes which covered me from head to toe. During this period, I was diagnosed with manic depression.

As a young teenager I didn't think about race or identity. I wanted to be a fashion designer and a singer, and I was very focused on that. It was not until I was eighteen and me and my brother moved to Iran for about eight months that I really started thinking about my identity. Iranians would point at us on the streets and laugh, calling us 'blacks' in Farsi. This was the early 2000s. It was so embarrassing. I hated the experience. I couldn't understand why people would see us as different and other us in such a public and mean manner. One of my Iranian aunties advised me to get married to a white man so my kid would be lighter-skinned than I was. I started hating Iranians even though I had previously felt very Iranian. I haven't been back to Iran since then. I think the level of rejection we faced is the reason for that.

By the time I got back to Britain, I saw the world completely differently. You can say it was in Iran that I became black. For the first eighteen years of my life, I had felt Persian, but my Iranian experience forced me to reassess my identity. This affected my art, too. I became more of a conceptual artist than a fashion designer. The activist in me was ignited by that trip. It was a difficult and humiliating experience for my father as well. We went on a road trip in Iran and he had wanted to take us inside some of the sacred temples in Shiraz. But they wouldn't let us in. They told him me and my brother weren't Iranian so we couldn't enter those temples.

My dad had always seen us as Iranian because we were his children. To be told we weren't was a huge blow to him. My dad was incapable of thinking of his children as black, especially as he has some pretty racist views about black people. I've told him this to his face. He tells me I don't understand and complains he suffered racism at the hands of black people in Britain.

Black men had often reacted very negatively to the sight of him and my mum walking the streets in the 1980s. He told me how at a Notting Hill Carnival, some black guys had pulled apart his hand from my mother's hand once. Some would look at them with disgusted expressions on their faces. My mum's dad didn't speak to her for years because she married outside her race.

So truth is, my dad has some very racist views about black people and once said something so racist to my brother that they don't speak to each other today. He has never been able to accept the idea we are black as well as Asian. He sees us in his own image. But that experience in Iran shattered the image he had created in his head; it highlighted the fact his own society saw his children as black. That was very painful for him. I once asked him why he married a black woman if he felt that way about black people. He said he was forced into the marriage, that it wasn't something he had chosen. When he says thing like that, he always tries to add the caveat that me and my brother are the best thing that ever happened to him.

Between the ages of eighteen and twenty-five, I spent most of my time making performance art. I was also in a music band. These were vehicles for me to express myself, using race as a subject matter for art form. I went to Brighton University where I did an undergraduate degree in visual arts performance and a postgrad in post-colonial cultural policy. The problem at Brighton was that there were no academics around who seemed familiar with theories relatable to my experience. One tutor finally pointed me in the way of Frantz Fanon and that led me on the path of discovery of post-colonial theorists.

But I couldn't believe how little knowledge there was of anything that wasn't white or revolving around the white experience at university. I don't expect anyone to know everything, but I would expect that if students are paying for your services, you should have knowledge reflective of their interests and educational needs. The Brighton student population was quite racially diverse, but the knowledge of Brighton academics was not. They were perfectly nice people and I got along great with them, but they just didn't have knowledge about things non-white.

A key breakthrough with my black identity came when I visited New York in my early twenties and stayed with one of my black aunties for three months. New York was where I first saw you could be black and like indie rock, which I'd always been into. Now there's music like Afro-punk, but when I was growing up in the 1990s and early 2000s, that didn't exist. Back then, there was really just one way to be black in the UK – the inner-city urban way – listening to rap music and R & B. It was in New York I first saw versions of blackness I could see myself reflected in. I met so many interesting and varied black people there, it was awesome.

Until New York, I never referred to myself as black. Now I see my racial identity in three parts: blackness, Middle Easternness and a third space that exists between those two. Previously, blackness was something I never felt I could claim. I've never agreed with the idea mixed-race people need to choose a side. I need to be both black and Middle Eastern to be myself, a mixed-race person. My mixed-raceness is the one thing that keeps me anchored, it's the one thing people can't deny me because it's biological. I know my mixed-race experience would have been different if I had one white parent, if I was half-white British. I have many mixed-race friends who are half-white, and I know this is an incredibly tricky and confusing terrain to cover. I just had a glimpse of that in Iran.

My mum experienced a year of reawakening when I was in my

third year of university. She was diagnosed with schizophrenia and went into a bit of psychosis. I think it was the best thing that ever happened to her. While Western medical science sees psychosis as something inherently negative, a lot of African cultures see it as part of a rebirth of your soul.

And indeed, my mum has now started to connect with her blackness in a way she never did before. She is now more accepting of her identity. She even wears baby dreads these days, something she would never have dreamt of doing before. When I was growing up, she'd always emphasise to me that when she'd gone to interviews in her natural hair, she'd never gotten the job. But when she'd gone in a weave, she did. Back then, she truly believed she had to kill whatever part of herself might become an obstacle to assimilation in Britain. But she no longer thinks like that. She is now like a full person. That really makes me happy.

I have focused on the experiences of mixed-race people, not their parents, but when Sereena spoke about how her Iranian father was incapable of thinking of his children as black, it really struck me how complicated mixed-raceness can be from the point of view of the parent of a mixed-race child. Especially one who has a strong sense of their own racial identity such as Sereena's father. That must also be one incredibly tricky role to play. When you see yourself as one thing, you probably assume your children will be seen as that thing, too.

It must be very painful for a parent to see their child rejected or meaningfully othered by their own society. What a feeling it must have been for Sereena's father to have his children associated with blackness, about which he himself feels quite negative. It doesn't get more conflicted than that. I was angry for Sereena when she told me about her experiences in Iran but not surprised. There is a strong focus on the stigma still attached to blackness in Western societies, so it is easy to forget that it can often be much stronger elsewhere, in places which are much less politically correct.

Stories of what mixed-black children still go through in Asia and the Arab world can be pretty horrifying. I would definitely rather be mixed black in Britain than anywhere else in the world outside Africa. The black stigma is sustained by the racial hierarchy I spoke of earlier, which is in turn sustained by the global economic hierarchy. As a result of her experiences, Sereena has gone from strong identification with Iranianness as a young girl to now perceiving herself in terms of 'blackness, Middle Easternness and a third space that exists between those two'. A real multiplicity of identities.

# Chapter 22

# Islam gives me something race doesn't

I have always had a special fascination for identical twins: two people born to the same parents who look the same and grow up in the same home at the same time. Yet as anyone who is close to a pair of twins will attest, they always seem to have completely different personalities and can in fact often be virtual opposites in terms of character. Despite growing up the same, it's as if they were born different. So I wondered how the twin dynamic might play out in terms of mixed-race identity. Since physical appearance and upbringing clearly play huge roles in how mixed-race people identify, I thought it would be interesting to find out how mixed-race twins who grew up under the same roof might end up feeling about who they are. I was fortunate enough to find Dania and Aliyah, identical twins born to a Pakistani father and Lebanese mother in London, who agreed to speak to me. I met with Dania first.

Despite the fact I'm twenty-seven years old it is only recently I've started examining my experiences through the lens of being mixed race. Before that, I always felt only people of mixed black and white heritage had the right to that label. Now I know that's not true, and that people like me with a Pakistani father and Lebanese mother also have a right to it.

My parents met in 1980s London when my dad was a student at the School of Oriental and African Studies. When my Lebanese grandfather heard my mum was involved in a serious relationship with a man she'd met who was not Lebanese, he asked one question: 'Is he a Muslim?' Once that had been answered in the affirmative, he voiced no objections to the relationship.

I find it very interesting that all my Lebanese grandfather cared about was whether my dad was a Muslim. Lebanese people are very nationalistic. Though interracial marriages can be common, Lebanese society maintains tight control on who can actually call themselves 'Lebanese'. Even though my mum is from Lebanon, I can't even claim Lebanese citizenship because you are only entitled to it if your father is Lebanese. Moreover, in practice, you are only considered truly Lebanese if both your parents are from Lebanon. Nevertheless, as my parents' case suggests, among Lebanese Muslims, Islam still acts as a strong enough unifying factor that my grandparents had no problems with her marrying a Pakistani man.

We visited Beirut every summer when I was growing up and I absolutely loved the place and identified with the people. But I was always conscious Lebanese people would never accept me as Lebanese. Over there, they make you learn your place very quickly. Society's dividing lines are drawn clearly and unmistakably. The Lebanese don't recognise the concept of 'mixed race'. You are either full-Lebanese or you are not Lebanese. Once I opened my mouth and people heard my British-accented less than fluent Arabic, I was marked as foreign. 'Ajnabi' is the term used for foreigner in Lebanon. It is not a neutral term, but one often used as a slur and I was called that several times. This definitely heightened my feelings of otherness in my mother's homeland. I identified with Lebanon, but I can't really say I felt Lebanon identified with me.

Aside from that, though, I really enjoyed visiting as a teenager. Beirut has a hedonistic feel to it – the nightlife there never stops. Life has long been a fragile experience in Lebanon because of all the conflicts the country has experienced, so people have a 'tomorrow we may die, may as well enjoy today' attitude. Beirut's nightclubs are packed full every day of the week. There is a sweet freedom in the air there that's difficult to describe, an almost lawless feel to the place. I've been to my dad's homeland of Pakistan, too. But I'd say Lebanon is definitely more liveable and progressive than Pakistan. Even my dad prefers visiting Lebanon to Pakistan.

But in our home both cultures were represented equally in terms of things like food. We'd eat a Lebanese dish one day, a Pakistani one the next. Thanks to Islam, there was a cultural equilibrium in our home. Islam is a shared value system that unites my parents and our whole family. It provides us a common moral compass, a shared foundation. My parents did not attend mosque very regularly; I wouldn't describe them as religiously devout. But they are both very culturally Muslim. I think our home would have been more conflicted if we had not had that shared focal point of Islam.

Though my parents were educated, I would describe our socio-economic status as working class. My father was a teacher. I went to working-class schools in Camden, which is where we lived. The schools were predominantly white, but there were also black kids and Asian kids. I never fitted in with any of these groups. I didn't really fit in with the South Asian girls because I didn't know Bollywood movies, Asian songs or how Indian, Pakistani and Bangladeshi weddings worked. I'd be with a group of Asian kids, someone would be telling a story about their parents and say, 'You guys know what Asian parents are like.' At such moments, I'd always think, *Hmm . . . well, actually I don't.*

While both my parents were culturally Muslim, there wasn't really much Asianness in our home apart from Pakistani food and a few minor cultural elements. My dad is a very progressive sort who basically feels British and is not attached to or even interested in Pakistani culture. As for my mum, like most Lebanese people, she is fiercely proud of her culture and heritage, very nationalistic. For her, Lebanon will always be home. But she is also quite Western-oriented in her everyday life.

Because of my lack of rootedness in Asianness and Arabness, virtually all the men I've dated so far have been either black or white. I haven't really dated Asian or Lebanese men. I always think if I date such men, they will figure out I'm a fraud. That sounds insane, no? I once went on a date with an Indian guy and he says to me, 'You're not really Asian, you're Arab.' Black and white men don't understand my heritage at all – to them I'm just someone other. The good side of that is they do not feel entitled to tell me what I really am, the way Asian or Arab men do. They accept whatever I tell them I am. But a Lebanese man would know I don't have the trappings of what it takes to be considered Lebanese. If he started talking about Lebanese cultural rituals in any detail, I'd probably just sit there with a blank look on my face. I want to avoid such situations.

Anytime I meet members of my extended family on either side, I realise how limited my understanding of both countries is. I only know a few elements of my parents' cultures. Hence, I seek out men who are from completely different backgrounds so I don't have to perform a role I don't genuinely feel.

However, while in the sphere of dating I don't feel in my comfort zone around people from my parents' cultures, in my journalistic career I draw on both my identities effortlessly. Being mixed race means constantly being on the periphery, observing things from the outside. From a distance. That is very helpful in journalism. So while it can be difficult to often feel the odd one out in everyday life, not fitting in can be a big asset in some careers.

Generally speaking, though, I feel really different from the girls in Britain's Asian community. I have a Chinese friend who is extremely well-educated, but she tells me if you're not married by thirty in China, you're considered old and useless. Despite all her degrees, she is under huge pressure from her parents to get married before thirty or else no Chinese man will want her. I can't imagine my parents, whose Islamic orientation doesn't stop them from being very liberal, coming to that kind of conclusion. Things like that make me feel very different from people of Asian heritage.

But my cultural background also makes me view some things differently from how English girls view them. In Lebanon, a woman's worth lies in her virginity. The longer you stay a virgin the higher the status of your eventual partner. Here in Britain, once girls enter their teenage years, casual sex is seen as no big deal.

When I was at university, the English girls would go all out to have as much casual sex as possible. It was seen as the obvious thing to do; you're young, enjoy life, get it out your system, duh. If I hadn't had my experience of Lebanese society, I would have also just assumed this is the obvious thing for girls like myself to do at that age. But I knew there was a different, less casual, way of treating sex.

I'm not saying there is a right or wrong way of viewing sex. What I'm saying is that when you are immersed in a single cultural world, you simply assume the way things are done there is the way things should be done. But when you are privy to different cultural worlds, you can juxtapose them and see there isn't just one way of doing things or viewing things. I love being able to see the world through different lenses. It is a privilege to have that.

When it comes to sex, I think I've found a nice middle ground. Sex is not viewed as something negative in the Islamic world, as often suggested, it is viewed as something to be celebrated. There is nothing in the Quran saying women are the property of men or that men should decide what is proper and not proper when it comes to sex. But it is definitely something seen as belonging in the realm of married life.

Islam has given me a sense of community that race hasn't. Especially during periods like Ramadan, you feel the invisible threads that bind you to other Muslims, irrespective of where their parents come from. It is difficult for me to imagine myself marrying a man who is not Muslim. I was once in a serious relationship with a Christian guy and I really liked him. He ticked all my boxes. But one day, I asked him how it would work with religion if we were to have children. He said they would attend both church and mosque. *That will never happen*, I thought to myself. And I ended things with him.

It's not like I expect a man to convert to Islam for me or else. But can I really have a future with someone who doesn't share my religion or who doesn't even have any faith at all but is just a nominal Christian? Perhaps I could, but I find it difficult to imagine today. Many British Muslims have complex relationships with their faith. I have met extremes. Some are extremely devout and overly conservative, but then some are too liberal and laissez-faire for my liking.

I am not here to judge others, but that doesn't mean I will ignore things that are important to me. Nowadays, it's considered old-fashioned to talk about God in Britain. But my faith gives me resilience. If one door closes, I believe it is God's way of pushing me in another direction. Ultimately my faith came first in my decision to break up a relationship with a guy I quite liked. At the time, I found it interesting that it came to that. It told me something about myself.

There is a difference between Islam as religion and Islam as culture, especially in its most conservative manifestations. The religion is ultimately about being a good person, but in a lot of Asian cultures today, Islam is weaponised against women to monopolise and control them. Men want to police female sexuality as if the female body is their property. There is no religious grounding for this, but of course it is sold this way. In the sphere of women's rights, Lebanon is definitely way more tolerant than most other Muslim countries in the Middle East.

I lived in Dubai for a while and the situation for women there is extreme. You could go to prison if you are caught with a man who is not your husband in a hotel room. The authorities often turn a blind eye when it comes to tourists and foreigners because they want to maintain Dubai's image as an open international city where people can do business and spend money. But the situation for locals is very different. Even as a foreigner, anytime I went to the hospital, doctors would ask me when I had my last period. Sometimes they even touched my belly to see if I was pregnant. It is actually enshrined in law that they could lose their licence if they find out a woman is pregnant and don't report it. That's scary stuff. These kinds of things should clearly not be happening in the twenty-first century and those parts of the Islamic world where they are will have to find a pathway forward from them.

I find it interesting that everywhere outside Britain I am seen as British, including in my parents' homelands of Lebanon and Pakistan. But when you actually live in Britain as a person of colour it's not like you can fit in effortlessly. When I was growing up in the early 2000s, I felt Britain was still by and large sceptical to the idea of people of colour being truly British.

While by then most people would no longer say out loud 'there's no black in the Union Jack', I think many still agreed with the general sentiment behind that saying. That's been changing recently. I think a lot of this change comes from the fact people of colour have mobilised themselves culturally. There are many books being written by writers of colour. Social media like Instagram have made us more visible in the public sphere. We are now being heard on our own terms.

When I was growing up, we were all just lumped together as 'ethnic minorities'. Now there is more recognition of the vast differences between us, but there is still a long way to go with that. Even when it comes to mixed-race people, there is this implicit assumption we all basically share the same stories. But my experiences are completely different from those of someone born to black and white parents, for instance.

It is frustrating many Britons still instinctively assume a mixed-race identity to be limited to people of black and white heritage. I was virtually force-fed this idea growing up. If you see an interracial couple on TV, they will usually be a black and white couple. If you see mixed-race people on TV, they will usually be mixed black and white. That is as far as the idea of 'mixed race' goes in the imagination of Britain. This is problematic as it leaves little room for more inclusive discussions about mixed Britishness.

We never see mixed white-Indian or mixed white-Chinese people on TV. Meanwhile, mixes outside black and white are not as unusual as some may think. Unfortunately, all the recent noise around Meghan Markle just ends up regurgitating this idea there is only one kind of mixed-race type, which is one of the reasons I avoid news about her like the plague.

My parents have never understood the intricacies of what it is like being mixed race. Sometimes, I'd try explaining some stuff I was going through to my mum and she'd virtually roll her eyes as I was speaking. She couldn't get what I was on about. My dad likewise. They are both very pragmatic people who believe you just get on with things. They came to Britain during the Thatcher era and they have a 'put up or shut up, just make it' attitude to life.

What they did often bang into my head was that as a person of colour, I would have to work three times harder than white people, which is something many non-white parents tell their children. Some people really believe Britain is a meritocracy. This is true to some extent, but it is a different kind of meritocracy for people of colour than it is for white people. One where more is expected of the former than the latter to get to the same place. If the gatekeepers don't let you in, your race can still hold you back.

In the world of journalism, being a person of colour still makes things very much an uphill struggle. The newsrooms are predominantly white with a smattering of people of colour who went to private schools. You quickly get the message you don't belong there until you've convinced them you've earned it.

I think people of colour in Generation Z are really lucky. Back in my school days, most teachers had very low expectations of, and aspirations for, people of colour. We were generally not expected to do too well academically bar the odd genius among us. It was also strikingly rare to see a person of colour at my university in Sheffield. The people who looked like me were often from London, meaning not many young people of colour from Sheffield went to university at the time. These low expectations and the demotivating effect they had on minorities seem to be dissipating in recent years.

It's funny, when people find out you're mixed race, they often ask you whether you feel more this or that. Truth is, some days I feel very Desi, some days I feel very Arab, other days I don't feel any of those. Sometimes, I feel nothing in connection to both my parents' cultures. Perhaps there are some mixed-race people who consistently feel more this or that, but that's not how it works for me.

I've come to realise mixed-race Londoner is what best describes me. 'British' is my nationality but I don't feel very British. I've especially not felt very British ever since the Brexit vote. What I definitely feel like is a mixed-race Londoner. There are sayings I can share with other Londoners no outsider would get. Like when one of the contestants on *Love Island* (Amber) called another contestant (Joanna) a 'dead ting'. People all over England started googling what 'dead ting' means. But every Londoner knew what it meant. We basically have our own language and way of life. London is a nation on its own.

Mixed-race people have always been defined by how others want to perceive us or box us. That is the mixed-race experience. It is why we get each other, why there is a silent understanding between mixed-race people even though we all have very unique individual experiences.

I'd advise any young teenage girls struggling with being mixed race today to be . . . patient. You don't have to make a decision today about who you are. You literally have all the time in the world to do that. It wasn't until I was twenty-five I decided I would call myself mixed race. When the anxiety of identity confusion calls, just drop the rope. Evacuate.

When you are a mixed-race teenager, you can get a nagging feeling something isn't quite right, but you don't have the words to articulate it and don't even know where the feeling is coming from. But you don't have to feel so distressed or conflicted just because something doesn't feel right. That feeling won't last forever. And even when it's there, it's important to remind yourself that, as a mixed-race person, you have two or more different worlds you can inhabit. Not many people can say that. Don't allow yourself to feel forced to choose an identity label. Understand that you will feel different in different places among different people. You just have to accept that.

# Chapter 23

# Always outside the bubble

I'm Aliyah, Dania's twin sister. Like her, it was not until I was in my mid-twenties that I started thinking of myself as mixed race. I also previously assumed that was a category reserved for people with black and white parents. However, unlike my sister who has always identified more with our Lebanese heritage, I have always seen myself as more Desi or Pakistani than Lebanese or Arab.

It is not like I don't think Lebanese culture shapes some aspects of my behaviour. For instance, being warm and hospitable is a huge deal for Lebanese people. They are very family-oriented and spend loads of time in each other's houses, hanging out and eating lots of food. I like that kind of lifestyle. I am quite homely. I like cooking, and I like to think I'm very hospitable.

Moreover, my mum definitely did more to teach both of us about her Lebanese culture than my dad did to teach us about Pakistani culture. This wasn't deliberate on his part. He was simply too busy working long hours when we were growing up. However, despite my mum's best efforts, I don't identify as Lebanese or Arab in any way.

I think this is mostly down to pure coincidence. As it happens, early on in life, I got more explicit signals from Lebanese people that they didn't consider me one of them than I did from Pakistanis.

Like my sister, I always enjoyed our summer trips to Beirut, but I never felt Lebanese. I remember us once walking down the streets of Beirut with a Bengali maid who worked for a family relative. Me and Dania looked particularly tanned that summer because it was very hot. A Lebanese guy saw us and started hurling racial abuse our way, assuming we were all Bengali or from some other South Asian country.

My sister got so upset she punched him in the face. This was quite a dangerous thing to do considering Lebanese men often carry guns. Luckily for us, this guy wasn't. His behaviour was outrightly racist, but I remember instinctively thinking we should never have gotten so tanned in the first place. Then we wouldn't be called names on the streets. That's a crazy thing to think, isn't it?

People of darker skin colour often experience this kind of treatment in Lebanon. In general, racism towards darker-skinned people is very common in the Arab world. It is not subtle either, but very much in your face. I witnessed it first-hand when I lived in Dubai as well. Thanks to these regular childhood visits to the Middle East, I understand that some Arabs can be anti-Black. While I know I will never be in the bubble myself, I can see clearly what is inside it.

However, while I have always identified more with my Pakistani heritage, I am well aware that Pakistanis do not see me as one of them either. The only difference is that, as coincidence would have it, it took longer for me to get this message from Pakistanis than from Lebanese. It took two romantic relationships with Pakistani men in my adult life to really open my eyes to this reality.

In the first relationship, despite dating the guy for quite a while, I noticed he seemed very reluctant to introduce me to his mother. I thought this was strange. One day I asked him why. 'Because she won't count you as Pakistani,' he replied shortly. I was taken aback by the finality with which he said this. There were no ifs or buts, just a decisive statement of fact that gave me no room for negotiation.

In the second relationship, before I even asked, the guy told me flat out that his mum wouldn't like me because I'm not Pakistani. 'But I'm half-Pakistani, doesn't that count?' I asked. 'Nah, that won't count,' he replied as decisively as my previous boyfriend. I basically stopped dating Pakistani guys after that. If I had that kind of experience once, I would have written it off as coincidence. But twice in succession was starting to look like a pattern. To cap it off, this second guy I had dated eventually ended up marrying a full-Pakistani girl. *So that's how it works*, I thought to myself when I heard.

I remember thinking how crazy it was that people could perceive me so differently from how I perceived myself. I felt very angry and frustrated because while I considered myself very similar to Pakistanis, they clearly disagreed. This difference between how you perceive yourself and how others perceive you can be quite jarring. I felt like my identity could be contested in so many ways. Such feelings engender self-doubt. *If my right to claim a Pakistani identity is being questioned by Pakistanis, then maybe I am not really as Pakistani as I think as I am*, I remember wondering. It was a very unsettling experience for me to see myself reflected this way in other people's eyes.

As a result of these experiences, my current boyfriend is white. I had earlier dated him for a couple of years but broke off our relationship because I thought I should be dating a guy from my own culture. But I had such bad experiences with South Asian men I decided I am better off dating white guys. If you won't introduce me to your mum even after we've been together for a while, what is the point of our relationship?

I know white families, too, will see me as other, but at least they won't contest my identity. They won't tell me I'm not really Lebanese or not really Pakistani. My current boyfriend's family have been very kind and welcoming to me. They couldn't be kinder.

Dating can be a very irritating experience when you are mixed race. On your first date, guys often spend the first few minutes trying to show you they can work out the particulars of your heritage by peering intently at your face with squinted eyes. 'No, wait, don't tell me, let me guess. At least one of your parents must be X, no? But you also look like you have a bit of Y in you. Am I right?'

Or guys will be so desperate to know where your parents are from, even if you try to evade the topic, they'll just keep on asking, 'Where, where, where?' If you just say you're half-Lebanese, half-Pakistani, they want to know which parent is from where. I know this is often just plain curiosity, but that doesn't make it any less tiring. On a first date, I want us to try to get to know each other better, not spend half the time talking about my family's roots.

When I was in primary school my friends were predominantly white. Growing up I usually found it easier to get along with white people than with Asians or Arabs because the latter were always questioning my identity. However, generally speaking, school was quite an isolating experience for me as I was never really able to fit in with any group. Some people have had positive experiences being mixed race. I would say my experiences have been mostly negative.

The most negative experience I had connected with looking the way I look was during my time at the University of Kent. Even though the primary and secondary schools I went to were predominantly white, Camden where we lived was a diverse neighbourhood with lots of Bengalis, Indians and Pakistanis. Kent, on the other hand, is a very white environment, as is the university there. I went from racial diversity to white suburbia. There were some students of colour at the university, but they all instantly formed into groups along racial lines, none of which I could join.

It is not that I had difficulties generally getting along with my white peers in Kent. We got along quite fine, but there were so many little everyday things they'd say that I found extremely frustrating. Things white people in London wouldn't say. I'd be having a conversation with a fellow student and they'd say something like, 'Wow, you sound just like my Muslim friend, you guys are exactly the same.' *Er . . . no, we probably aren't exactly the same,* I'd think to myself.

However – and I know this will sound petty – what was really key to my Kent experience was that I wasn't deemed as physically attractive as I'd been deemed in London. And it wasn't just me. I met a Pakistani girl in my second year, and we agreed we had identical experiences. Guys were always interested in me in London. This Pakistani girl I met at Kent, she was drop-dead gorgeous, the kind of girl guys would kill for in London. Yet in Kent we both became redundant. It was like we were invisible to the (mostly white) guys. They clearly didn't view us as physically attractive women.

I probably looked the best I'll ever look in my life when I was in Kent, considering my age back then. When I think about it today, I feel quite annoyed I spent some of the best years of my life in a place which didn't value me. Those kinds of experiences are especially damaging for a young woman. After something like that, when some guy gives you a bit of attention, you're so easily flattered you find yourself tolerating all sorts of rubbish just to hold on to that feeling of being wanted. This was exactly what happened to me. I dated some truly awful guys in my years after Kent just because I got off on the attention. *Finally, someone sees me,* I'd think to myself.

My Pakistani friend in Kent became so depressed at the lack of male attention, she stopped going to classes. She eventually transferred to Leicester University just because there was a big Asian population there. I remember feeling envious she'd now be in

Leicester while I had to stay in Kent. Luckily for me, during my studies I was able to go to Miami for a six-month exchange programme. Once again, I could feel like an attractive woman as I can't complain of a lack of male attention there.

To be fair, I realise every culture has its own specific beauty ideals, not just (white) British culture. The Arab beauty ideal, for instance, is very specific. As a woman, you are expected to be groomed 24/7. You should be completely hairless everywhere apart from your head. You should be slim but slightly curvaceous. You should have great hair, great eyebrows and generally use heavy make-up. Arab beauty ideals are quite far removed from how I see myself and how I want to look on a daily basis. Still, knowing beauty ideals differ from culture to culture doesn't mean feeling unattractive in Kent sucked any less.

In Miami, people called me 'London' because of my accent. I felt quite British there. When you're mixed race, so much about how you are perceived depends on which part of the world you are in. After university, I lived in Dubai for a while, which was quite an interesting experience. I'm a journalist like my sister. I wrote for an exclusive magazine there, reviewing restaurants, hotels, nightclubs, that sort of thing.

Whenever I'd be in a taxi with a Pakistani driver taking me to go review some new six-star hotel, I remember often feeling quite guilty. Here I was with someone from 'my side', but we had completely different lives simply because of where I'd been born. On the other hand, while I was British by passport and definitely had privileges thanks to this, the Brits in Dubai's 'expat community' didn't really seem to consider me *British* British.

I remember once attending one of the 'expat' events the British community there organises quite regularly. After a few minutes, it was obvious there was a clear hierarchy in the room. The very few people of colour like myself were instinctively positioned at the bottom of this hierarchy by the white Brits. People's eyes would just glaze over when they saw me. I could tell they felt I was definitely not one of the people worth hanging out with. It was like reliving the worst moments of university. I remember feeling annoyed I'd even bothered to try. Why had I put myself in a situation to be treated so dismissively, naively thinking I'd be welcomed to the fold as a fellow Brit away from home?

The big irony is that because of my job, I probably had the most power in that room in terms of access to Dubai's most exclusive places. I could get a table in any restaurant or nightclub, not an easy thing in a city full of billionaires and celebrities. Dubai had opened up to me, but the British community hadn't. It never crossed their mind I might be someone worth knowing. They just assumed I was inconsequential.

In general, white Britons in Dubai treated everyone a shade darker – Filipinos, Indians, Pakistanis – very condescendingly. Interestingly, white South Africans got a pass, so there was definitely something very racial going on there, not just a First World/Third World divide.

They would set up these online forums which I read out of journalistic curiosity. There were constant comments along the lines of 'we Westerners' do things in such and such a way, 'We're not like these Filipinos who sleep three or four to a room.' British people renting out flats would put out vacancy adverts, saying 'For British girls only' or 'For Westerners only.' There was really an awful colonial-style way of thinking in that community.

While I sometimes agreed with the general sentiments of what they said with regards to the way Emiratis behaved, for instance, I would never adopt the 'we are obviously so much more civilised' tone that came so naturally to the white Brits. Such experiences definitely have a negative effect on the way I perceive Britishness. Like Dania, I too consider myself a Londoner, not a Brit.

I don't speak to my parents about the issues I face being mixed race. They just wouldn't get it. Or they'd say that I was born and raised in Britain, so I shouldn't have any issues here, a common attitude many children of immigrant parents often complain about. I don't blame my parents for not understanding my situation. My personal experiences and how I feel about them are so unique sometimes even my own twin sister doesn't understand every feeling I try to explain to her. If she can't understand some of the things I feel, how can I expect anyone else to?

On the plus side, like in her case, my mixed-raceness has worked for me in my journalistic career because I have always observed in-group behaviours from a distance. In some respects, being Muslim was also an advantage because I was able to access communities that other journalists were often not able to.

Thankfully, I'm now at a place where I can pick to write about issues other than those directly related to being brown or Muslim in Britain. In my professional environment, apart from my sister, I've yet to meet anyone quite like me in terms of racial background. The world of journalism is, of course, predominantly white. But even the few people of colour there are usually Arab, Asian or black, but never quite like me.

My sister is definitely more religious than me. Islam does play a role in my life, but nowhere near as significant a role as it does for her. I think she finds it easier to identify with Muslims because there is a lot of common ground she can easily establish with them, including things as banal as not eating pork. Meanwhile, race is so complex and tricky, identification does not always come easy when you're mixed.

I remember once when my mum came to visit me at university. There was this Syrian girl in my hostel. Immediately she saw my mum, she stopped her, and they struck up a conversation in Arabic. It was so natural. So effortless. Watching them together was like watching two old friends even though they were from different generations, different countries and had just met. I knew that girl would never have stopped me to strike up a conversation based on an instinctive 'we are the same' sentiment. Only a mixed-race person would understand the sense of perpetual otherness I felt watching that conversation.

I was intrigued by the unifying role Dania recalled Islam playing in her household growing up. Due to the virtual non-existence of religion in (white) Western life today, many have forgotten its huge potential to unite people of different races and cultures in a way few other things can. When we speak of Islam in the West, it is usually in the context of terrorism or its perceived incompatibility with Western values. Its enduring ability to bring together people of very different backgrounds and cultures hardly ever gets talked about. This is by no means a banal ability.

I felt a twinge of envy when Dania spoke about how Islam had united her parents. I wished my parents had shared some kind of value system that had the power to overshadow their vast cultural differences – some common 'moral compass' as Dania described the role of Islam in their home. But there was nothing like that in our home. No final authority to defer to, no shared Ten Commandments, just two people with very different views of how the world should work. A home in more or less perpetual conflict. I envied Dania the peaceful household atmosphere she described.

Both sisters did not really feel they ever fitted in either with South Asians or Arabs. Clearly the 'not fitting in' experience is not just a black-white issue or an Asian-white issue, it is a mixed-race issue. However, fascinatingly, Dania has ended up identifying more with her Lebanese heritage than her Pakistani roots while the opposite is the case for Aliyah. 'Coincidence' is what Aliyah believes has led to this.

Coincidence doesn't usually rank high on the list of things we believe lead people to identify one way or the other. We like to think of our identity as a destination we arrived at sitting in the driver's seat. This stems from our general need to feel in control of the most important aspects of our lives. In reality, how we identify, just like our career paths or the spouse we end up marrying, is often down to happenstance. If just a single major event in our lives had happened differently, we could have ended up in a completely different place.

Sometimes we consciously develop our identities in a certain direction, sometimes events develop them for us – like someone telling us at a young age that we will never really be considered Lebanese or Arab. Even though Aliyah would later learn the same thing about her chances of being seen as Pakistani, the particular sequence of events in her life meant she had definitively resigned from laying a stake to Lebaneseness much earlier on. No two people in this world can share the exact same identity experience, not even twins.

When Dania said she avoids dating Arab and Asian men not to get figured out as a 'fraud', I knew exactly what she was talking about. It highlights a popular but wrong perception people have of the abilities of mixed-race people to switch identities at will. It really depends before which audience. When I tell white people my dad is a Yoruba, I can see from their eyes they assume I know a lot about Yoruba culture and traditions. I usually don't disabuse them of this assumption. Why should I? It's advantageous to be seen as someone familiar with numerous cultural worlds. As long as I don't lie outright, there's no reason for me to be voluntarily reducing my unique selling points, is there?

But a Yoruba person would sniff out in a minute that my knowledge of Yorubaness is highly superficial. Like Dania, I wouldn't pass the authenticity test. I can convince anyone in the world that I know a lot about Yoruba culture, expect a Yoruba person. We might be able to pull off various identities before third-party observers, but cultural insiders know an amateur when they see one. We can't fool them. Unfortunately.

I liked what Dania said about not feeling consistently more Pakistani or Lebanese, but some days feeling more of one identity than the other and on other days feeling 'nothing in connection to both my parents' cultures'. I can definitely relate to that as well. There are moments and situations in which I feel very Nigerian. Other times, I feel decisively mixed race. And while I can't honestly say I have ever felt like a Polish man, I do have moments when I identify strongly with the Poles.

For example, when I watch movies showing how much Poland suffered during the Second World War, I feel its historical pains on something decisively deeper than an intellectual level. At such moments, I do feel a sense of oneness with Poles. The same goes for when I'm listening to Polish rap songs. I get into them. I get them. Sometimes, when I'd be with a group of Nigerian friends in Poland and we'd all be complaining about Polish racism, a time would come in the conversation when I'd feel like introducing some historical context.

I'd start talking about how Poland had been decimated by the Second World War and then suffered Soviet-imposed communism for the next half a century, trapped behind an Iron Curtain it had never wanted. And how before that it had been literally wiped off the map for 123 years when it was partitioned by the Austrians, Prussians and Russians in the eighteenth century. I'd try and explain how all these historical experiences had helped make Poles a very closed nation, instinctively suspicious of foreigners, especially those they didn't understand. My Nigerian friends were usually unimpressed by these history lessons. They would say something like, 'Ah, we forgot! Your mother is a Polish woman. You're like one of them too.' I could see it sounded to them like I was trying to justify Polish xenophobia, which I wasn't. I was just trying to explain it. At such moments, I did feel quite Polish. It's all very fluid really.

# Chapter 24

# Half-Indian, half-Jamaican makes no sense!

Eajaz is seventeen. His father is Indian while his mother is Jamaican. We met in Birmingham where he lives.

My parents met in Derby during their university years. When they started becoming serious about their relationship, my mum introduced my dad to her family. They were not too bothered he was Indian. Some of her brothers had white wives so interracial relationships were not new to them. But my dad's family was much less open to their relationship. When my parents decided to get married, most of my father's family members didn't turn up for the wedding. Some of them still don't speak to my dad today because he married a Jamaican woman. They see Indian and Jamaican cultures as incompatible.

A couple of years after I was born some members of my dad's family started becoming friendlier towards my mum. But developing a relationship with them has been a slow and difficult process for her considering the initial rejection she experienced. For a long time, she never accompanied me and my dad to his family events. At Indian weddings, women are usually seated separately from men, so my mum knew she would not be sat next to my dad but to female members of his family she did not feel comfortable around. Only recently has she started coming with us to his family events. The way it works now is my Indian aunties who are favourable to us make sure they seat my mum next to friendly family members who won't be mean to her or ignore her.

Weddings were my greatest peek into Indian culture as a child. I started attending them with my dad around the age of four but it took me about ten years to start understanding them. Before that, I never really got what was going on and would notice people looking at me funny, which made me nervous. I always felt very uncomfortable whenever my dad went off somewhere and left me on my own, even if it was just for a few minutes. Every minute he was gone seemed like forever. But nowadays I feel quite comfortable and don't wait anxiously for my dad to return anytime he wanders off. The same goes for Indian movies and Indian music; for many years I didn't get them, but now I've started enjoying them.

It helps that I recently started reading about India, trying to learn about the country. My Indian grandmother tells me stories about how it was for her when she came to Britain, how she spoke little English and felt very isolated. My dad occasionally speaks Gujarati to me so I know some words and can understand the language. Funnily enough, I've never been to a Jamaican wedding, so I have no idea what that's like. But I've always had good relations with my mum's family. My Jamaican grandparents have always been very welcoming.

During my earliest years we stayed in Halesowen, a town in the borough of Dudley, roughly thirty minutes' drive from Birmingham's city centre. We lived in a mostly white neighbourhood and even as a young child I could sense my mum didn't like it there. She felt isolated and complained she was cut off from her family. She didn't really have friends because she stopped working when I was born and didn't get out much.

I went to three different primary schools. The first one in Halesowen was a nice experience and I really enjoyed it. But then we moved to Dudley proper. There, between the ages of five and eight, I went to a semi-private primary school attended by mostly middle-class white kids from families much better off than ours. At the time, my dad was at the beginning of his engineering career and my mum wasn't working, as I mentioned. The only ethnic kids there were me and a half-Filipino, half-English boy who became my best friend.

This was where I first experienced racism. One day some kid just came up to me and called me a nigger. I was quite confused. I told my mum about it when I got home. She was really upset and called the school to complain, asking how this could be happening. She said I should never let anyone say that to me again but warned me not to retaliate if it did happen. She said I should just walk away. I clearly remember watching the film *The Color Purple* around this period. I was too young to understand it, but I remember connecting with it because of that boy calling me a nigger. I was desperately trying to understand what was going on here. Why had he said that to me?

In my new primary school, I got racial abuse from the white kids at least a couple of times a week. I couldn't understand it. I'd always been quite a popular kid, the kind who makes friends easily and who people tend to like. This made the name-calling even more confusing as it felt odd having others lash out at me. My unusual ethnic mix only made things worse. The kids would ask where my parents were from. When I'd say I was half-Indian, half-Jamaican, they'd say, 'What? That doesn't even make any sense!' Or they'd have disgusted expressions on their faces. I told them half-Indian, half-Jamaican does make sense because I am here. But I really felt awful when they'd say things like that to me. The disgust I'd see on their faces was especially painful for me.

My half-Filipino friend was also treated horribly. The white kids thought they were better than us not just because they were white but also because their families had more money than ours. We were both constantly bullied. We'd report to the teachers and they'd be harsher on us than on the boys calling us names! They'd tell us those kids didn't really understand what those bad words meant. They generally downplayed what was happening to us and tried to brush everything under the rug.

We felt really angry they were not doing anything about it. It was worse for my friend. At least I could count on my parents' support. But my friend's dad was white English and completely unable to understand how he was feeling. He let my friend know he didn't consider any of this a big deal. This made him feel like he was this weak kid, this cry-baby moaning over nothing. He felt really isolated and I know he had suicidal thoughts.

Things got so bad my parents finally withdrew me from that school. They placed me in a more diverse school, which was a much happier place for me. There were loads of Asian kids there and I felt a sense of belonging I had never felt in my previous school. But for a long time I felt very bad for my friend because I had left him there and knew he would now be facing all that hell on his own. I have no idea what happened to him.

My new school was mostly working-class kids, white kids and ethnic minority kids. The white kids there were completely different from the middle-class white kids in my previous school. They didn't see colour. They really tried to integrate, some of them even learnt a bit of Urdu just to be able to mix with the minority kids. I noticed that when our parents were around they didn't cluster along racial lines either but mixed with each other very freely. This felt good to see.

I think the shared economic struggle is what united everyone in that school, children and parents. Most of the families were not doing well financially. We all had similar lunches and similar toys. This was very different from my previous primary school where the better-off kids always showed off their expensive toys, making the rest of us feel quite poor. In the new school we shared our lunches and played with each other's toys. It was really cool. The kids reacted positively to my ethnic mix. While they did find Indian-Jamaican surprising, no one made disgusted faces. They'd be like, 'Oh wow, so what food do you guys eat at home? Which language do you speak?' Or they'd ask me which side I identify with more.

After that school, I went to a grammar school which was predominantly Asian. This, too, was a very different experience. Here, too, there was racism but in a different direction. The Indian and Pakistani kids who were in the majority regularly called black kids 'niggers'. Not behind their backs either, but to their face. Even though they knew I had a Jamaican mum, I think there must have been something they saw in my eyes, perhaps an aggression from the trauma of that primary school in Dudley, I'm not sure, but for some reason, they never called me that.

I thought it was disgusting the way they treated the black kids. There were two African boys in my class – one from Nigeria, the other from Ghana. The Asian kids called them 'nigger' non-stop. I asked the Nigerian kid why he allowed it. He said Asian kids got a pass because they were brown.

He even told me to stop telling them not to call him 'nigger' because my complaints were affecting his friendship with them. I thought that was crazy. I think he just made up that stuff about them getting a pass because they were brown to provide himself an excuse for not reacting. In truth, he didn't really know what to do about it. Or perhaps he was just willing to pay any price to have 'friends'. The Ghanaian kid admitted he wasn't happy being called the n-word but couldn't think of how to stop kids calling him that.

The Indian and Pakistani kids felt perfectly comfortable making racist comments about black people in front of me. They'd say I wasn't 'that black', that I was different from 'them', meaning the black kids. *I actually am that black, you just don't see it*, I'd think to myself.

There was a difference in the way the Indian kids used the n-word from the way the Pakistani kids used it. The Pakistani kids used it playfully, like how it's used in hip-hop culture. They felt it was acceptable because everyone else uses it in rap songs. But the Indian kids said 'nigger' with malice. They were often genuinely racist and felt superior to the black kids. I know from my dad how negatively many Indians view black people. You don't hear about Indian racism in Britain, but it's there. The reaction of my dad's family to him marrying my mum was no coincidence.

Why didn't I react when the Indian and Pakistani kids said racist things about black people in front of me? Because I wanted them to feel free around me and reveal their true feelings about black people. I would never have gotten this inside information if I'd shut them up. I do the same thing around white kids when it comes to Muslims.

The kids in school know I'm half-Jamaican, half-Indian, but they never quite imagine that I'm also Muslim. And I don't advertise it. I don't dress like a traditional Muslim, so people just assume my dad is Hindu. But our family is Muslim; my mum converted to Islam after marrying my dad. However, if I announced my Islamic faith loudly, I'd never learn what my peers really think about Muslims. I like observing groups from the outside. I think my horrible experiences in primary school taught me I needed to be observant of people and understand how they think.

I've noticed that when prejudiced comments or jokes are made about Muslims in a group, it's never all the kids who make the comments or laugh at the jokes. It's always just one or two kids. You can see others in the group feel uncomfortable and think it's wrong, but they just don't feel they have the social currency to tell those one or two kids to stop. When it comes to whether prejudices will end up getting spread or not among young people, a lot depends on what the kids who feel most confident about their social standing do. The confident kids dictate the atmosphere. The rest will usually just play along.

I've also noticed that when people make racist comments to your face, what they really want is for you to get angry and feel bad. So nowadays when someone says something racist to me, I just laugh in their face. This usually gets them quite confused. *Why is he not getting angry?* I can see them asking themselves. If people see their insults have no effect on you, they become confused. I'm not saying people should be allowed to say 'nigger' and things like that, but on the other hand, it is a kind of mental slavery if the words of other people can affect you so negatively.

In terms of how my mixed-race heritage played out at home, I've been quite blessed. Both my parents have always pointed out the positives and negatives in their cultures. Neither my mum nor my dad try to suggest their culture is the better one or the one we must follow. Because of that there are no cultural tensions at all in our home. In terms of food, it's an almost fifty–fifty experience. We eat a lot of European dishes because they are simpler to make. But we also often have a curry or something Jamaican.

I don't feel more Indian than Jamaican or the other way round. I have a friend who is half-Pakistani, half-Swiss. When she was younger she embraced her Swiss side fully mostly thanks to her Pakistani father who is quite self-hating. However, because she is currently surrounded by more brown people than white people, she has done a 180 and is now anti-white. That kind of thinking is strange to me. I want experiences from both sides. I plan to visit Jamaica in two years' time, and India in four.

I think one of the reasons some other mixed-race kids my age might be having problems with identity is because their parents did not properly educate themselves before getting into an interracial marriage. My dad grew up in close proximity to Jamaicans in Gloucester, where he was raised. He understands Jamaican culture. My mum started learning about Indian culture once she started dating my dad. But some other interracial couples just wing it, hoping things will work out somehow.

The couples themselves then end up having problems understanding each other while the kids get stuck in the middle, all confused. A lot also depends on the parenting skills of the interracial couple. How parents react to issues the mixed-race child raises is key; if they brush them off like my Filipino friend's English father did when he was getting racially abused, then that child is bound to grow up having issues. Parents of mixed-race kids need to take seriously the issues they raise with them. But mixed-race kids need to educate themselves as well, find their own sense of worth. They should ask their parents about their cultures and life experiences. You also need to develop your social skills because they play a big part in how confident you feel. And confidence is key.

I've never had black kids tell me I'm 'not really black', which I know some other mixed-black kids sometimes get told. Perhaps this is because I'm not half-white, but full-ethnic. I think only mixed-race kids who are half-white get told they're 'not really black' by black kids. Also, because I have friends from West Africa, I try to read about that part of the world. This helps me get involved in conversations and shows them I know something about where they come from. Things like that make people warm to you because they see you've made the effort. Then they look at me and think I'm just like them.

Britain doesn't feel like home to me. And white Britons don't feel like my people. Ethnic minorities feel like my people, it doesn't matter where they're from. I feel a sense of togetherness with them. It's strange to be born in a country and not feel a connection to it. But that's how I feel. I know when I travel abroad, people see my mannerisms, hear my accent and consider me British. But I don't feel British.

Would I like to feel British? Because I'm Jamaican-Indian not mixed British, I really don't feel the need to feel at home in Britain. The fact I don't feel British doesn't make me feel sad or rejected. I am happy being a Muslim who is Indian-Jamaican and happens to live in Britain for now. When I visit Muslim countries like Turkey or Morocco where people are brown like me, I feel connected to them and to those places. My parents are not that religious, but they instilled Islamic values in me. Always treat people with respect. Understand before reacting. This has worked for me and I definitely identify with Muslims.

But I also realise being lighter-skinned helps me move more freely among white people. Especially as they usually assume I'm half-white, so when they see me they see whiteness, safety. I've noticed it's harder for white kids to feel comfortable around black kids than around mixed-race kids. This is down to their own prejudices and fears. It is not the black kids' problem to solve, it is for the white kids to understand why they feel like that and break those habits. I would like people to see me as me, without race being involved. But I understand mixed-race people are still not that common in Britain, especially my kind of mix, so I really don't mind when people ask me questions about my racial heritage. It's natural for people to be curious.

I wish I'd been as mature and perceptive as Eajaz at seventeen. He pretty much seems to have life all figured out. I had to control myself from gasping out loud when he said the reason mixed-race kids his age might be having problems with identity 'is because their parents did not properly educate themselves before getting into an interracial marriage'. Nigerians would call Eajaz 'an old man', meaning someone far wiser than his age.

It is difficult to dispute his logic that for an interracial marriage to work, especially one involving people from different cultural planets like his parents, it is crucial for them to both understand and show respect for each other's cultures. Just seeing this alone is also beneficial for their children, who are likelier to grow up identifying with both their parents' cultures the way Eajaz does rather than perhaps seeing one as inherently better than the other. Not feeling any pressure from his parents to 'choose' a side is also definitely better than the contrary.

I have to say I was quite shocked at the kind of racist experiences Eajaz and his part-Filipino friend went through in their primary school as well as the lack of reaction on the part of his teachers. Considering he is just seventeen, we are talking about events within the last ten years, not in the 1970s. That this kind of behaviour is still being tolerated in some schools in Britain is something I find quite inexplicable. Of course, what made things even more difficult for Eajaz in his Dudley primary school was his unusual racial mix.

While Britons of mixed black and white heritage often said their peers saw them as 'cool', the situation can often be different for those who represent more non-standard mixes. David, the twenty-eight-year-old son of a Ghanaian dad and Bangladeshi mum, told me: 'Even though I grew up in multicultural London, I almost always gets weird looks when I say where my parents are from. People will say things like, "that's a strange mix". Comments like that always annoy me. What's so "strange" about two human beings falling in love with each other? If my mum was white, everyone would think my mix was cool. But Ghanaian-Bangladeshi, what's that all about? That's not seen as cool.' A common complaint I heard was that when Britain wants to 'show off' its mixed-race faces to prove how multicultural it is, those faces virtually always represent the standard mix. 'It's like we don't exist,' I heard on several occasions. But exist they do, and it's high time Britain started noticing there is a whole multitude of mixes in mixed-race Britain.

Another worrying theme in Eajaz's story is the 'Indian racism' he said we 'don't hear about' in Britain. Apart from Eajaz's account of how some Indian kids treated black kids in his school, stories of Indian families virulently opposed to the idea of their family member marrying someone not Indian do seem a bit too common to be explained solely by the cultural anxieties I argued people have the right to experience.

We should not be sensitive to racism only from white people, and we should not pretend we can't see or hear once it's black or brown people being racist. Eajaz, of course, talked not just about Indian kids but also about Pakistani kids feeling free to call their black peers the n-word because they knew children of Asian heritage were in the majority in their school and they could get away with it. Clearly, they also felt the unfortunate human need for domination. It is important for us to approach such behaviour as, again unfortunately, human, if we truly want to develop the right psychological response to tackling it. Pretending only white kids can feel the need to dominate and put down others is to ignore the human root of the problem. If we want to fight racism, we need to fight our need for domination. This, of course, is a particularly big problem among males and stems from the reality that men who dominate tend to be rewarded by society.

There are significant material and psychological rewards to be gained from being seen as a dominant male. You are likely to be seen as 'strong' and 'confident', qualities young boys will often hear people are looking for in leaders, be it in business, politics or sports. Until dominating others stops paying off, it is difficult to see how we can effectively tackle racist behaviours that are fundamentally a tactic for achieving a strategy of domination.

I found intriguing that Eajaz said that because he's 'full-ethnic', he's never been told by black kids he's 'not really black'. He thinks only mixed-race kids who have a white parent get told that by black kids. I guess that makes a kind of sense. The Indian–black relationship in Britain doesn't have all the historical emotional and psychological baggage of the black–white relationship nor its implicit status as a relationship of opposites in the eyes of many. If one sees black and white people as opposites, then I guess it is more difficult to imagine the offspring of black and white parents as black than the offspring of black and Indian parents. Plus, I'm assuming ethnic minority solidarity plays a role here, too. If you are someone who mentally divides Britain into a country inhabited by 'them' white people and 'us' ethnic minorities, then the offspring of a black parent and another ethnic minority parent is an us-and-us mix while the child of a black and white parent is an us-and-them mix, so someone that much further from us.

I also found it interesting that Eajaz said because he is 'Jamaican-Indian not mixed British' he doesn't 'feel the need to feel at home in Britain'. I personally have a similar stance being Polish-Nigerian and not having grown up here. Even though I do feel at home in Britain, I would be perfectly fine if I didn't, considering I lay no claim to Britishness. I am fine thinking of myself as an outsider here. But I was surprised to hear Eajaz, who was born and raised here, expressing similar sentiments. Perhaps his bad experiences at primary school have something to do with this. Or perhaps, as he suggests, it boils down to the fact that he seems to consider his father Indian and his mother Jamaican rather than see either of them as British, hence his lack of a need to see himself as British.

Chapter 25

# That mixed-race buzz

Hamid was born to an Iranian father and mixed-race British mother. He is thirty and grew up in Sheffield, where he currently lives.

My father came to Britain in the mid-1970s when he was seventeen. His parents sent him to join his siblings who were studying here. The plan was for him to learn English and eventually study, too. But he ended up in Sheffield where he met my mother. Even though she is technically Nigerian-English, my mum was raised very British here in Sheffield. She's never even been to Nigeria. Growing up, I always thought of her as simply British. My parents met on a night out and started a relationship. They had my older sister five years before me. I was born in 1989.

My dad has worked in Asian takeaways ever since I can remember, so he usually did nights and slept during the day. But whenever he was free he'd often have his Iranian friends over. Most of them had English wives so my mum liked them coming to our place because it meant company for her, too. I thus spent my earliest years around quite a lot of Iranian people. My dad taught my mum how to cook Iranian food, so when his friends came over our home would be abuzz with Farsi, loud laughter and the smell of Iranian dishes. I used to like being around all this.

My dad wanted me and my sister to feel a strong connection to Iran – he even registered us for Farsi classes on Saturdays. But all this ended when my parents got divorced. I was eight at the time. After that, we stopped having contact with Iranian people apart from my dad, who me and my sister would sometimes meet on weekends. But then we'd just go for some fast food or to a shopping mall, so no contact with Iranian culture or anything like that. One of my biggest regrets today is that I stopped taking those Farsi classes as I'd be able to speak the language today. As it is, I can't really connect with my Iranian heritage. It would be nice if I could. When I was a teenager I wasn't bothered with things like that. But the older I get, the more I'd like to visit Iran and learn something more about the country.

Growing up in Sheffield, I didn't think about identity much. By the age of seven or eight I was definitely aware there weren't many other mixed-race kids around, and certainly none of my kind of mix. But while I was conscious I was a bit different from everyone else, I never saw that difference as a negative. I always thought it was kind of cool being mixed race. Nobody gave me any problems because of it. I think this was key. Because everyone around me used to think being mixed race was cool, I thought so, too. I've always vibed off the mixed-race buzz, to be honest.

I grew up in a predominantly white neighbourhood of Sheffield and went to predominantly white schools. My secondary school was more diverse, but in my primary school there were maybe one or two black kids, a couple of North African kids and that was it. My friendship groups in both primary and secondary school were very white. But I don't remember ever thinking, 'Wow, I'm the odd one out here, I don't fit in. Should I be looking for some black friends or maybe some Middle Eastern friends?' I never felt that way. Maybe some of it had to do with my personality. I've always been a rather chatty and sociable person. I've always got on very well with my peers. I did quite well in school so I was quite pally with a lot of my teachers as well. I think a lot of my generally positive attitude towards people is down to my mum.

I have a lot of respect for my mother. Despite being a single mum, she made sure I and my sister had everything we needed, including love and security. At the time my parents got divorced, my mum worked as a dinner lady. But when my dad left she realised she wasn't going to be able raise two kids on her wages. So she went back to school in her mid-thirties. She got a degree in psychology and a postgraduate degree in education. And she did all this while raising two kids, making sure we never went without food or clothes on our backs. So my mum is my role model.

She is a very gentle and tolerant person, quick to look for the good in others rather than the bad. Quick to give people the benefit of the doubt. I try to emulate her. I'm always inclined to give people the benefit of the doubt. I think that's why the 'where are you from?' question has never really bugged me. I didn't get asked this very often growing up. People saw me and immediately knew I was mixed race, but they rarely asked details. On the rare occasion they did, when I'd say my dad was Iranian and my mum was British with some Nigerian roots, they'd usually be like 'Wow, that's cool.' I liked that reaction so, to be honest, I kind of liked when people wanted to know more details about my racial background.

The one thing that teed me off a bit growing up was that it took some people a while to learn how to pronounce my name properly. But aside that I never really felt my racial identity playing a negative role in my life. Which doesn't mean I never experienced racism growing up.

I used to play under-fourteen Sunday league football and some-times we'd have games in rough white working-class neighbourhoods further out of Sheffield. In those kinds of places I'd sometimes get racist abuse during games. I've always felt the closer you are to the city centre in Sheffield – where the universities and all the international students are – the more multicultural and tolerant it is. But the further you venture from the city centre, the less diverse it is and the more likely you are to encounter racism. Maybe it's not a rule but that was my experience anyway.

While I would get upset after such incidents, I don't think they affected me that much. I know some people get really down after these kinds of situations, which is very understandable because racism is disgusting to experience. But I think they affected me less because I felt loved and secure at home. I could always talk to my mum after such incidents. She'd put her arm around me and say the standard things parents say in such situations: 'What an idiot. It's ignorance. That's how he's been brought up' and so on. This always made me feel better and before long I'd be thinking, *Well, we won the game, that's what really matters.* If I came back to an unstable home where I couldn't count on support, these incidents would probably have affected me more. Aside from the football racism, there were a couple of mothers of some of my white friends who I sensed were wary of me at the beginning because I was a bit different. I think they feared I might be a bad influence on their sons or something. It would usually take them a few months to get to know me but, once they did, everything would be fine.

When I got older and started reading sociology literature on race, I began thinking a bit more about these kinds of things, like people asking where you're from. I started thinking maybe it is a bit annoying that people ask these questions. But ultimately my instincts have remained to give everyone the benefit of the doubt unless it's obvious from afar that you mean malice. I am confident those who ask me the 'where are you from?' question usually don't mean anything malicious.

I've always liked being a bit different and I don't remember ever having an identity crisis. When answering the ethnicity question in forms, it always tickles me to tick 'any other mixed background' as there is obviously no separate category for mixed British-Asian-African. But practically speaking, I identify British more than anything else. It's where I'm from, it's the place that has shaped my cultural values. I've also always identified mixed race because that is one of the first things people have always noticed about me.

My mum didn't talk much about race when I was growing up. She never sat me down to tell me people would treat me differently because of my race. That would have just made me paranoid. She wanted me to feel a part of Britain, and I did. It was my dad who used to talk about race quite a bit when I'd meet him. Because his job is in takeaways and for a long time he worked near Hillsborough stadium where Sheffield Wednesday plays its matches, he's had many bad experiences with drunk racist football fans. He's been physically attacked, too.

By the time I was in my teens in the early 2000s, I'd say people of Middle Eastern descent had it tougher in Sheffield than black people, mostly because they were constantly being demonised in the press over the terrorism issue. Add to this the fact my dad is a very patriotic Iranian who believes the West is out to destroy his country, and he definitely has some strong views and ideas about how the West sees people like him. I think he has influenced some of my political views and it is probably no coincidence I wrote my university thesis on depictions of Muslims in right-wing British media. I studied sociology at the University of York.

While my dad worked in rougher neighbourhoods than the one I lived in, I think he also told me these stories about his experiences with football fans so I would keep my wits about me and be careful of where I go and when. I definitely agree with him that people from the Middle East are often portrayed very negatively in the British media, especially by the tabloids, of course. But despite some of his views undoubtedly having some influence on my views, I wouldn't say I'm really close to him. Nor do I feel Iranian or worry there's something I'm missing by not feeling Iranian. I am interested in Iran and in learning more about it, but I don't feel something is amiss because I don't feel connected to it. I guess that's sad, really, but it's the way I feel.

When I was in York, which is a very white city, I really buzzed off my mixed-race status. It was a real winner with the girls there. I was unique in York and I enjoyed the benefits of that. I remember this one incident, though. Some of us students were all sitting chatting in a group. There were some guys and girls from Europe, so everyone was talking about where their parents were from and whatnot.

When I told them my background, this girl from the south said in a very matter-of-fact voice, 'You're a bit of a mongrel, aren't you?' Some people in the room froze, wondering how I'd react. I had every right to react very negatively as many people probably would have. But I laughed it off because I sensed she didn't mean anything malicious by it. She was actually a lovely girl and we later became good friends. Like I said, I always focus on people's intentions.

All the mixed-race people I know hate being called 'half-caste'. But I have worked with people from older generations who still use that term. This too doesn't bother me once I sense they are not saying it in a bad way. However, I usually warn them that while it's no big deal for me, they should avoid using that term around other mixed-race people because they might end up causing serious offence.

When it comes to how prejudice might have affected my life in Britain, one thing I sometimes wonder about is how many job interviews I might not have gotten because my first name is Hamid and my surname is Iranian. One experience in particular got me thinking about this. A few years ago, I worked part-time in a House of Fraser in Sheffield. On my first day, one of the girls who worked there said to me, 'When we heard you were coming and saw your name, we thought you'd turn up in a turban or something.'

I found that absurd. But it made me think about the reactions recruiters reading my name on job applications might have had. I've noticed that whenever I've managed to get an interview, 95 per cent of the time I'd get the job. But there'd be periods I'd send loads of applications and never get any interviews. I am not assuming there must be a connection, but there certainly might be. It is only at interviews people can see that despite being a Hamid, I am personable, enjoy a pint and a night out, and love football. And that's British culture, really. So when they meet me, they know I can fit in with the team. But before meeting me, they might assume I won't. I guess this is why some of my Iranian cousins here have given their kids English names to make things easier for them.

I have a one-year old son. Me and my missus (who is English) decided to call him Benjamin. Simple English name, it doesn't get simpler than that. I love my name, but it always teed me off when people struggled to pronounce it right. So I decided to give my son an English first name. But, of course, he has my Iranian surname. Benjamin looks really white, so I think it will be cool when people find out a Benjamin who looks as white as he does has an Iranian and Nigerian heritage. Of course, in his case, these identities will be very theoretical. I think my son will feel even less of a connection to Iran and Nigeria than I do. He'll just see himself as British like me.

I do think being mixed race and lighter-skinned has helped me embed myself in British culture more easily. It's been easier for me to integrate in Sheffield than if I were 100 per cent black or 100 per cent Iranian. There's quite a sizeable Somalian community here and some of my Somalian friends have experienced bad racism. Somalians get really bad press because their country is so war-torn.

I feel a particularly strong connection to Sheffield. I lived in London for a while and absolutely hated it. All that hustle and bustle. I'm happy I came back here. You're near the countryside but you also have your inner-city concrete jungle nearby if that's what you feel like. These days, I work in a large accounting firm where I've been for two years now. No issues with race. And most important of all, everyone says my name right.

I found it very interesting when Hamid said that, growing up, he considered himself different from others around him but never saw that difference as a negative thing – on the contrary. I think this is crucial. There are, of course, various levels of different. There is different as in a different-kind-of-one-of-us and different as in a definitely-not-one-of-us. The former, which is the kind of different Hamid was describing, is a far less alienating kind of different than the latter. The Somalian friends of whom he spoke who have experienced bad racism in Sheffield would probably be seen in the latter category, for instance. Especially if they were not born here and don't have British accents. Nevertheless, there are people in Hamid's category of different who would also associate their feelings of difference with alienation and marginalisation. In these kinds of cases, I think the difference in experience often boils down to personal psychology. Some will develop very self-conscious attitudes to their difference while others such as Hamid will revel in it, especially if they perceive it as bringing them benefits, such as being considered 'cool'. Or the flattering female attention to which Hamid alluded. But ultimately, personality will play a significant role here.

One of the things that struck me when I was speaking to Hamid was that he did not use the term 'white people' even when he was clearly referring to white folk. He simply used the word 'people'. It was so consistent it was noticeable, and I think this says a lot about the fact he does not instinctively separate himself from white people as a separate category of human beings.

He's been around white people so long he just sees them as people. Despite having experienced some racist incidents, Hamid was clearly one of those mixed-race people who are effortlessly British. He is so confident in himself even someone calling him a 'mongrel' didn't make him react defensively. He actually laughed heartily when he told me this story. Oh, to be a happy man!

# Conclusion

A few things struck me in particular while writing this book. Most importantly, mixed-race Britons clearly see issues around race and identity for what they are: complex spheres of our contemporary world that defy easy Manichean divisions of humanity into good tribes and bad tribes. When you are raised in an interracial home, you are likely to have experienced both positive and negative interactions with people of various shades of skin colour within your own family.

You learn pretty early on in life that there is no good race, only good people. That the world is divided into those who have an open-minded inclusivist approach towards other human beings and those who have a closed-minded exclusivist approach. And it is not even to say that the latter are always bad people, sometimes they are simply driven by cultural beliefs and value systems they hold dear and believe they are protecting. Of course, sometimes, they *are* just malevolent racists.

Another thing that stood out for me is that mixed-race Britons of all skin shades and configurations are no longer content to be assigned their identity by society, they want to assert it on their own terms. As their numbers grow, so does their confidence in being themselves. This is a sea-change in attitude from the twentieth century when the mixed-race identity was a defensive identity.

In most countries, mixed-race people were but a tiny minority with little choice but to adapt to the rules set by monoracial majorities. The 'one-drop' rule introduced by white America and practised all over the Western world was a classic example; the offspring of black and white parents had no say in the matter. You were black, period. Your identity was decided for you. One of the major mental adjustments monoracial British society will have to undergo this century is getting used to an increasingly assertive mixed-race population that will insist on the right of its individuals to identify the way they feel rather than how the rest of society feels they should. They will want to be left free to draw on their multiple identities without feeling pressured to 'choose' one and without being considered only 'half' of an identity. In other words, we are tired of always having to adapt to monoracial society: it is time monoracial society started learning how to adapt to us. It is time the mixed-race experience started being accorded its rightful place as a unique identity experience, rather than a slight variation of the monoracial life journey. We *are* different.

But we have more than just demands of society. We also have something very valuable to offer in today's atmosphere of racial polarisation. Growing up mixed-race is a life experience that lays the groundwork for an inclusive open-minded attitude towards others, including those of a different skin colour from us. The circumstances of our mixed heritages and upbringing make delving into the perspectives of various others come somewhat naturally to us because it is what we had to do to fit in growing up. We had to learn how to observe and how to pick up various racial cues. And we of all people know just how messy and complicated this whole race business can get. Because it is complicated inside us. We don't just bring *a* different perspective to the issues of race and identity; we bring all the different perspectives that exist *within* us.

Everybody wants to be understood. To be got. Most people do not demand others see the world exactly the way they see it, all they want is for you to give them a chance to explain why they see it that way. Because a readiness to understand signals a readiness to accept. And us mixed-race folk know a bit about what it's like wanting to be understood and accepted. I have no doubt Barack Obama's biracial life experience is one of the reasons he was so brilliant at making different kinds of people feel comfortable around him. As someone who had struggled with acceptance all his life, he had an acute understanding of the human craving for it.

Aside the need to be listened to, people also want to be treated as the unique individuals they are, not as nameless members of this or that race or ethnic group. We all want to be viewed as individuals, not as 'black people', 'white people' or 'mixed-race people.' So, we need to approach others as we would like to be approached: as complex human beings full of so many contradictions any label deployed to define us is inevitably a gross simplification.

We all have our beliefs, our logics, our sacred stories. Stuff that makes sense to us but might not to anyone else. Or only to those who have had similar life experiences to us. They are what help us make sense of this world, give it meaning. They are the building blocks of what we refer to as our 'identity'. But just as our stories seem the realest and most sensible to us, others think the same about theirs.

What matters is that we respect the right of individuals to their own stories. Not because of a cynical belief that there is no such thing as 'truth', only 'narratives', but because we know the human mind is a maze of thoughts and feelings, each designed with different passageways. That is why even twins experience the world differently. This is why we must never let the individual's story get lost in all the group commotion.

It is also important that as we respect the right of others to tell their own unique experiences, we work too on developing overarching stories of inclusion that transcend racial boundaries. Stories that connect us rather than divide us. National stories. Global stories. Human stories. There is room for all sorts of stories to co-exist. Even in each of us as individuals. Much more so in the infinite universe of our collective imagination.

# Acknowledgements

A huge thank you to all the mixed-race Britons who agreed to tell me their stories for this book. Without you, this would never have happened, and I am eternally grateful.

Big shout-out to Andreas Campomar who believed in this project from the start and was incredibly supportive throughout the process. Jo Wickham, Claire Chesser and the rest of the team at Little, Brown who worked on this book with me, you guys are awesome. Love you all!